HF
5415.3
.F598
1987

Forbes, J. D.
(James D.), 1932-

The consumer
interest

$63•00

THE CONSUMER INTEREST

THE CONSUMER INTEREST

Dimensions and Policy Implications

J.D. FORBES

Faculty of Commerce and Business Administration,
University of British Columbia,
Vancouver, Canada

CROOM HELM
London • New York • Sydney

© 1987 J.D. Forbes
Croom Helm Ltd, Provident House, Burrell Row,
Beckenham, Kent, BR3 1AT
Croom Helm Australia, 44-50 Waterloo Road,
North Ryde, 2113, New South Wales

Published in the USA by
Croom Helm
in association with Methuen, Inc.
29 West 35th Street
New York, NY 10001

British Library Cataloguing in Publication Data

Forbes, J.D.
    The consumer interest.
    1. Consumer protection
    I. Title
    381'.34   HC79.C63
    ISBN 0-7099-1063-0

Library of Congress Cataloging-in-Publication Data

Forbes, J.D. (James D.), 1932–
    The consumer interest.

    Bibliography: p.
    Includes indexes.
    1. Consumers. 2. Consumer protection. I. Title.
HF5415.3.F598 1987   381'.34   87-12947
ISBN 0-7099-1063-0

Printed and bound in Great Britain by Mackays of Chatham Ltd, Kent

CONTENTS

PREFACE

Although consumers' concern over a particular problem may be quite simple to understand, it is a difficult task to define and describe the unique significance and the scope of the rising tide of consumer consciousness. An analytical framework which adequately allowed a logical evaluation of the political and economic activity affecting the consumer interest in Western pluralist democracies did not exist when this book was first begun in 1973. While some of this deficit has been filled since then, there is still not, to my mind, an adequate exposition of what the "consumer interest" comprises nor of what are its many dimensions. This is particularly so at the margin where the consumer interest is in conflict with the interests of other groups in society.

Consumer activist groups have had a difficult problem in defining their role in the advocacy process. Consumerism and consumer pressure groups are not well understood by consumers themselves, by business groups, by policy makers nor by students. This lack of understanding has had a variety of consequences. Business has often responded inappropriately to consumer concerns and has seen negative publicity and increased regulation as a result. Consumers, both individually and as pressure group members, frequently only partially understand the functions of their organized pressure groups. Policy makers do not understand the constraints under which such groups operate nor their potential use in helping develop and implement effective consumer policy. Finally, students first starting to study consumers and their role in society are usually hard pressed to fit the things they learn about consumers and the consumer interest into an inclusive framework. I hope this book provides some help in these areas.

I hope also the book may be of help in the advocacy process, as well as in courses in consumer behaviour, political science and law.

Preface

The seeds of this study are contained in Chapter III of the report on *Consumer Interest in Marketing Boards*, published in 1974 by Consumer and Corporate Affairs Canada. (Forbes, J. D., Arcus, P. L., Loyns, R. M. A., Oberg, S. M., Ouellet, F., Veeman, M. M., Veeman, T. S., and Wood, A. W. Ottawa: Canadian Consumer Council, Consumer and Corporate Affairs Canada.) In that study we were forced to define the consumer interest in order to be able to evaluate the effects of agricultural marketing board regulatory activity on consumers. We found that defining the consumer interest in its many dimensions was both difficult as well as a problem which had not received much attention. Almost everyone who had commented on the subject believed that every reader knew what that interest was. Most of what had been done lacked rigour and was not based on existing research on interests and interest representation. To date, this is the first concerted attempt to define that interest in its many dimensions that I have discovered, although some authors have devoted attention to parts of the problem and thereby facilitated the task to some degree.

In its earlier stages this book had two authors, Stan Oberg and me. He first encountered the problem of defining the consumer interest when working as part of the team preparing the report on the consumer interest in marketing boards. The two of us worked together for about four years on previous drafts at which time Stan stepped aside to assume increased university duties. However, since stepping aside his support and enthusiasm for the project has not diminished. I cannot express adequately my thanks to him in words.

Dr. John Evans, former Director, Consumer Research Branch at Consumer and Corporate Affairs Canada, was instrumental in providing monetary support for starting this study. However, he contributed in more than just a monetary sense, especially by allowing us to look in breadth at the problem. The division of labour in the project started with Mr. Abdul Wahab, a doctoral candidate at the

University of British Columbia, spending the summer months of 1976 performing a detailed literature review and recording the results of his work in September of that year. I appreciate his intense labours over those three months. A revised and expanded draft of that original work was published by the Consumer Research Branch, Consumer and Corporate Affairs Canada under the title of *Defining the Consumer Interest*. Consumer Research Report No. 1, February 1977.

The present volume is a culmination of further, intermittent work on the book; work interrupted by several other projects, but projects which widened my understanding of consumer problems of advocacy and representation.

Additional support for work on the project is most appreciated. A further research grant by the Consumer Policy Directorate of Consumer and Corporate Affairs Canada in 1984 and 1985 provided funds to expand the scope of the study to include consumer policy in the OECD countries; evidence of Canada's continuing support of the efforts of that organization to expand its consumer policy activities. My thanks go to Tom Gussman of the Department for his encouragement and support. In addition, work study grants from the Province of British Columbia and grants from the Canadian Social Sciences and Humanities Research Council between 1981 and 1985 contributed to research assistance which was most useful and instrumental in completing research for the book.

A number of individuals were most helpful in expanding my understanding and perspectives of consumers and the consumer movement. Among those are Scott Maynes, Tom Recter of Consumentenbond, Lars Broch and Ruth Vermeer of IOCU in Den Haag, Tony Venables and his staff at BEUC in Bruxelles, Professor Norbert Reich and his colleagues at the University of Bremen, Erich Linke of the OECD in Paris, Eirlys Roberts, Daphne Grose and Maurice Healy in London, and Iain Ramsay in Newcastle. Their insight, gained of long experience in various national and international consumer activities were freely shared and I value them highly.

I want to thank others who contributed to the completion of this book. First, thanks are due to consumers whose concerns sparked our efforts in the first place. Further thanks are due to Louise Heslop, Sheila Brown, Stan Shapiro, Scott Maynes, Bill Stanbury, Greg Kane, Barbara Sulzenko, Peter Gall, Fred Thompson and Jim Brander. Special thanks go to Susan Burns, Judy Marriott, Steve Arnold, Hugh Walker, Scott Fraser and Nancy Forbes whose editorial comment and conceptual contributions significantly added to the completion of the manuscript. The list of names of persons contributing typing skills over many years is too long to remember, let alone list. They are most appreciated, if not individually listed.

Thanks are due the Computing Centre of the University of British Columbia and to Peter Van Den Bosch who provided support, suggestions and advice for processing the text into its present form.

I am particularly grateful to Croom Helm Limited and Peter Sowden for encouraging the completion of the manuscript they saw several years ago and for providing the vehicle for publishing it.

Finally, I want to thank my wife Nancy for her understanding and encouragement over the many years and drafts necessary to bring the task to completion.

J.D.F.
University of British Columbia

1. DEFINING THE CONSUMER INTEREST

In today's increasingly pluralistic society, in what appears to be a more formal and structured balancing of the interests of competing groups in social, political and economic decisions, consumers feel their interests are being eroded by special interest groups.

The range of situations in which consumers believe they have interests that need stronger consideration range from the desire to have prices and ingredients prominently displayed on a can of string beans, to the environmental impact of nuclear power and alternate forms of energy on the quality of their lives. Indeed, the number of situations which individuals may wish to classify under the aegis of "consumer interest" may be infinite. Because this interest appears to be so broad, many people, including politicians, government officials, business people, and consumers, frequently experience problems in differentiating the "consumer interest" and the equally ill-defined but commonly used term, the "public interest."

PURPOSE

The purpose of this book is to provide a clarification of the meaning, the scope, and the dimensions of the consumer interest. The task is not trivial, especially to those who have to delineate the difference between the many interests vying for consideration in public and private policy decisions.

There is sufficient awareness that there is a "consumer" interest for most countries in the OECD to have established government ministries or departments that are charged to represent at least some of the interests of consumers in policy matters.[1] Every country in the OECD also has at least one, and frequently many, groups outside government whose *raison d'etre* is to represent consumer interests in the many areas of economic, political and social life of their countries in which consumers have an interest. In recent years, business firms in many countries have formed separate departments whose duties are to deal with consumers and consumer groups. These departments are often responsible for representing their employers in dealings with government regarding relations with consumers and the governments' development of consumer policy and legislation.

The Organisation for Economic Cooperation and Development was chosen as the unit of analysis because it is the largest grouping of countries for which consumer policy information is collected. Data for non-OECD countries is sparse, to say the least.

METHODOLOGY AND STRUCTURE

Different groups of people have viewed the consumer interest in a variety of ways, much like the proverbial blind men who viewed an elephant by touching it. One of the men, feeling the leg, believed the elephant to be very much like a tree. Another, feeling the tail, thought the elephant a snake, and so forth. The methodology used for describing and defining the consumer interest in this book uses a similar technique. It analyzes the consumer interest as described by various activist groups and academic disciplines. The final chapters bring these ideas in an overview and discussion of the policy implications and future directions for consumer policy.

The methodology is in the historicism tradition which is very useful in analyzing complex, socially and time-bound systems, where statistical data is impossible to come by since things happen only once. It uses empiricism, where possible, to shore up the inferences necessary in this type of research.[2] This chapter provides a background and overview of the consumerism movement and illustrates how complex that interest can be. Chapters 2 and 3 describe how consumer activists and business have viewed the consumer interest and consumerism. Chapter 4, analyzes the consumer interest from viewpoint of microeconomics, consumer behaviour and information theory, while Chapter 5 discusses consumer interest from the perspective of industrial organization theory. Chapter 6 structures the consumer interest from the point of view of the national and international consumer law. Chapter 7 views the problem through the eyes of the political scientist as a political process. The penultimate chapter presents a framework within which to analyze consumers' interests and to develop consumer policy. The final chapter considers future directions of consumer policy and the consumerism movement.

CONSUMERS IN HISTORICAL PERSPECTIVE

Legislation to protect consumers' interests spans thousands of years. For example:

- Mesopotamian legal codes, Codex Hammurabi, 1750 B.C., contained regulations regarding credit, rents, quality of goods and services, prices and weights and measures.
- Hittite legislation, 1200 B.C., regulated food safety and wholesomeness.
- Hebraic laws, Deuteronomy 25:15, counselled "...thou shalt have a perfect and just weight, a perfect and just measure..."
- Indian laws around 200 B.C. had laws against food adulteration, especially grains and oils.
- The United Kingdom, 1202 A.D., had laws against short-weight and adulterated bread. The Magna Carta, a few years later, further stipulated standards for weights and measures.
- In 15th Century Austria, the seller of adulterated milk had to drink all of the adulterated product.
- Sixteenth Century French were allowed to throw rotten eggs at those who had sold them.[3]

Two English authors date the beginning of modern organized action by consumers in Britain to the start of the consumer co-operative movement, when the first consumer co-operative was formed in the back streets of Rochdale, in the Midlands near Manchester, in 1844. The weak bargaining position of poor, unorganized workers/consumers in relation to all powerful suppliers, who were also mill owners, was highlighted in acute forms; payment in kind by employers, chronic indebtedness, adulteration of food, wide variations in product quality and monopoly pricing.[4] The beginning of the consumer movement in North America may be dated from the formation of Consumers' League in New York City in 1891. In 1898, local groups joined in a national federation, the National Consumers' League and by 1903 the national organization had grown to 64 branches in 20 states.[5]

Both Herrmann and Kotler[6] divide the consumer movement into three eras: the early 1900s, the mid 1930s and the mid 1960s. I have added a fourth, the late 1970s to the present, to assist understanding the evolution of present day consumer activism and concern about the consumer interest.

Consumerism is defined as the *organized reaction of individuals to inadequacies, perceived or real, of marketers, the marketplace, market mechanisms, government, government services, and consumer policy.*[7]

The First Consumerism Era "Turn of the Century"

The first consumerism era occurred mainly in the United States. It was fuelled by such factors as rising prices and Upton Sinclair's *The Jungle,*[8] which exposed widespread adulteration and unsafe practices in the U.S. meat industry. The gain to consumers in the U.S. was the passage of the Pure Food and Drug Act of 1906, the Meat Inspection Act of 1906 and the creation of the Federal Trade Commission and a variety of anti-monopoly laws. Following the U.S. lead in its fight to reduce the power of large monopolies, Canada passed anti-monopoly legislation in the late 1890s. In Europe, Sweden appointed an Ombudsman in 1899, some of whose efforts benefited consumers. We have been less than successful in finding many other consumer events in Europe during this time. However, on both continents, the pressures of World War I dampened the flames of consumerism for the time being.

The Second Consumerism Era "The Mid 1930s"

The second era of consumerism, in the 1930s, was the result of a combination of factors which included the publication in 1927 of Chase and Schlink's best selling book *Your Money's Worth*,[9] an upturn in consumer prices in the midst of the depression, the sulfanilamide scandal, and a widely imitated Detroit housewives' strike. Many people believe that Chase and Schlink's book, which highlighted many of the ways in which consumers were being exploited at the hands of the business interests of the country, served as an inspiration for some of Franklin D. Roosevelt's reforms during the New Deal era following his election as U.S. president in 1933. They also believe that the book continues to serve, even today, as the intellectual underpinning of consumerism. These factors resulted in the strengthening of the Pure Food and Drug Act and the granting of more powers to the Federal Trade Commission to regulate unfair or deceptive acts and practices in the United States.

Schlink formed Consumers' Research Inc., in 1929, to do product testing on a large scale.[10] In 1936, because of Schlink's apparently poor labour relations skills and a dispute over a union, a group of disgruntled employees broke away from Consumers' Research and formed Consumers Union, the publisher of *Consumer Reports*.[11] While Consumers' Research still exists, it is widely acknowledged that Consumers Union has provided the model for other consumer groups around the world to follow. The first mention of Canadian consumers as a political interest that we have been able to find is in the "Consumer Manifesto" presented at the 1933 Canadian Commonwealth Confederation convention in Winnipeg.

The European scene at the time was less salubrious for consumers. Hitler's rise to power was well underway. European business cartels were rampant. These situations, combined with war clouds on the horizon, left little room for concerns about consumer interests. It is interesting to note that runaway inflation in Post World War I Germany, with its devastating effects on German consumers, was a major assist to Hitler in his rise to power. His promises to reduce the rate of inflation, which had wiped out consumers' bank accounts, and the rising incomes which resulted from military spending, are credited with some of Hitler's popularity. In addition, the rest of the world was coming out of a major depression where having a job was more important than improving the lot of consumers.

The Third Consumerism Era "Post War to Late 1970s"

Consumerism might have gained more momentum in the late 1930s had the second World War not diverted the public's attention to the problem of national survival. That conflict, however, did have at least one positive consumer benefit in that the present Consumers' Association of Canada, Canada's national consumer advocacy organization, evolved from the Wartime Food and Prices Commission.[12]

This period was the consumers' heyday in Europe, but born out of the severe problems consumers were facing in the aftermath of the war. In the United Kingdom, less than acceptable quality of some products, and the lack of availability of comparative testing led, after some preliminary activities, to the publication of the first issue of *Which?* in October of 1957, putting the Consumers' Association, the British equivalent of Consumers Union, on its way.[13] There was a dramatic increase in consumer organizations in the other OECD countries as well, as documented in Chapter 7. It was these organizations which provided the political impetus for an explosion of government departments representing consumers in Australia, Canada and Western Europe over the next decade. With the advent of the European Economic Community (EEC), the consumer organizations in the member countries joined together to form the Bureau Europeen des Consommateurs (BEUC) to act as spokesperson for all consumers in the EEC and to hold a place on advisory committees within the EEC organization dealing with consumer matters. The International Organization of Consumers Unions was founded during this period to bring together activist organizations the world over in an effort to improve the effectiveness of consumer pressure groups.[14]

During the 1950s Vance Packard's *The Hidden Persuaders* (1957) and *The Waste Makers* (1960)[15] created considerable interest in consumer problems in the U.S. But the focal point of the third era is usually identified as John F. Kennedy's Consumer Message to the Congress in the Spring of 1962, where he presented his well known *Consumer Bill of Rights* which consisted of the right to safety, the right to be informed, the right to choose, and the right to be heard.

Among subsequent events which spurred the development of a stronger consumer movement in the U.S. were the birth of thalidomide deformed babies, President Johnson's creation of and appointment of Esther Peterson to the White House position of Special Assistant for Consumer Affairs in 1964, the publication in 1965 of Ralph Nader's best selling book *Unsafe at Any Speed*, the high rate of inflation during the mid-sixties, and the publication of *The Poor Pay More* by David Caplovitz in 1963.[16] Through the efforts of consumer and other organizations, a variety of legislation was passed which included the Highway Safety Act of 1966, the Truth in Packaging Bill of 1966, and the Truth in Lending Bill of 1968. "Congress enacted more than twenty-five consumer, environmental, and other social regulatory laws between 1967 and 1973."[17]

The Fourth Consumerism Era "The Late 1970s and the 1980s"

Election of right-wing governments in the United States and the United Kingdom, a general shift to conservatism throughout the developed world, another world wide depression and intense pressures on public budgets all combined to reduce consumerists' activities during the latter half of the 1970s and into the 1980s. A concerted lobbying campaign by business and the news media in the United States resulted in the defeat of a bill to establish a Department of Consumer Protection.[18] In the U.K., the Thatcher government's ideological love affair with Milton Friedman's policies of deregulation resulted in the demise of many Quangos, quasi-governmental organizations. Interestingly, those which represented consumers' interests survived and appear "alive and kicking."

The consumerism movement has matured. National and international networks of consumer groups have honed their research, organizational and political skills. The press depends upon them to provide objective product and service information which benefit not only consumers but help reporters "get" stories which include articulate consumer viewpoints. The consumerism movement in Europe effectively organizes campaigns by its member organizations to put pressure on governments, both domestically and at the EEC level, to consider the consumer viewpoint on issues.

With this brief historical perspective of consumerism we now look at the consumer interest at a general level. A more in depth discussion of the consumerism movement and its political dimensions is in Chapter 7.

POLICY DECISION ENVIRONMENTS

A definition of what constitutes the interests of consumers, the limits to pressure group activity on their behalf, indeed the purpose of economic production and the quality of life, is completely bound up in a particular society's attitudes about these complex matters. That the sole purpose of economic production is consumption as Adam Smith wrote in his famous theorem (1776), is seldom questioned in the assumptions under which the consumer interest is championed. In some democratic societies, such an assumption may quite rightly represent reality. However, in other types of political regimes, maintenance of political power, enrichment of the ruling power group, imposition of one political or religious ideology over another, or other reasons may constitute the rationale for economic production. Obviously, even in democratic societies the situation is far from clear. Adam Smith's doctrine is too general and simplistic except for the most simplistic and politically naive of analysts. Indeed, Professor Smith did not intend his model to be used as the cornerstone of modern welfare economics. What is clear is that without production there is little consumption, and trade-offs between the two make for difficult societal choices.

Therefore, it is impossible to separate societal decisions on consumer interests from policies affecting income levels, income distribution and from matters where it is felt that market mechanisms are inappropriate or where political or social welfare considerations override economic concerns. Some choices tend to increase consumer welfare and choice, while others tend to restrict individual choice and circumvent or distort market mechanisms as depicted in Figure 1-1.

Some of the restrictions in consumer choice illustrated in Figure 1-1 are instituted by governments to redistribute income, to ensure universal access to goods and services, to ensure a minimal level of service to all its citizens or to institute other societally desired measures. Most of such activities result in income re-distribution to some degree. Examples of each activity include government food stores or food stamps, subsidization of basic

Figure 1-1 Continuum of Consumer Choice

Individuals, Marketplace Choice of Goods/Services		Public Choice of Goods/Services
Market End of Continuum		Public End of Continuum
Resources under individuals' control to allocate to a specific basket of goods/services. Market signals indicate preferences.		Involves complex societal goals and concerns over distribution and access by citizenry to goods/services. Political mechanisms are used to indicate preferences and effect change.
(Resources available to individuals are not independent of government policies on income levels, income distribution, taxation, etc.)		(Often used as an income redistribution mechanism. e.g., subsidized consumption of goods -- food, rent, transportation, medical services, education, etc.)

consumption items such as housing through price fixing or regulation of rents and housing prices, postal service, government insurance schemes (unemployment, pension funds, automobile, medical), universal medical care and publicly supported education.

While some of these examples may be controversial, many are widely accepted as socially desirable in most Western societies. It can be seen that some consumers may benefit from these measures while others will become relatively worse off. The same consumers may not be affected equally by each of the measures which restrict their individual range of choice.[19] These concerns become societal decisions about justice and equity.

This discussion and illustration lead to the conclusion that there can only be a definition of the consumer interest and the acceptance of the legitimacy of consumer interest group's activity in a particular societal/cultural context. Such is the case for most important, real world issues. Even within a specific society or culture it is impossible to precisely define concepts such as the consumer or the public interest. While there may be broad societal support for the preponderant aspects of a definition, the marginal issues are frequently contentious and less broadly accepted by some groups. The public interest and its components discussed below obviously are completely bound up in these societal considerations and must be viewed in that light.

THE CONSUMER VS THE PUBLIC INTEREST

James Madison, writing in *The Federalist* in the late 1700s, recognized that the most common basis for interest group action is economic when he stated:

... the most common and durable source of factions has been the various and unequal distribution of property. Those who hold and those who are without property have ever formed distinct interests in society. Those who are creditors and those who are debtors, fall under a like discrimination. A landed interest, a manufacturing interest, a mercantile interest, a moneyed interest, with many lesser interests, grow out of necessity in civilized nations, and divide them into different classes, actuated by different sentiments and views. The regulation of these various and interfering interests forms the principal task of modern legislation, and involves the spirit of party and faction in the necessary and ordinary operations of government.[20]

Ben Lewis (1938) provided a simplistic but useful analytical structure when he defined the function and process of governments to be the advancing of the public interest. He defined the public interest to include three major economic groups: the owners of capital, the providers of labour, and consumers.[21] Governance involves weighing and balancing these interests, the goal being whatever is agreed upon by societies' power groups (my expansion of Lewis' definition). Although not in any manner mutually exclusive, capital and labour may be viewed as the input sides and consumption as the output side of the socio-economic process. Figure 1-2 depicts the parties' relationships.

Each of these three elements of any society is concerned that the government represent and protect their collective and individual interests in the generation and distribution of a standard of living. In this context, standard of living is meant to convey the totality of consumption including goods and services purchased individually in the marketplace, public goods and services provided by governments, as well as the consumption of an environment, both physical and mental, all of which contribute to satisfying consumers' wants. While many consumption items are difficult to define and measure, and while measuring consumer satisfaction is complex, difficult to interpret and apparently a function of the gap between aspirations and actuality, the consumer interest must include the totality of all consumption if one does not wish to end up with a partial analysis.[22] Throughout the remainder of the book it is assumed that all aspects of consumption are legitimate concerns for consumers. This is in contrast to what has often been assumed -- that consumerism is concerned solely with privately purchased or government provided goods and services.[23]

The crux of the consumer interest problem is the limited ability of governments to represent these broadly based and often difficult-to-define interests against the more specific interests of owners of resources and providers of labour. The nature of the differences in representing broad versus more specific interests is crucial to understanding the sources of consumerism and the problems facing consumers and consumer pressure groups. The complex subject of

Figure 1-2 Major Elements of the Public Interest

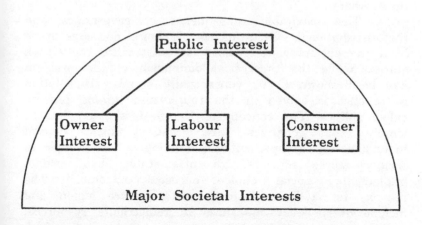

Major Societal Interests

SOURCE: Adapted from Lewis, Ben W. (1938) "The 'Consumer' and the 'Public' Interests Under Public Regulation," *Journal of Political Economy*, 46 (Feb.), pp. 97-107.

interest representation is discussed in greater detail in Chapter 7.

Even more critical at this stage of the analysis are the global problems of social choice and governance which have faced societies from time immemorial. While we will not solve these problems, we can at least point out how these problems affect the definition of the consumer interest and the challenges which these considerations pose for researchers and policy makers.

PROBLEMS OF SOCIAL CHOICE

The instant that individuals voluntarily decide to band together for self-governance, problems of social choice arise. When rules of behaviour are prescribed, such as voting, the representation of individual interests through various forms of government, the method of assessing taxes and the relationships between economic, political and social units (church and state, schools, business and the like), the rules invariably result in some individuals and groups benefiting more than others.

This inevitable consequence of governance and the distributional effects of social choice decisions have been the subject of discussion at least since the Greek states. While the theoretical dimension of the problem has been shown to be conceptually simple, its solution in practice is solved in the rough and tumble process called politics. The concept of Pareto Optimality, stated simply that changes are made which benefit individuals or groups without making other groups in society worse off, is an often-stated but seldom implemented social choice decision outcome.[24] The reasons for a lack of implementation are legion and include overt policy measures to redistribute resources, such as progressive taxation, policy alternatives which are neither infinite nor continuous (minimum economic size, political and administrative realities of implementation), and difficulties of or failure to evaluate and measure differential distributional effects of alternative policy choices.

The problems, theoretical and practical, of social choice decisions are not unique to defining or representing the consumer interest but encompass all interests in a society. However, there are concerns of consumer representation in governance which, while not unique, are characteristic of large "latent interest" groups to which consumers are described as belonging.[25] These characteristics are described at the end of this chapter and addressed in greater depth in Chapter 7.

DEFINING THE CONSUMER INTEREST

In spite of many years of research, the process by which the desires of the electorate are transformed into reality is poorly understood. Indeed, many observers of the political process, in effect, believe that the public and consumer interests are always subordinated to smaller, politically powerful special interests.[26] That is, that general interests of a society are a conglomeration of special interests, rather than evidence of the collective desires of all its citizens. Indeed, this is inevitable in a multi-party democracy. The goal of politicians is making acceptable trade-offs among the special and the general interests of its citizens.

While noting the lack of a complete model to describe how democratic governments transform the electorates' wish into action, there is most likely enough theory, methods and data to create models to better understand the process.[27] Although the question of governance is neither completely nor well understood, it must be recognized that representing any interest takes place in a complex process, where even if one is able to identify inputs and observe outputs, understanding the process which produced those outcomes is usually not simple. Further, the consumer interest is only one of many clamoring for attention in the political process of a particular jurisdiction. On reflection, it should be clear that the consumer interest is not an absolute waiting to be discovered. Rather, it is an agglomeration of individual preferences concerning the economic, political, and social benefits derived from a particular decision.

For example, the widely stated bill of consumer rights, attributed to President John F. Kennedy, of the right to choice, to information, to be heard and to safety, while generally accepted in principle, faces widespread conflict in its application. The consumers' "right" to information is one whose problems of implementation has spawned much research and for which there is evidence of poorly designed policy. It is well known that the complex listing of the nutritional contents of processed foods required by law in the United States has limited if any value in helping consumers make better food choices. How to think through the goals of public policy such as this, and how to relate the desired goals to the research on how consumers use information, in order to develop rules of behaviour (laws) which will achieve those goals, is not a simple task.[28]

The discussion above indicates that there is no generalized consumer interest. Rather, there is a need to evaluate the distributional effects of each of the many areas of public policy affecting individuals in their various roles as consumers, laborers and as owners of both financial and intellectual capital. An illustration of the diversity and inclusiveness of the consumer interest in public policy, developed at a Research Conference on Consumer Policy at the University of Guelph, is presented in Table 1-1. One of these policy areas, electronic funds transfer systems, has been selected to illustrate the types of considerations which arise when defining the consumer interest in specific situations.

CONSUMER INTERESTS: THE EFTS EXAMPLE

Electronic funds transfer systems (EFTS) provide a concrete and current example of the complexity and conflicting interests involved in defining and representing consumer interests. Banking systems are going through revolutionary changes in the way in which funds are transferred between buyers and sellers and consumers are in the midst of this revolution. Credit cards are old hat for many of us by now, and automated teller machines (ATMs) are springing up in a variety of locations, including convenience stores, airports as well as associated with banking institutions. It appears that in the not too distant future electronic point of sale (EPOS) systems will have evolved to the point where a consumer will use a plastic card at a retail store to purchase goods and the consumer's bank account will be debited directly and the retailer's account credited in the same transaction. In the United Kingdom, consumers connected with the British Telecom's *Prestel* viewdata service, with appropriate devices, can order merchandise via cable television.[29] Along with a large nation-wide experiment with many types of electronic services transmitted over the government-owned

Table 1-1 Public Policy with Consumer Interest Implications

POLITICAL REPRESENTATION
ECONOMIC WELL-BEING
JUSTICE
EQUITY
PRIVACY
TAX POLICY (cross-subsidization)
SAFETY
HEALTH
ENVIRONMENT
ACCOMMODATION
ENERGY
EXCHANGE TRANSACTIONS
EDUCATION
FINANCIAL SERVICES
FOOD
LEISURE
TRANSPORTATION

SOURCE: Developed by Consumer Interest Seminar, Conference on Consumer Policy Research, Department of Consumer Studies, University of Guelph, Guelph, Ontario, June 20-24, 1982.

telephone system, including an all electronic telephone directory, a number of French financial and retailing institutions have been running tests of a variety of EFT possibilities.[30] A non-network system also being tested in France is the debit card concept, where a positive balance is put on a card and the retailer debits the card at the store, negating the need for an electronic connection to the banking system.[31] British telephone users may already use such a card which works on this same principle. Canadian banks have joined in a nation-wide network of automatic teller machines, which is a precursor of a national EPOS system.[32]

EFTS are essentially comprised of two interrelated but distinct needs for moving money electronically through the system.[33] One relates to the wholesale or inter-institutional transfer of funds among financial institutions, and between financial institutions and other large money users such as governments and major corporations. The other relates to payments made at retail level -- between individuals, financial institutions and the sellers of goods and services. The material which follows focusses on the retail aspects of the system which affect consumers most directly.

The two main types of EFT arrangements on the individual consumer side of things are the Automated Teller Machines (ATM), which are already in use, and Electronic Point of Sale Terminals (EPOS) which are still in the planning, design and testing stage.

These two, ATM and EPOS, represent the best defined components of retail EFTS, but there are other EFT possibilities on the horizon that will extend the systems. These others include participation in EFTS by households, retailers, manufacturers, credit card companies and non-deposit financial institutions to buy and sell a variety of goods and services. Some of these transactions are planned to take place over home electronic systems utilizing television cable systems.[34]

EFTS - The Actors

A good way to understand the various relationships and interests in EFT systems is to break the system down into its major actors and to outline the interests of these actors *vis a vis* consumers.

Financial Institutions - Banks and other financial institutions, who are in fear of drowning in paper and people with the manual paper system which requires a large number of low-skilled, white-collar workers to process numerous, repetitive transactions, have the greatest interest in developing EFTS. Their three main objectives are (1) to reduce the high costs of the present paper payment system where processing each cheque costs from $ .50 to $1, down to a more manageable 1 to 10 cent range;[35] (2) to increase the productivity of their workers by enabling a greater volume of business per employee and (3) to reduce processing errors.

Employees - Union and non-union employees alike are concerned about the possible loss of employment opportunities that may arise because of EFTS. As these clerical bank workers are predominantly female, women's groups will also be concerned about the employment implications of EFTS.

Suppliers of EFTS Systems - Suppliers of system components and operating materials, whose customers are the system owners and operators, have an obvious interest in the system.

Wholesale Users - Major wholesale users of EFTS are assumed to be interested in advancing the interests of their institutions and, by definition, these transfers have few consumer interest implications.

Sellers of Goods/Services - Sellers are obviously interested in collecting payment from consumers. Their interests coincide with consumers' to the extent that consumers are not driven away by the use of EFTS.

Governments - Since banking and money systems are fundamental to the operation of any economic system, and since banks in all modern societies operate under government legislation, governments' policy role is evident.[36] The amount of influence a government chooses to have in the development of EFTS is not predictable. Obviously, they will want to retain control over and protection of their ability to implement and control economic policy. Once this goal is insured under EFTS, governments will react to pressure groups in their normal way. That reaction will vary, by jurisdiction, and is based on a complex interaction of considerations which include the particular society's and government's attitudes and methods of accommodating pressure groups.

Consumers - Consumer interests in EFTS are both simple and complex. Simple in that, to the extent that the EFTS benefits of cost savings, convenience and increased efficiencies are passed on to them, either directly or indirectly through a more efficient economic system, consumers benefit. However, there is no guarantee that this will happen. In fact, since financial institutions in all countries are at least oligopolistic in nature, due in part to natural scale economies as well as to government regulation, and since the cost of moving one's bank account is seldom trivial, there is an obvious consumer interest in ensuring that consumers have effective representation in the evolution of EFTS.

The complex nature of the consumer interest lies in the fact that no single point of view completely represents the interests of all consumers. For example, under the present system, consumers who pay by cheque benefit from the float created by the two to three day delay between making a payment and having their accounts debited. This group of consumers would therefore stand to lose the credit value of float which would be eliminated under an instantaneous EFTS. But there are many consumers -- mostly low-income or otherwise disadvantaged -- who are outside the present checking system and who pay cash for purchases and therefore do not benefit from a float. It has been estimated that in the United States, 20 to 25 per cent of households have no chequing accounts. Similarly, consumers living in rural areas may not be served by EFTS but they may incur some of the EFTS costs.[37]

There are a number of other issues of consumer interests which which are bound to arise in EFTS development, but which can only be briefly noted here. The two general concerns are who represents consumers' interests and who pays and who benefits from EFTS developments. They are examples of the classic representation and distribution problems of large, latent interest groups in their relationships with the more narrowly focussed special interest groups.[38] Specific concerns include how consumer privacy will be ensured. Will there be adequate choice of payment methods (cash, cheques, etc.), given possible monopoly/oligopoly control of payment systems. Who will spot and correct system errors and ensure adequate paper record keeping (such as cancelled cheques) so that individuals will not lose the ability to monitor, manage and audit their own financial affairs? Who will ensure that EFTS will be able to accommodate disadvantaged groups such as low income earners, children, the elderly, people with low education levels and the mentally or physically handicapped? Who determines legal liability for the performance of EFTS and legal protection and redress procedures for the consumer in conflict situations because of unequal power and size between large institutions and individual consumers? Since government will legislate and regulate EFTS, consumers may worry that EFTS will provide an opportunity for increased government intervention in the everyday lives and activities of consumers -- the Big Brother syndrome.

On the continuum of who pays and who benefits, who has the responsibility and who pays for the education costs necessary to change to the new system? How much of the cost of legal and security provisions of the systems will be borne by the consumer? Who pays for the loss of float for current cheque users when their payments for goods and services are instantaneously debited from their accounts, especially when goods may not have been received? Who insures consumer redress and who pays for the costs of redress, such as stop-payment procedures on cheques drawn to pay for goods not received or which have been returned to the sender? Who determines the distribution of the benefits of cost-reductions inherent in EFTS to its participants (consumers, banks, wholesale users)? Back-up systems will be provided to allow EFTS to maintain service to consumers during periods of system failure (downtime). Who pays costs of the downtime or the secondary effects of these types of failures, such as transactions which fail or penalties incurred because a payment could not be made at a specific time? Will consumers in rural and remote areas be excluded from the mainstream of EFTS, or will they have to bear extraordinary costs of being included in, or excluded from, the main payment system?[39]

Governments have normally been charged with the responsibility of representing the public interest and, within it, the consumer interest. However, examples are legion where, because it is in the interest of special interest groups (financial institutions and wholesale users in our present example) to put their case effectively, because they have resources and because the potential returns from such resource use can be large, the broader consumer interest is not effectively represented. This is not a condemnation of government nor an indictment of special interests. Rather, it is a statement of fact supported by an expanding body of literature about pressure groups, politics and the process of governance (discussed in depth in Chapter 7). The consumer interest is to see that these concerns are dealt with in the process of developing EFTS.

CONSUMER INTEREST CHARACTERISTICS

Below are five characteristics of consumers and their interests which explain why consumers' interests have frequently not been represented as well as other interests.

1. Diffusion of Interests

An important difficulty in defining consumer interest is its diffusion. "The consumer interest is the objective interest of the entire public".[40] A member of the public is a consumer at the dinner table but a producer, a farmer, a worker or a business person during the hours of the day before dinner. An interesting elaboration of the diffuse nature of the consumer interest was stated as follows:

> Everyone must consume in order to survive .....
> since all people are consumers ..... However, ...
> most individuals must be gainfully employed ..... in
> order to ..... finance their consumption, implying
> that most people are also producers. As a result,

there is no single, well-defined pattern of actions which uniquely and universally determines consumption behaviour. Therefore, while everyone is a consumer, it is also true that no one is solely a consumer.[41]

Another aspect of diffusion is that purchasing is diffused over many products. When the consumer buys infrequently, purchasing expertise does not develop. In addition, the consumer interest is diffused over such a wide range of concerns, especially in complex, high standard of living societies, that the ability to gain expertise or to be able to devote one's efforts to resolving problems with any given item of concern is difficult.

2. Intensity

A second important difficulty in defining consumer interest is the variable intensity of the interest. All people are consumers, but their self-awareness as consumers is generally lower than their awareness of their other roles. This makes consumer interests an issue that most people do not care very much about.[42] They are only confronted with this truism when something occurs in their role as a consumer which they cannot resolve. It is often only then that recognition of a particular power imbalance in the market place or vis-a-vis government-provided goods and services becomes intense enough to elicit concern, or, even more infrequently, an overt response.

3. Organizational Difficulties

Consumers are not as well nor as effectively organized as are specialized groups (for example, business or labour). The common interests that result in the forming of groups and organizations are less compelling than for the more specialized interest groups, because of the low intensity levels and the low potential returns from joining consumer groups.[43]

4. Conflicting Interests

Conflict refers to a situation in which a person is motivated to engage in two or more mutually exclusive activities.[44] A conflict emerges whenever two or more persons (or groups) seek to possess the same objects, occupy the same space or the same exclusive position, play incompatible roles, maintain incompatible goals, or undertake mutually incompatible means for achieving their purposes.[45]

We are both producers and consumers. Our interests as producers are immediate and obvious, but as mentioned earlier, our interest as consumers almost always is more distant and diffuse. As a result, the two often come into conflict.[46] As one lawmaker said,

...we are especially sensitive to the dilemma of conflict in consumer interests. In the area of farm commodities, many consumer advocates have worked for lower farm prices with the goal of maintaining lower food prices for consumers ... (On the other hand) when the market signals a surplus through low prices, farmers are forced to cut back production, which increases the prices."[47]

Everyone in their consumer role wants more variety, lower prices, and better quality. At the same time, everyone is a producer of goods or services or owner of capital. And in these roles we want a larger share of the national income through higher prices for providing labour and capital. The benefits of lower prices for a product or service are diffused over the whole buying population. The benefits of higher prices, wages or rates of return accrue directly and in large measure to the producer, wage earner or owner of capital.

5. Specificity of Special Interests

It follows from the previous concern that the interests of consumers is broad and diffuse while those of other groups are much more circumscribed and focussed. The owners of labour or capital have much more direct and specific interests in their producer/capital role. Similarly, the sellers of automobiles have a direct and special interest in influencing regulations affecting their product. Higher safety standards and testing procedures for an automobile, for example, may seriously affect an automobile company's competitive position so that there is direct and pressing concern within the industry to organize and represent that interest.

There is no simple solution to the conflict between producers and consumers, nor does it always have to be an "either/or" situation. However, in the final analysis, economically, politically and socially, individuals, in their collective roles, are the final judges in the conflict through the marketplace and through the government. The debate is age old but no easier to decided for all that.

CONCLUSIONS

Illustrating the consumer interest in the context of electronic funds transfer system provided a classic example of a constantly recurring situation for consumers the world over: the attempt to ensure the consumer interest is represented in the development of policies which affect them.

At its broadest level, the consumer interest may be defined as *the balancing by government of the interests of individuals in their roles as consumers and the interests of individuals and organizations in their roles as providers of labour and capital in the economic system. It is an element of the overarching public interest and, therefore, is a political concept.* Society defines, molds, changes and defines the power relationships and distribution of resources and rights among societal groups through the political process. Such decisions involve complex problems of social choice. And consumers, being a major but difficult to represent societal group, must compete for attention with other groups in the rough and tumble of the socio/political milieu called governance and politics.

As such, the consumer interest is not a truth nor an absolute waiting to be discovered. Rather, it is defined in the context of governing. Dimensions of the consumer interest are more complex than this, however. In the chapters to follow, a variety of the aspects of the consumer interest touched on in this introductory chapter are expanded.

NOTES

1 The OECD is an organization of twenty-five western countries and Yugoslavia (as an associate member). They include Australia, Austria, Belgium, Canada, Denmark, Finland, France, Germany, Greece, Iceland, Ireland, Italy, Japan, Luxembourg, the Netherlands, New Zealand, Norway, Portugal, Spain, Sweden, Switzerland, Turkey, the United Kingdom, the United States, and Yugoslavia.
2 Fullerton, Ronald A. (1987) "Historicism: What It Is, and What It Means for Consumer Research," in Paul F. Anderson and Melanie Wallendorf, eds., *Advances in Consumer Research*, Vol. *XIV*, Association for Consumer Research, forthcoming.
3 Vermeer, Ruth (1981) "The Consumer Protection Movement." Penang: International Organization of Consumers Unions, draft outline, mimeo; Roberts, Eirlys (1966) *Consumers*. London: C. A. Watts & Co. Ltd., pp. 38-39; King James version of *Holy Bible*; Friedman, Hershey H. (1984) "Ancient Marketing Practices: The View from Talmudic Times," *Journal of Public Policy & Marketing*, 3, pp. 194-204.
4 Martin, John, and Smith, George W. (1968) *The Consumer Interest*. London: Pall Mall Press, p. 18.
5 Herrmann, Robert O. (1970) "The Consumer Movement in Historical Perspective." State College, PA: Department of Agricultural Economics and Rural Sociology, Pennsylvania State University, (February), reprinted in Day, George S., and Aaker, David A. (1978) *Consumerism: Search for the Consumer Interest*. New York: The Free Press, pp. 27-28.
6 1971, pp. 10-17, and Philip Kotler (1972) "What Consumerism Means for Marketers". *Harvard Business Review*, (May-June) pp. 48-49.
7 Forbes, J. D. (1985) "Organizational and Political Dimensions of Consumer Pressure Groups," *Journal of Consumer Policy*, 8, pp. 105-106.
8 New York: Viking Press Edition, 1946.
9 New York: Macmillan.
10 Herrmann 1970.
11 Silber, Norman Issac (1983) *Test and Protest: The Influence of Consumers Union*. New York: Holmes and Meier, pp. 19-23.
12 Dawson, Helen Jones (1963) "The Consumers' Association of Canada," *Canadian Public Administration*, 6 (March), pp. 92-118.
13 Roberts, Eirlys (1966) *Consumers*. London: C. A. Watts &

Co. Ltd., Chap. V.
14 Roberts, Eirlys (1982) *International Organization of Consumers Unions: 1960-1981.* The Hague: International Organization of Consumers Unions.
15 New York: David McKay Company, Inc.
16 Nader, Ralph (1965) *Unsafe at Any Speed.* New York: Pocket Books Special; Caplovitz, David (1963) *The Poor Pay More.* New York: The Free Press.
17 Pertschuk, Michael (1982) *Revolt Against Regulation: The Rise and Pause of the Consumer Movement.* Berkeley: University of California Press, p. 5.
18 *Consumer Reports* (1978) "Business Lobbying: Threat to Consumer Interest," 43 (Sept.), pp. 526-531. Also see a description of this campaign at the end of Chapter 7, pp. 258-261.
19 There is a wide literature on social choice. Of special interest is Rawls' concept of the "social contract" in which society is considered to have an implied contract with each of its members to provide a basic minimum of goods and services. Once that minimum is provided, individuals are to be free to earn and allocate their resources unencumbered by government. (Rawls, J. (1971) *A Theory of Justice.* Cambridge, MA: Belknap Press of Harvard University.) While too broad a subject for the present book, the decision that a government should provide basic levels of income and goods/services has within it many basic societal values. This has been an area of much academic and philosophical discussion since the time of Plato. Obviously, many areas of consumer legislation fall within this sphere of dialogue, but their discussion is outside the scope of this book. Nevertheless, the reader should be aware that many of the ideas discussed in this book have elements of social choice. See, for example, Arrow, K. J. (1967) "Values and Collective Decision Making," in E. S. Phelps, ed. (1973) *Economic Justice.* Baltimore, MD: Penguin Education, pp. 117-136; Buchanan, James M. and Tullock, Gordon (1962), *The Calculus of Consent.* Ann Arbor, MI: University of Michigan Press; Hirschman, Albert O. (1970) *Exit, Voice and Loyalty.* Cambridge, MA: Harvard University Press; and Little, I.M.D. (1952) "Social Choice and Individual Values," *Journal of Political Economy,* 60, pp. 422-432.
20 Madison, James (ca 1788) *The Federalist: No. 10,* in *Great Books of the Western World.* Chicago: Encyclopaedia Britannica, 1952, p. 50.
21 Lewis, Ben W. (1938) "The 'Consumer' and 'Public' Interests under Public Regulation," *Journal of Political Economy,* 46 (February), pp. 97-107.
22 See Tse, David K. C. (1984) "A Model of Consumer Post-Choice Processes." Berkeley: School of Business Administration, University of California, unpublished doctoral dissertation, for a current review of this area.
23 Koopman, Joop (1986) "New Developments in Government Consumer Policy: A Challenge for Consumer Organizations," *Journal of Consumer Policy,* 9, pp. 271-272.
24 Blomquist, Ake, Wonnacott, Paul, and Wonnacott, Ronald (1983) *Economics: First Canadian Edition.* Toronto: McGraw-Hill Ryerson, p. 488.

25 Olson, Mancur (1971) *The Logic of Collective Action.* Cambridge, MA: Harvard University Press.

26 Alford, Robert R., and Friedland, Roger (1975) "Political Participation and Public Policy," *Annual Review of Sociology,* pp. 429-479; Lowi, Theodore J. (1969) *The End of Liberalism.* New York: W.W. Norton and Co. Inc.

27 Burstein, Paul (1981) "The Sociology of Democratic Politics." *Annual Review of Sociology,* 7, pp. 291-319.

28 Mazis, Michael B. et al. (1981) "A Framework for Evaluating Consumer Information Regulation," *Journal of Marketing,* 45:1 (Winter), pp. 11-21.

29 Office of Fair Trading (1982) *Micro-electronics and Retailing.* London: Office of Fair Trading (Sept.).

30 Mayer, Robert N. (1986) *Videotex in France: The Other French Revolution.* Salt Lake City, UT: University of Utah, Family and Consumer Studies (September).

31 Hunter, Mark (1985) "The Smart Card Earns Its Credentials in a French City," *International Herald Tribune,* Electronic Banking: A Special Report, June 11, p. 9.

32 Howlett, Karen (1985) "B of M joins teller network," *Globe and Mail,* Oct. 17, p. B6.

33 Humes, Kathryn H. (1980) "EFT and the Consumer: An Agenda for Research," in Kent W. Colton and Kenneth L. Kraemer eds., *Computers and Banking.* New York: Plenum Press, pp. 55-65; Lambie, J. (1979) *Electronic Funds Transfer Systems in Canada.* Ottawa: Consumer and Corporate Affairs Canada; Morrison, James F. and Wagstaff, Stanley W. (1984) "The Videotex Dimension of Marketing." Burnaby, BC: Department of Business Administration, Simon Fraser University, unpublished MBA Research project (March); and Rose, P. S., and Bassoul, H. G. (1978) "EFTS: problems and prospects," *The Canadian Banker and ICU Review,* 85:3 (May-June), pp. 24-28.

34 Morrison and Wagstaff 1984.

35 Rose, P. S. and Bassoul, H. G. (1978) "EFTS: problems and prospects," *The Canadian Banker and ICU Review,* 85:3 (May-June), p. 26.

36 Examples of governments investigating the consumer interest in EFTS include Lambie 1979 and Office of Fair Trading 1982.

37 Humes 1980, p. 63.

38 Olson 1971; Terry M. Moe (1980) *The Organization of Interests.* Chicago: University of Chicago Press; J. D. Forbes (1985), "Organizational and Political Dimensions of Consumer Pressure Groups," *Journal of Consumer Policy,* 8, pp. 105-131.

39 Mitchell, George W. (1980) "Problems and Policies in Making EFT Available to the Public," in Kent W. Colton and Kenneth L. Kraemer, eds., *Computers and Banking.* New York: Plenum Press, pp. 141-146; National Commission on Electronic Fund Transfers (1977) *EFT and the Public Interest.* Washington, DC: U.S. Government Printing Office; Rose and Bassoul 1978; Office of Fair Trading 1982; Lambie 1979.

40 Nadel, Mark V. (1971) *The Politics of Consumer Protection.* Indianapolis: The Bobbs-Merrill Company, Inc., p. 235.

41 Loyns, R. M. A., and Pursaga, Alex J. W. (1973) *Economic Dimensions of the Consumer Interest.* Winnipeg:

Department of Agricultural Economics, University of Manitoba, p. 5.
42 Nadel 1971, p. 235.
43 Olson 1971; Moe 1980; and Forbes 1985.
44 Murray, Edward J. (1968) "Conflict: Psychological Aspects." in David L. Sills, ed., *International Encyclopaedia of Social Sciences*. New York: The Macmillan Company and The Free Press, p. 220.
45 North, Robert C. (1973) "Conflict: Political Aspects." *International Encyclopaedia of Social Sciences*. New York: The Macmillan Company and The Free Press, p. 226.
46 Fulop, Christina (1968) *Consumers in the Market*. London: Institute of Economic Affairs, pp. 11-12.
47 Dole, Robert (1975) "Hearings before the Committee on Government Operations." Washington, DC: United States Senate, Ninety-Fourth Congress on S.200, U.S. Government Printing Office, p. 251.

2. CONSUMERISM AND CONSUMERISTS

Irate consumers, demanding that something be done to force the butcher, the baker, or the manufacturer of a product to give fair value, are not a new phenomenon. This chapter traces how the dimensions of the meaning of the consumer interest evolved with the growth of the consumerism movement. As the movement grew and became vocal, helped by some famous muck-raking journalistic investigators and consumer advocates, and as failures of the market system to serve the consumer were documented and used by consumer activists to spur both government and business to action, consumers were better able to articulate their views of the consumer interest.

The first section of the chapter presents a series of statements, some by activists and others by academics studying consumerism, about failures of the marketing system to provide for consumers. These statements serve as background to pressures which were behind the evolution of the consumerism movement. Consumerism is defined in the next section of the chapter. The final portion of the chapter is devoted to an analysis and discussion of how consumer activists and researchers have defined the consumer interest.

THE EVOLUTION OF CONSUMERISM

The litany of most business people, many politicians and government officials and many economists is that the invisible hand of competition works so that consumers are optimally served if the marketplace is allowed to operate unrestricted. Yet the happenings in the marketplace belie the conclusion that the guiding hand of competition is all that is needed to adequately serve consumers' interests. Many consumers believe that firms are guided more by avaricious, rapacious, and exploitative self-interest than by consumer interest.[1] The reality is somewhere between these two polar positions. The material which follows is selected as representative of statements more to the end of the spectrum favouring consumers because it is obviously from these situations, where the system was believed to be deficient, that impetus for consumer action originated.

Kallet and Schlink, the authors of *100,000,000 Guinea Pigs* criticized the system as early as 1933. "Using the feeble and ineffective pure food and drug laws as a smoke-screen, the food and drug industries have been systematically bombarding us with falsehoods about purity, healthfulness, and safety of their products, while they have been making profits by experimenting on us with poisons, irritants, harmful chemical preservatives, and dangerous drugs."[2] Another author, referring to Kallat and Schlink, said, "[t]oday, nearly forty years later, the situation is worse, not better. Every new advance seems to have brought with it a more than equal share of danger. New hazards are more subtle, more sophisticated, more deadly than those of the less regulated days of the early thirties ... It is [the thirties] all over again - multiplied by logarithms."[3]

Ralph Nader, referring to the 1970 Hearings of the U.S. National Commission on Product Safety, wrote,

The Commission estimates that manufacture of hazardous products costs our society over $5.5 billion each year. Each year as a result of incidents connected with household products, 20 million Americans are injured seriously enough to require medical treatment or be disabled for a day or more. This includes 585,000 hospitalized, 110,000 permanently disabled, and 30,000 who are killed.[4]

Consumers in Europe face similar problems. But they also have problems which were endemic in North America until several years ago when the airline industry was deregulated.

Europe has a sophisticated air transport market oriented mainly to the interests of airline staffs and ill adapted to the needs of users. [F]ares [are high] and [the system] discriminates between (sic) passengers. Where lower fares are available ..... choice is severely limited [by restrictions on lower fare users]. A market dominated by State owned airlines ..... where [the] airlines and their governments protect themselves from competition by a "cartel" which limits capacity and fixes fares in relation to the least efficient airlines ..... without regard to the efficiency of ..... management [or] the interests of the users of air transport or the general population.[5]

These first five statements overstate the case if taken literally. However, there are large components of truth in each of them. Furthermore, they illustrate the types of problems which frustrate consumers and cause them to question the way the system operates. These doubts that unfettered and unregulated markets always serve consumers most likely can be traced back to a comment about the motives of business persons by Thorstein Veblen, the famous economic and social philosopher, to the effect that "[the] businessman's place in the economy of nature is to make money, not to produce goods. The production of goods is a mechanical process, incidental to the making of money; whereas the making of money is a pecuniary operation, carried on by bargain and sale, not by mechanical appliances and powers."[6]

Failure of competition, proliferation of products, and impersonal buying are mentioned as other causes of consumer dissatisfaction.

Since the productive process was so prolific, goods poured into the marketplace in a torrent in which the most competitive aspects of marketing were spawned. However, out of the by-ways of competition also crept fraud, deception, shoddy goods, shabby practices. Deceit, usury, and guile were not new in the world ..... there was a bonanza of all the things we had done without:

tires, flatirons, refrigerators, etc. Moreover, there was a great burst of goods we'd never seen before: detergents, nylons, TVs, plastics and frozen foods.[7]

A report prepared for the Organisation for Economic Cooperation and Development (OECD) mentions the growth of mass production, acceleration of technical progress, the increase in purchasing power, and the widening of markets as four important reasons creating difficulties for consumers in decision making. The report states that,

While these developments have brought benefits to the consumer, he has in the process been confronted by a vastly greater range of goods, more complex and designed to meet a great variety of specific uses, produced in anticipation of demand rather than in response to it, promoted by more vigorous and sophisticated selling techniques, and bringing into play a more elaborate range of services. In such conditions it has become increasingly difficult for the consumer to identify dangers which may arise from the goods on offer, to recognize deceptive practices before they have induced him to buy, to choose the goods most suited to his particular needs, and to ensure that his wishes are adequately conveyed to and reflected by the supplier.[8]

Another important factor contributing to the dissatisfaction of the consumer is the expectation of perfection from technology. "..... society has been thoroughly conditioned to expect perfection from its technology. Moon landings, miracle drugs, organ transplantations, and jet transportation make the housewife wonder why zipper manufacturers cannot make one that will not jam."[9] Another writer called it, "..... a revolt of rising expectancy ..... the public is staging a revolt arising from frustration. Customers today expect products to perform satisfactorily, to provide dependable functional performance and to be safe. This threshold of acceptable performance is steadily rising."[10]

Some businessmen think that consumerism is an invention of politicians. However, a well known commentator on American business thinks otherwise.

A good many of my friends in business have been telling me over the years that consumerism is an invention of the politicians, and that there is no support for it in the marketplace. And I am willing to believe that up to a point. But I've been around long enough to know that politicians don't flog dead horses - they can't afford to. They are in a much more competitive business than we are, and if there is no support for something they go elsewhere very fast.[11]

Another train of thought is that the modern complexities of products and services reduces the consumer's ability to make intelligent decisions.

The consumer's dilemma is that he wants goods. He needs goods. But the fact is that technology is spawning such a torrent of new and improved goods, marketing is creating such complicated packages and deals, and advertising is so misleading, uninformative, and so riddled with half-truths, that it is difficult for the consumer to choose wisely and to be an effective decision maker.[12]

The statements of the authors just cited have some substance in fact. More important is the fact that consumers believed that the problems occurred with sufficient frequency and were of sufficient importance to require action. The evolution of the consumer movement and consumerism are due, at least in part, to those problems as summarized in Table 2-1.

DEFINING CONSUMERISM

Consumerism means many things to many people. Vance Packard used the word to mean "voracious,

Table 2-1 Factors Leading to Consumer Activism

---

1. Complex, difficult to assess products and services.
2. Deceptive marketing practices.
3. Deteriorating balance of power vis-a-vis sellers in the buying situation.
4. Increasing remoteness of consumers from manufacturers through lengthened channels of distribution.
5. Proliferation of product/services.
6. New technologies increasing chances of long-run dangers to safety and health.
7. Rising levels of unsatisfied expectations.
8. Fear that advances in communications technology allow greater seller influence over consumer purchases.
9. Higher standards of living resulting in more choices in a given time period.

---

wasteful, compulsive," consuming.[13] An analysis of the various researchers' definitions of consumerism uncovered eighteen articles on the subject and about ten varying definitions. Those definitions contain many of the ideas incorporated into the definition I have chosen to use, which is based on the analysis of consumer groups contained in this chapter and in the chapters on law and on the political process which follow.

Consumerism was defined previously as the *organized reaction of individuals to inadequacies, perceived or real, of marketers, the marketplace, market mechanisms, government services, government, and consumer policy.*

While this definition may strike some readers as overly "negative" in character, it is assumed that if each individual in society were content with his or her consumer role and rights, no reason would exist for consumer interest groups nor for consumerism to have developed. Citizens would have saved their energies for other purposes. The operative words in the definition are "organized reaction," which is the subject of Chapter 7.

THE CONSUMERISTS' DEFINITIONS

This next portion of the Chapter presents five of the best articulated statements of the consumer interest we were able to uncover in our research. The statements are interesting, not only in their own right, but because they appear to have been the objectives which have guided in some degree governments and consumer groups in their consumer policy activities. Both the Kennedy and the OECD statements fall into this category. Many consumer groups have used these statements, especially the Kennedy one, both in Europe and North America as statements of their policy objectives.

The first reasonably complete statement of consumers' interests appeared in a 1939 issue of the *Harvard Business Review*. The article reflects the business community's patronizing tolerance of the consumer in those years, but also recognized responsibilities that business firms and associations owed to its customers and the difficulties inherent in the buying process. Recognizing no simple solution, it concluded as follows,

> ..... consumers will gain from (1) cooperation with existing business channels, (2) securing unbiased useful facts on the kind or quality of things they buy, (3) securing facts behind the price they pay, (4) continuous study of consumer buying problems, and (5) support of efforts (government and business) which aid the consumer to buy quality goods at reasonable prices.[14]

The second and probably most widely cited statement of the consumer interest is President Kennedy's Special Message on protecting consumer interests sent to the Congress on March 15, 1962. In this message, the first ever delivered by a President on this topic, he took note of the important role played by consumers in the American economy and the challenging problems that confronted them. While addressed to an American audience, this statement is applicable to consumers everywhere and has been used as a statement of rights by consumer advocates in many countries. In the message, President Kennedy included the following as consumer interests:

1. *The right to safety* - to be protected against the marketing of goods which are hazardous to health or life.

2. *The right to be informed* - to be protected against fraudulent, deceitful or grossly misleading information, advertising, labelling or other practices, and to be given the facts needed to make an informed choice.

3. *The right to choose* - to be assured, wherever possible, access to a variety of products and services at competitive prices, and in those industries in which competition is not workable and government regulation is substituted, an assurance of satisfactory quality and service at fair prices.

4. *The right to be heard* - to be assured that consumer interests will receive full and sympathetic consideration in the formulation of Government policy, and fair and expeditious treatment in its administrative tribunals.[15]

These four rights of consumers, although broad, are useful, guiding principles. However, their major fault is that they are stated as absolutes, without concern for costs nor efficiency in their implementation. Some of these definitional deficiencies have been improved upon in other definitions.

Day and Aaker, considered the following as the major consumer interests:

1. *Protection against clear cut abuses* - which encompasses outright fraud and deceit that are a part of the "dark side of the marketplace", as well as dangers to health and safety from voluntary use of a product.

2. *Provision of adequate information* - which concerns the economic interests of the consumer. The question is whether the right to information goes

beyond the right not to be deceived. The two polar positions are the business view that the buyer should be guided by his judgement of the manufacturer's reputation and the quality of the brand, versus the view of the consumer spokesmen that information should be provided by impartial sources and reveal performance characteristics.[16]

3. Protecting consumers against themselves - "Some of the thrust behind consumerism comes from the growing acceptance of the position that paternalism is a legitimate policy. Thus, the [U.S.] National Traffic and Motor Vehicle Safety Act of 1966 is not concerned with the possibility that the buyer has an expressed but unsatisfied need for safety, and emphasizes instead that carelessness may have undesirable consequences for innocent participants. There is a strong justification for the protection of inexperienced, poorly educated, and generally disadvantaged consumers. More controversial by far is the extension of this notion to all consumers on the grounds that manipulated preferences may be disregarded when the consumer is not acting in his best interest."[17]

4. Consumers' ecological interests. - "Today, consumerism is becoming increasingly concerned with the quality of physical environment and the impact of marketing practices and technology on the ecology. It is a recognition which has finally emerged from our long standing concern with built-in obsolescence, and all the attendant problems which contribute to pollution in a "disposable society" and a "throw-away culture"."[18]

The next statement is that of the OECD Committee on Consumer Policy, which classifies consumer interests either as physical or economic. The consumer interests in the physical sense include safety and health, which are considered so important in OECD countries that "at the present time, even Member countries which do not have a general consumer protection policy do have a fairly full range of measures whose purpose is to safeguard consumers' health and safety".[19]

Table 2-2 Interests - 1985 UK Consumer Congress

Ageing and the elderly	Education - general and consumer
Maternity concerns	Political representation
Health - including patients' rights	Housing
Product/service standards	Financial matters (instruments, institutions)
Real British ale	Transportation
Poverty - ages and sexes	Relations with EEC
Co-operatives	Bicycling
Protection/use of rural England	Physically/mentally disabled
Energy	Family social services
Equal status for females	Environmental protection
Trade practices and standards	Consumer law
Civil liberties	Working women
Pedestrians	Postal services
Tenants' rights	

They identify the protection of consumers' economic interests as the protection from "fraud and deception by unscrupulous traders ..... control of aggressive sales methods, banning of deceptive or misleading sales techniques, and inaccurate or misleading advertising, and measures for controlling consumer credit."[20]

Under the auspices of the National Consumer Council, a government organization which represents consumer interests in legislation development, implementation and enforcement in the United Kingdom, an annual Consumer Congress is held to discuss its member organizations' concerns. The list of the major concerns and aims of the member organizations shown in Table 2-2 illustrates, in a very pragmatic way, what actual participants in British consumer policy believe falls within the realm of the consumer interest.

THE CONSUMER INTEREST - A SYNTHESIS

The statements presented above provide the background to a synthesis of how consumerists and researchers have defined the consumer interest. They are discussed under the headings of safety and health, information, environmental and voice and redress. It should be pointed out here that a good deal of theoretical support from a number of academic fields of study, presented in chapters to follow, provide a basis for the concerns presented in this section.

1. Consumers' Safety and Health Interests

Ensuring consumers can obtain products and services that are safe and not injurious to their health is an obvious and long standing goal of consumerists. However, there are questions relating to how much safety and the imposition of safety and health standards which should be discussed here.

One concern is how much should consumers be protected from themselves. The question which must be asked in such situations is how much consumer policy should concern itself with legislating against activities such that, except for the probability of serious personal injury, involve the invasion of individual liberty. The answer is as much ideological as any other thing and decided only in the political context and jurisdiction in which it is faced.

The question of where to draw a line when safety is involved is difficult to answer. Numerous examples of free choice and safety, such as wearing of safety belts by motorists and motorcycle helmets by motorcyclists, can used as examples. When Ford Motor Company tried to sell safety belts as optional automobile equipment in the 1950s, buyers did not respond. Many who had them in their cars did not use them. A similar debate continues today regarding the mandatory requirement to install protective air bags in automobiles. In those jurisdictions where safety legislation is mandatory, especially where there is universal medical care, one argument in support of the use of mandatory auto safety devices is that since the general population has agreed to underwrite medical care, there is a concomitant responsibility of individuals to protect themselves and others from injury. Protection from injury is felt to be a minimal and necessary infringement on individual freedom to this end. However, everyone does not agree with this concept.

In reply to some of these concerns, it can be said that safety and health hazards are not individual problems. It is society which ultimately bears the cost of lost-working days, medicare, police and court time, insurance costs, and unemployment and welfare payments.[21] The question, of course, is one of who assumes risks and the political acceptability of controls. In the final analysis, whether or not such types of prohibitions are instituted rest on their political acceptability and on the degree to which the governed accept the restrictions on their freedom.

2. *Consumers' Interest and Information*

There are at least two aspects of information which consumerists and researchers have identified as important: the aspect of the consuming family unit and its decision making ability as pitted against the expertise of sellers; and characteristics of information itself, its availability, distortion and similar concerns.

In 1912, Wesley C. Mitchell wrote a classic piece on the difficulties which housewives face, buying a myriad of products which allowed little specialization in developing purchasing expertise. He contrasted this with the specialized nature of businesses who concentrate their efforts in the production of a narrow range of products or services.[22] Holton expressed it this way, "..... specialized professional seller meets the amateur part-time buyer in the market place ..... [such that] the consumer is disadvantaged."[23] This concept of consumer buying units pitted against business lies behind the value which some consumers place in the objective buying advice and expertise provided in consumer testing magazines, about which more is said later at several places in this book.

The second aspect of information is that consumers are interested in being able to evaluate the suitability of products and services so that they may most efficiently and effectively consume a chosen lifestyle. This may mean optimising the consumption of goods and services, or it may mean living in a frugal, non-materialistic manner and optimising savings. That decision is generally left to the individual. While several of the persons quoted previously referred to this as 'economic interest', on reflection what is really being said is that consumers should be able to individually evaluate how they wish to allocate their consuming power (wealth and income in economic terms, but the concepts here are more than economic). The concern is that information and the ability to analyze such information is necessary to make informed choice. Consumers believe that there is a basic right in this area.

As shall be shown in Chapter 4, information theory and the theory of consumer buying behaviour confirm the pivotal role of information in helping consumers effectively exercise their rights in the marketplace. The consumerists' cited in this Chapter did not need the theory tell them this.

3. *Consumers' Environmental Interests*

Consumers are showing increasing interest in their total environment. The term is used here to mean the use of both their physical and mental environment. What this means to each consumer may take a variety of forms which would include the consumption of that environment in the form of agreeable, unpolluted physical space, both chemically and visually -- no noxious chemicals nor unsightly billboards -- to freedom from noise pollution, mental anguish and fear of such things as nuclear war and similar types of catastrophic events that can be controlled by man. To some readers, such a definition will be overly broad. However, in the consumerist literature this concern for the environment is widespread. One must leave each reader to define the scope of this interest as each sees fit.

In one survey, eighty-five percent of the respondents from the general public considered pollution to be America's number one problem, and three out of four thought it industry's responsibility to clean up the environment. The feelings about ecology are growing to the extent that a California banker has suggested that top executives of companies that pollute the environment be sent to jail for up to five years.[24]

Air, water, and noise pollution have become an important part of consumer interests. More recently, consumerism has become identified with the widespread concern with the quality of the physical environment. The problem of air, water, and noise pollution have become increasingly salient as the tolerance of the public for these abuses has decreased.[25]

An economist who was one of the earlier environmentalists stated that "..... we are discovering ecology -- that the rivers are not infinite sources of clear water, that the ocean itself is not an infinite receptacle for our garbage, and that the air is exhaustible too."[26]

The Club of Rome, a group of concerned scientists from around the world, published a polemic highlighting the effects of pollution and the unrestrained use of natural resources on the world and on the quality of life. A later *Global 2000* report to the President of the United States was a similarly overstated treatise on the hazards of ecological mismanagement, which, if nothing else, shows that the concerns of the 1970s are still with us today.[27] No knowledgeable person believes that man can be profligate in the exploitation of the environment and its pollution without significant negative consequences on consumption and the quality of life.[28] However, one must exercise caution in stating precisely the reality and common sense dimensions of the problem.

Consumers themselves are a big source of pollution. The role of personal consumption in the deterioration of our environment is of growing

concern.[29] Indeed, Holsworth shows that a good deal
of consumer rhetoric about environmentalism is
inconsistent unless consumers wish to change their
lifestyles, because environmentalism means changes in
consumption habits and a reduction in consumption.[30]
Such logical inconsistencies serve to point out the
difficulties in even defining the interrelationships of
complex modern consumption choices.

4. Consumers' Right to Voice Concerns and to Redress

The evidence of misuse of market power presented
above, is cited as an indication of the difficulties of
consumers in exercising their rights in the
marketplace. A second aspect of this right is for
consumers to have access to the political process and
to legislators and civil servants who design, modify
and implement consumer policy. Consumers are denied
their rights if they are not able to participate in the
political process to represent their interests as
consumers. Chapter 7 is devoted to this topic. Some
of the seminal work in this area include Nadel's *The
Politics of Consumer Protection*, Lucy Black Creighton's
Pretenders to the Throne, Michael Pertschuk's *Revolt
Against Regulation*, Laura Nader's *No Access to Law*,
When Consumers Complain, by Arthur Best, and Reich
and Micklitz's *Consumer Legislation in the EC
Countries*.[31]

SUMMARY AND CONCLUSIONS

A working definition of consumer rights which evolved
in this chapter included consumers' right to safety and
health, to information and its effective use, to voice
concerns on matters affecting their ecologically fragile
environment, and to be able to voice their concerns to
government and business on a wide range of
consumer concerns. The interest of consumers in
consumption of the environment adds a dimension to
the consumer interest which is difficult to delimit.

NOTES

1 Markin, Rom J. (1971) "Consumerism: Militant Consumer Behavior - A Social and Behavioral Analysis." *Business and Society*, 1:1 (Fall), p. 61.
2 Kallet, Arthur, and Schlink, F. J. (1933) *100,000,000 Guinea Pigs*. New York: Grosset and Dunlop, p. 4.
3 John G. Fuller (1972) *200,000,000 Guinea Pigs*. New York: G. P. Putnam's Sons, p. 10.
4 Nader, Ralph (1971) *Beware*. New York: Law Arts Publishers Inc., p. 7.
5 BEUC (1985) *Report on Air Fares*. Brussels: Bureau Europeen des Unions de Consommateurs, July 11, pp. 1-2.
6 Veblen, Thorstein (1920) *The Vested Interests and the Common Man*. New York: B. W. Huebsch, Inc., p. 92.
7 Prior, Faith (1971) "Today's Consumer Movement." in Loys L. Mather, ed., *Economics of Consumer Protection*. Danville, IL: The Interstate Press, p. 2-3.
8 OECD Committee on Consumer Policy (1972) *Consumer Policy in Member Countries*. Paris, p. 5.
9 Buskirk, Richard H., and Rothe, James T. (1970) "Consumerism - An Interpretation," *Journal of Marketing*, 34 (October), p. 63.
10 Wells, Robert C., quoted in James Bishop and Henry W. Hubbard (1969) *Let the Seller Beware*. Washington, DC: The National Press, p. 14.
11 Drucker, Peter F. (1969) "The Shame of Marketing," *Printers' Ink*, 299:8 (Aug.), pp. 60-61.
12 Markin 1971, p. 7.
13 Packard 1960, p. 25.
14 Dameron, Kenneth (1939) "The Consumer Movement," *Harvard Business Review*, 18:3 (Jan.), pp. 271-289, as reprinted in Ralph M. Gaedeke and Warren W. Etcheson, eds. (1972) *Consumerism: Viewpoints from Business, Government, and the Public Interest*. San Francisco: Canfield Press, p. 78.
15 Executive Office of the President (1963) *Consumer Advisory Council, First Report*. Washington, DC: U.S. Government Printing Office, pp. 5-8.
16 Bauer, Raymond A., and Greyser, Stephen A. (1968) *Advertising in America: The Consumer View*. Boston: Graduate School of Business Administration, Harvard, p. 345, as cited in George S. Day and David A. Aaker (1970) "A Guide to Consumerism," *Journal of Marketing*, 34:3 (July), p. 15.
17 Day and Aaker 1970, pp. 13-14.
18 Day and Aaker 1970, p. 14.
19 OECD (1972) *Consumer Policy in Member Countries*. Paris, p. 6.
20 OECD 1972, p. 7.
21 Furuhashi, Y. Hugh, and McCarthy, E. Jerome (1971) *Social Issues of Marketing in the American Economy*. Columbus, OH: Grid, Inc., pp. 28-37.
22 Mitchell, Wesley C. (1912) *American Economic Review*, 2 (June), pp. 269-281, as reprinted in Gaedeke and Etcheson 1972.
23 Holton, Richard H. (1967) "Government-Consumer Interest: Conflicts and Prospects," *Changing Marketing Systems*. Chicago:

American Marketing Association, Winter Conference Proceedings, pp. 15-17, as reprinted in Gaedeke and Etcheson 1972, p. 234.

24 Rockefeller, David (1971) "Environment: Beyond the Easy Answers," *Wall Street Journal*, (July 7), p. 10; *Wall Street Journal* (1971) "Leaders of Firms Who Pollute to Prison," (April 19), p. 23.

25 Day and Aaker 1970, pp. 13-14.

26 Lerner, Abba P. (1972) "The Economics and Politics of Consumer Sovereignty," *American Economic Review*, 62 (May), p. 265.

27 *Global 2000 Report to the President.* (1980) Vols. I, II, III. Washington, DC: U.S. Government Printing Office.

28 Simon, Julian L., and Kahn, Herman (1984) *The Resourceful Earth.* Oxford: Basil Blackwell.

29 Kinnear, Thomas C., Taylor, James R., and Ahmed, Sadruddin A. (1974) "Ecologically Concerned Consumers: Who Are They?" *Journal of Marketing*, 38 (April), p. 20.

30 Holsworth, Robert D. (1980) *Public Interest Liberalism and the Crisis of Affluence.* Boston: G. K. Hall & Co., p. 69.

31 Nadel 1971, Chap. 7; Creighton, Lucy Black (1976) *Pretenders to the Throne: The Consumer Movement in the United States.* Lexington, MA: D. C. Heath and Co.; Pertschuk 1982; Nader, Laura (1980) New York: Academic Press, Inc.; Best, Arthur (1981) New York: Columbia University Press; Reich, Norbert, and Micklitz, H. W. (1980) Berkshire, UK: Van Nostrand Reinhold Company, Ltd.

3. BUSINESS AND CONSUMERISM

Sir John Methven, late Director-General of the Confederation of British Industry, said in the foreword to a book on *Marketing and the Consumer Movement* that

> I have never believed there to be any real conflict of interests between suppliers and consumers. This was the view I took as a manager in industry and as the first Director-General of the Office of Fair Trading and it is a view which I hold just as firmly today as Director-General of the CBI.[1]

There is no doubt that suppliers and consumers have many mutual interests. However, because they are involved in exchange relationships, exchanging things of value which each desires, if both parties are not completely satisfied, and if one party tends to have greater power in a transaction than the other, then there is ready made potential for conflict. Sir John Methven, after serving both the Office of Fair Trading, an organization set up to develop and enforce policy between buyers and sellers in the marketplace, and the Council of British Industries, the largest and most powerful business trade association, should have understood that the potential for conflict always exists in such situations.

One of the major goals of the consumerism movement has been to change the power relationship between buyers and sellers. While there are no doubt situations where both parties, business and consumers, may profit from such types of improvements in power relationships in market transactions, there are obviously many areas where if one loses power the other gains it. Because this is the reality of environment within which business and consumers operate, and because business is the second party to consumer exchanges in marketplaces, it would be remiss if we did not evaluate the attitudes and activities of the business community in response to consumers and the consumerism movement.

BUSINESS PEOPLE ARE CONSUMERS TOO

We all have a multiplicity of roles. The vice-president of a large corporation is also a consumer. One's perception of problems in any area of endeavour, including that of being a consumer, changes with the role which is being played at a given time. Therefore, it is not enough to say we are all consumers. We are consumers in one role, but most of us are also producers in another.

There are a bundle of attitudes which each of us carry in our myriad roles. For example, since senior managers tend to be in upper social classes compared to blue collar workers, differences in attitudes and associations related to social class would be expected and, indeed, have been evidenced in studies of social class.[2]

There are also differences in attitudes about consumers and consumerism, and many other things in life, depending upon the industry with which one is associated. When one speaks with a person who sells automobiles, their perception of consumers and consumer decision making with regards to automobiles is different from that of the general population. Similarly, people in the clothing industry seem to view buyers of clothing differently from the general population, and so forth. Furthermore, there are a number of cultural differences which may affect one's attitudes about business and consumers. The seriousness with which Swiss businessmen view the world of business, as evidenced for example in the serious legal penalty for violating business secrecy in the Swiss banking industry, is well known. These attitudes are bound to carry over into people's attitudes about their role as consumers and the relationship of that role to business.

This chapter contains people's statements about consumers and consumerism from their position as business people, recognizing the natural conflict which may occur in that relationship. It is interesting to note that, in collecting data for this chapter, most of the statements in the United States press arose in relationship to a concerted business effort to defeat the passage of a bill which would have established a Consumer Protection Agency in the United States. Following the defeat of that bill, the number of articles appearing in the press about consumer groups and their interests fell almost to zero. This points out that many of the statements relevant to the business-consumer dichotomy are made when a conflict situation is occurring, and it is these situations that tend to highlight differences.

Yet, once removed from their specific business role, it has been my experience that the attitudes of business people tend to revert to that of consumers everywhere. Furthermore, it has frequently been the business person, with the experience and knowledge of how consumers have been exploited, who has pointed out many of the flaws in the system.

STATEMENTS ABOUT CONSUMERS AND CONSUMERISM

Statements about consumers, consumerism and consumer activists have been classified under six different headings in order to impose some structure and order to the wide-ranging comments on this complex phenomenon. The attitudes expressed by business people run the gamut from recognizing that there are legitimate concerns which are brought to light through consumerist activities to those that believe that consumer activism is stifling and subverting "representative democracy".

Legitimate Consumer Concerns

Recent statements by business people about consumers and consumerism recognize some legitimate complaints come from consumer advocacy efforts.

Most corporate consumer affairs specialists acknowledge that business would seldom have moved as fast -- or as far -- in improving their products. Several of the consumer affairs executives say that consumerism can produce significant dividends for the company that "works with instead of against it." (Consumer affairs specialists surveyed agreed with this position by more than the 220 to 1.) The corporate specialists credit the advocates for helping in three prime areas. 1. Promoting improvements and products and service quality. 2. Helping to sensitize managements to the importance of consumer concerns. 3. Delineating the positions of consumers on various product, service, and economic issues.

"As hard as we try to market perfect products", says Nell W. Stewart, director of consumer relations at Texize, "we cannot always determine all the possible effects of them in day to day use..... Consumer advocates don't solve complaints", points out R.H. Janssen, director of consumer affairs for Culligan USA, "but they do force companies to take measures to solve individual problems."

While believing that advocates are occasionally "out-of-step" with the consumers' interests, Coca-Cola vice-president Dianne McKaig points out that "they are sometimes in the forefront of identifying issues ..... [and] it is useful to listen -- and sometime to act -- on such subjects as a more comprehensive response to the consumer's right to know."[3] Peter Bunt, Head of the Environmental Affairs Department at Metal Box Ltd., a UK-headquartered multinational that makes containers and packaging says that there ..... is a "dissatisfaction" with the affluent society. "A lot of people don't like modern society," he says. "They have found that affluence has not brought fulfillment ..... Perhaps we have failed to explain the virtues of packaging ..... Many of the industrial relations problems today are caused by the poor management of them in the past ..... We now have a chance to do better with industry's relations with society."[4]

Do Consumer Activists Have a Constituency?

A consistent and recurring attitude expressed by business people is that consumer activists do not represent the average consumer. Ralph Winter, writing for the American Enterprise Institute for Public Policy Research, called the consumer advocate, "the self-appointed vigilante of the economic system."[5] David Vogel, a teacher of political science at the School of Business at the University of California at Berkeley and author of a book on lobbying by citizens groups for changes in business ethics, said in a summary of his findings that, "Most citizen challenges do not represent a clear constituency; it is difficult for executives to judge how seriously to take them."[6]

Irwin Stelzer, President of the National Economic Research Associates, presented a paper to a seminar sponsored and attended by members of power utilities in the United States with similar beliefs.

In the early days of the consumer movement, participation took of the form of appearances by real live consumers at rate and siting hearings, people telling about the effect on them of rate increases or of the location of plants close to their homes. Gradually, however, the consumer intervenor movement became institutionalized. In New York, for example, the grey-haired little old lady has been replaced by the state attorney general and his econometricians, supplemented by the Consumer Protection Board and whoever will testify to some of its positions.

Consumers serving on these [utility-appointed consumer councils] do not "represent" anyone, and may be as terribly out of touch with other consumers as utility executives fear themselves to be.

..... less willing to rely on representative democracy, consumers want to participate (intervene) directly in rate setting and other cases, rather than be represented by commission staffs.[7]

This questioning of the constituency of an advocate or pressure group is not unique to business people. Having observed and participated in interventions, normally on the consumer side, I have seen both business people and politicians continually require what is called in political science "legitimation" or confirmation of the constituency which a group purports to represent.

Consumerists are Negativists

The main thrust of this attitude is that balance is needed in looking at consumer problems rather than focussing on the negative aspects of risk which are inherent in everyday life. Ralph Winter succinctly articulated this concern.

..... the rhetoric of the consumer advocate leans towards measures which hinders the marketing of any product deemed "unsafe," with little regard to its potential benefit. Although there is considerable ambiguity as to what disposition should be made of common items like matches and knives, the consumer advocate is prone to subject new products to tests which require that safety be established before marketing, no matter what the potential benefits. The danger of a thalidomide being marketed is to him presumptively greater than the danger of a penicillin being suppressed.[8]

Bloom and Greyser cite Marc Leeson who criticizes Ralph Nader for being overly serious about problems which many people would deem minor. Leeson cites as an example Nader's efforts to organize Fight to Advance the Nation's Sports, FANS, a consumer group for sports fans.[9]

Unrealistic Norms

Another concern, again articulated by Winters, is as follows,

..... he [Nader] would outlaw the marketing of products which fail to meet particular quality standards. Stroganoff without a specified percentage of beef is not stroganoff and should not be called such. It is also a loophole in the law to permit a product which appears as salad dressing but does not meet salad dressing standards to be sold as a "whip." And he regrets that "in 1970 this gaping loophole in the law is still substantially available to manufacturers, allowing products such as Gatorade, the 'thirst quencher,' on the market. Since the law has no standards for 'thirst quenchers,' Gatorade can legally contain whatever the manufacturer chooses, although now he must list the ingredients on the label." The implication of such an approach is that the government is to draw up a list of permissible products with requirements as to the standardized structure and content. Anything not on the list cannot be legally purchased.[10]

Bloom and Greyser saw the same type of unrealistic standard behind the use of seat-belt interlocks, a device which causes an alarm in an automobile to continue to ring until a seat-belt is actually affixed to a person sitting in the seat. This requirement exists despite people feeling that the cost of the personal inconvenience was too high.

Infringing on Management Prerogatives

Vogel summarizes his research and interviews with corporate executives on citizen challenges to business by quoting from a *Fortune* Editorial in 1965 to the effect that:

..... There is no reason that management must tolerate all these obstructions to the proper conduct of company business ..... "Corporate democracy" derives from the hoary notion that the corporation is constructed on a model of a democratic political state, with the shareholders as the electorate and the board of directors, the legislature. In fact, however, a corporation is not a republic in miniature. It is a business organization in which the owners -- the shareholders -- have some clear rights. But those rights are not analogous in any important way to the rights of citizens in a democracy, and the board of directors does not really resemble a legislative body.[11]

Vogel interestingly comments on the fact that "the annual meeting may well be the only time when the corporation's chief officers interact with the public in a physical environment that is not totally planned and controlled by them. "..... it is the one time when corporate executives are a captive audience of their diverse publics; both "corporation" and "public" become, momentarily, real individuals, rather than abstractions."[12]

Ideological Conflicts

The final area, but by no means the least controversial nor smallest for potential conflict, is an attitude by some business people that consumerists and the consumer movement are attacks against the basic ideology of free market and *laissez faire* capitalism. For example,

Many top managers are deeply suspicious of the motives of consumer activists, believing that they are opposed to free enterprise and they make reckless and unjustified attacks on business. Executives and government officials believe that if *caveat emptor* (let the buyer beware) as a means of doing business is not already replaced by the concept of *caveat venditor* (the philosophy of let the seller beware), it is fast approaching such a situation.[13]

These individual statements of attitudes form the basis of a number of studies which have evaluated the attitudes of business people and at times compared them with other groups, such as consumers.

BUSINESS ATTITUDES ABOUT CONSUMERISM

The five studies discussed below provide a comparative analysis of attitudes between business and consumers. The first, by Stanley and Robinson, summarizes five different surveys, taken between 1971 and 1977, on a variety of consumerism issues. Next, Sturdivant looks at gaps and attitudes between business and social activist groups. In an international context, Ryans *et al* compare German, Swiss and U.S. marketing and advertising executives' attitudes, while Klein compares attitudes of Swedish and American consumers and business people. Finally, Dornoff and Tankersley provide an interesting commentary on areas of perceptual agreement and disagreement between consumers and business people.

In an analysis of five different surveys, Stanley and Robinson were able to glean perceptual differences among consumers and executives on five areas of mutual interest. The findings are summarized in Table 3-1.[14]

Through the use of a consumer attitude survey, which recorded the reactions of individuals to sixty-five statements about business, justice, social order and other topics, Sturdivant was able to show significant differences between social activist groups and managers. The survey, which recorded answers on a 6-point agree-disagree format, included statements such as: executives of toy producing companies should be subject to jail sentences for failure to inform parents that their products may be hazardous; a business should not hire a person if it suspects him of being a homosexual; government programs to aid the poor usually support those too lazy to work, and; many blacks would be executives of major corporations today if they had not been discriminated against in the

Table 3-1 Executives' - Consumers' Opinions on Consumer Issues

Product Quality	Consumers felt quality had been falling while executives believed it had risen.
Advertising	Both consumers and executives wanted false advertising to be forced to stop. However, executives believed it occurred less often than did consumers.
Consumer Information	Executives believed consumers had sufficient information to make adequate decisions and that government should not provide comparative product information. While 60-75 % of consumers interviewed believed that many consumer problems came from consumer carelessness, an even greater proportion felt information was inadequate.
Corporate Attitudes	While 75-80% of consumers believed competition led to fair prices they disagreed that business tried to honestly deal with complaints and felt profits came before serving consumers. Consumers saw needs for changes which executives did not.
Government Regulation	Seventy percent of consumers wanted minimum government quality standards while only 20% of executives wanted them.

SOURCE: Summarized from Stanley, J. and Robinson, Larry M. (1980) "Opinions on Consumer Issues: A Review of Recent Studies of Executives and Consumers," *Journal of Consumer Affairs*, 14:1 (Summer), pp. 207-220.

past. This management attitude survey was mailed to "organizations which had been classified by themselves or others as "committed to the resolution of social issues."" These included organizations such as the Sierra Club, the National Organization of Women, and the National Association for the Advancement of Colored People. It was sent also to a sample of business executives whose companies had been ranked on social responsibility by a previous study.[15]

It was found that, except for one crossover, all the social activist organizations' members' responses ranked more liberal on the scale than the responses of the members of business organizations. While not all the social activist groups were consumer groups, many of them were, including such groups as the

Center for Law in the Public Interest, Center for the Study of Responsive Law, Citizens Advocate Center, Consumer Federation of America, and Consumers' Research. While one is not able to infer that the consumer activist group is more or less socially active than other groups, this finding is a good indication that the activists tend to be more liberal than the business groups surveyed. One may be able to infer that there is a difference in attitudes between consumer activists and business groups from this data.[16]

Two cross cultural measures of business attitudes towards consumerism were discovered. One measured the attitudes of advertising and marketing executives in Germany, Switzerland, and the United States. The other compared Swedish and U.S. consumers and business people.

It is probably fair to draw the inference that German and Swiss marketing and advertising executives are less sympathetic to consumer groups than their U.S. counterparts. They believed consumers were less naive than did U.S. executives. Notice that in Table 3-2 both the Swiss and German responses are higher than the U.S. responses in each case, although there is some switching between high and low on the German and Swiss responses to individual questions. The European marketing and advertising executives tend to believe more strongly than their U.S. counterparts that the consuming public is not accurately represented by consumer groups.

In a matched sample of consumers in Uppsala, Sweden and Long Beach, California, Professor Klein looked at three issues: the need for consumer protection; the belief that product quality improved because of regulation; and the belief that one should be very skeptical about the truthfulness of packaging information. He found that Swedish business attitudes were more similar to the views of Swedish consumers than were the attitudes of U.S. business people to their consumer cohorts.[17] He attributed some of this difference to the fact that there is a more centralized, less fragmented, government supported consumer policy

Table 3-2 Views of German, Swiss and U.S. Marketing and Advertising Executives on Statements About Consumer Groups

	German*	Swiss*	U.S.*
1. Consumer groups accurately represent opinions of consuming public.	4.19	3.93	3.19
2. Consumer groups feel average consumer too naive to deal with many advertisements.	2.74	2.74	2.02
3. Consumers feel consumer groups have objectives other than consumers' interests.	2.48	2.70	2.25
4. Consumer groups have more credibility with government officials and legislators than business community.	2.43	2.96	2.39
5. Consumer groups favour legislation to restrict advertising content.	2.62	2.22	2.04
6. Consumer groups favour limiting amount of money firms spend on advertising.	2.76	2.65	2.50
7. Consumer groups feel advertising does not play a useful societal role.	2.57	2.61	2.27

* Mean value of responses based on a five-point scale. 1 = strongly agree; 5 = strongly disagree.

SOURCE: Ryans, John K., Jr., Samiee, Saeed, and Wills, James (1985) "Consumerist Movement and Advertising Regulation in the International Environment: Today and the Future," *European Journal of Marketing*, 19:1, p. 7.

in Sweden than in the United States and that Swedish business persons have seen that consumers fare better under the system. However, Swedish business people were less enthusiastic for their system than their U.S. counterparts. Klein attributed this to the fact that the Swedes expressed the feeling "that many business people feel stifled and/or intimidated" because of the high level of government intervention into Swedish industry.[18]

The final example of how attitudes of business persons and consumers may differ comes from an interesting piece of research conducted in Cincinnati, Ohio by Dornoff and Tankersley. They presented a series of situations involving a purchase conflict to a sample of consumers and retailers. The results showed a wide range of agreement as well as disagreement between the two groups. They are interesting from the point of view of perceptual differences.

Three situations out of a total of 14 reported by Dornoff and Tankersley were selected to show the range of agreement and disagreement which may come about. They are presented in Table 3-3. The first presents one where there was almost complete agreement between consumers and retailers. The second is one where the groups were about evenly split. In the third one, there was maximum disagreement between consumers and retailers. The study is interesting in its own right, being much richer than the three examples selected here to demonstrate the range of perceptual differences -- rather than real differences on substantive issues.

THE LOGIC OF CONSUMER-SELLER CONFLICT

Using a very creative experimental research design, Folkes and Kotsos have shown that because of the differing experiences in the buying process, there are good reasons why conflict between buyers and sellers arise. Sellers tend to see many more satisfied than dissatisfied customers, because a high proportion of products are satisfactory. Consumers who experience problems with products do not have the countervailing experience of satisfied customers to offset their negative experiences. The logical outcome is for sellers to underestimate product failure and buyers to overestimate it. Folkes and Kotsos' is the first experimental study of buyer-seller perception of satisfaction-dissatisfaction we found. Although these findings are tentative, they do tend to confirm both business and consumer experience in exchange transactions. Research of this type should continue and holds the promise of expanding our understanding of

Table 3-3 Examples of Consumer and Retailer Perception of Situations Involving Purchase Conflict

---

1. A customer calls the retailer to report that her refrigerator purchased two weeks ago is not cooling properly and that all the food has spoiled.

   Action: The retailer should repair the refrigerator at no cost.

	Agree	No Opinion	Disagree
Consumer	96	2	2
Retailer	88	9	3

2. A local retail store ran an ad in the Sunday newspaper announcing a sale on a well-known brand of high-quality men's slacks and stated that large quantities were available in a wide variety of sizes, colors, fabrics and styles. The enthusiastic response to the ad resulted in only 1/4 of the advertised merchandise being available after the second day of the sale.

   Action: The retailer continued to run the same ad each day for the entire week up to and including the following Saturday.

	Agree	No Opinion	Disagree
Consumer	36	7	57
Retailer	77	10	23

(Continued)

---

the bases of consumer-seller conflict.[19]

BUSINESS RESPONSE TO CONSUMERISM

In response to the rise of consumerism, businesses recognized the need for specialized personnel to interact with consumers and a number of other organizations and groups. These consumer specialists

Table 3-3 Continued

3. A retail grocery chain operates several stores throught the local area, including one in the city's ghetto area. Independent studies have shown that prices tend to be higher there and that there is less of a selection of products in this particular store than in its other locations.

Action: The day after the welfare cheques are received in that area of the city the store habitually raises its prices on all its merchandise.

	Agree	No Opinion	Disagree
Consumer	0	1	99
Retailer	57	20	23

SOURCE: Dornoff, Ronald J., and Tankersley, Clint B. (1975) "Perceptual Differences in Market Transactions: A Source of Consumer Frustration," *Journal of Consumer Affairs*, (Summer), pp. 97-103.

have been given titles such as manager of consumer services, corporate affairs officer, consumer affairs advisor and the like. These "consumer affairs professionals" have banded together into industry associations in the United States, Canada, the United Kingdom and an international one in the process of forming in late 1986.

The purpose of the Canadian association is

..... to foster and maintain the integrity of business in dealing with consumers; to encounter and promote effective communication and understanding between business and government and consumers; and to define and advance the consumer affairs profession.[20]

Members of The Society of Consumer Affairs Professionals do their jobs by becoming knowledgeable about consumers, their groups, government organizations involved with consumers, interacting with these groups, advising their employers on reactions and courses of action to take, both *vis-a-vis* consumers as well as governments, lobbying for new legislation or for changes to existing laws which best serve their clients but which also, if possible, serve consumer interests, and promote and conduct eduction programs, both within the firm and to consumers and other external groups. In general, they are the consumer experts and facilitate communication between business, consumers and government on consumer affairs. The U.S. organization has over 1,400 members representing over 400 companies and the Canadian group has 157 members representing 108 firms.[21]

CONCLUSIONS

Several billion exchange transactions take place between business and consumers in the OECD countries daily, most of them to the mutual satisfaction of both parties. However, there are general differences in attitudes about consumers and their organizations among business people and among consumers and their organizations. It should not be surprising that the direction of these differences and attitudes is towards the interests of each of the parties involved.

It is not unfair to generalize the major attitudinal differences being that business people believe consumer activist and consumer groups do not reflect the attitudes of most consumers, that consumer groups are impinging upon the ideology and the prerogatives of management under present business attitudes about the function of business in society, and that consumers want more government regulation than business would like. However, there are people who believe that many of the consumer concerns are legitimate and business can respond, to the firm's benefit, to a number of legitimate concerns.

NOTES

1 Methven, John (1978) "Foreword," in Jeremy Mitchel, ed., *Marketing and the Consumer Movement*. London: McGraw-Hill

Book Co. (U.K.) Ltd., p. vii.
2 Warner, W. Lloyd. (1963) *Yankee City.* New London: Yale University Press, one volume, abridged edition.
3 McGuire, E. Patrick (1980) "Consumerism lives ..... and grows," *across the board,* (Jan.), pp. 57-62.
4 Bickerstaffe, George (1980) "A New Direction for Consumerism," *International Management,* (Oct.) pp. 35-41.
5 Winter, Ralph K. (1972) *The Consumer Advocate versus the Consumer.* Washington, DC: American Enterprise Institute for Public Policy Research, pp. 1-16, as reprinted in Aaker and Day 1978, p. 78.
6 Vogel, David (1979) "Ralph Naders all over the place: citizen vs. the corporations," *across the board,* (April), p. 30.
7 Stelzer, Irwin M. (1980) "A Policy Guide for Utility Executives: "Know When to Hold 'em' Know when to Fold 'em," *Public Utilities Fortnightly,* (Oct. 9), pp. 64-65.
8 Winter 1972, pp. 81-82.
9 Bloom, Paul N. and Greyser, Stephen A. (1981) "The Maturing of Consumerism," *Harvard Business Review,* (Nov.-Dec.), p. 112.
10 Winter 1972, p. 82.
11 Vogel 1979, p. 30.
12 Vogel 1979, pp. 30-31.
13 *across the board* (1977) "The consumer confronts the business man," (Nov.), pp. 81-83.
14 The articles Stanley and Robinson summarized included surveys by Sentry Insurance (Fall 1976 - Winter 1977); Stanley and Robinson (Summer-Fall 1976); Gazda and Gourley (1977); Barksdale and Darden (Summer 1971); and Diamond, Ward, and Faber (Nov.-Dec. 1971).
15 Moskowitz, Milton (1974) "Social Responsibility Portfolio 1973," *Business and Society Review,* (Jan. 15), p. 1; Moskowitz (1975), "Profiles in Corporate Responsibilities," *Business and Society,* (Spring), pp. 28-42; and Moskowitz (1974) "46 Socially Responsible Corporations," *Business and Society Review,* (July 2), p. 8.
16 Sturdivant, Frederick D. (1979) "Executives and Activists: Test of Stakeholder Management," *California Management Review,* 22:1 (Fall), pp. 53-59.
17 Klein, Gary D. (1982) "A Cross-Cultural Comparison of the Attitudes of Consumers and Business People Towards Consumerism," *Developments in Marketing Science,* 5, Greenvale, NY: C.W. Post Center, Long Island University School of Business, pp. 45-54.
18 Klein 1982, p. 48.
19 Folkes, Valerie S., and Kotsos, Barbara (1985) "Buyers' and Sellers' Explanations for Product Failure: Who Done It?" Fullerton, CA: School of Business Administration and Economics, California State University, mimeo.
20 Canadian Society of Consumer Affairs Professionals -- CSOCAP (ca 1985) "Membership List." Toronto: Box 6338, Station A, M5W 1P7.
21 Telephone conversation, SOCAP, Arlington, VA, 14 April 1986, and CSOCAP ca1985. See also, Adamson, Colin (1982) *Consumers in business: How business has responded to the consumer interest.* London: National Consumer Council.

4. EXCHANGE AND THE CONSUMER INTEREST

Although consumer interests have been broadening in scope, the major activities and concerns of consumers and consumer groups in the OECD countries still lie in the problems encountered in the exchange process. The buying advice provided by consumer groups in their publications are a major source of their operating funds. These groups perceive their testing and buying advice as critical to the success of their other activities. Consumers the world over are interested in being able to make good consumption decisions and in obtaining fair value for their money.

Concepts and theories from microeconomics, consumer behaviour and information processing are used in this chapter to illustrate the consumer interest in the exchange process.[1] The chapter is structured along the lines of the analytical framework presented in Figure 4-1. The figure illustrates the four basic elements and interrelations of the consumer interest in the exchange process. Namely, consumers must determine their needs, understand the differences in products and services which may satisfy those needs, and determine the relative value among the alternatives available, all of which must be done through the use of information.

The process and its individual elements are interrelated. As one understands the relative values of differences among alternatives, one is likely to re-evaluate one's needs. One may reconsider the purchase of a Mercedes-Benz automobile, in spite of its beauty and prestige, when a Volkswagen is one-fifth the price. However, if one wins a lottery several weeks later, the change in circumstances may mean a Mercedes is well within the budget. Few of us face this type of decision. However, every winter shoppers decide that, even though they dearly like asparagus, at ten times the price of carrots or cabbage they may wait until the price comes down in the spring time. Consumer decision making is a

Figure 4-1 Exchange and the Consumer Interest - Analytical Framework

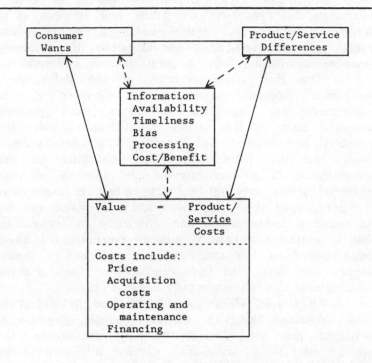

complex business, and, as we shall see, there are many aspects within that process where the consumer interest may be violated and where policy questions arise.

POLICY GOALS AND ASSUMPTIONS

Goals for policy on consumer interest in the exchange process are necessary for a focussed and relevant discussion. The consumer interest goals and assumptions, which have been expressed or implied by consumers, their groups, and by economists, are presented below. While one may take issue with parts of some of them, they provide a useful starting point for the discussion.

At the broadest level, consumers' policy goals in the exchange process may be viewed as having two components. First, consumers should be able to exchange their resources for goods and services at the lowest possible cost, within some limits of overall social policy. Second, they should obtain the maximum possible satisfaction from a given income endowment.

The first issue returns to the definition of consumer interests presented in Chapter 2, that consumers are interested in more than personal, material gain. In this sense, satisfaction includes both material and non-material benefits. Their satisfaction is based on the value that they attribute to their consumption of an environment and lifestyle of which material goods are but a part, albeit a major part. To paraphrase this, consumers attribute value not only to material consumption and efficiency in consumption but to equity and natural justice. Fairness, not having been duped in the exchange process, and a general feeling they have had fair treatment in their exchange transactions are all important considerations.

Of course, efficiency, equity, and natural justice mean different things to different people. Because the concepts are not always mutually compatible, · they imply normative tradeoffs which will vary from individual to individual. But over time, society experiences a convergence of opinion on what constitutes acceptable bounds for these goals. And as those bounds change and evolve, or if they are violated consistently, reaction may well lead to a change in policy. While it is usually at the societal or aggregate level where these elements encourage policy changes, we should not ignore them at the individual level. Rather, because individuals recognize that their satisfaction is inextricably linked to that of other individuals in society, and that more satisfaction can often be derived from foregoing material benefits to the benefit of another member of society, it is important to recognize that people consume more than economic goods. Most societies decide to forego current consumption to pay for educating children. Most OECD countries have adopted universal medical care, where the healthy forego consumption to provide care for the sick. At the family level, family members often forego personal gain in the interests of other members.

So what exactly are these elements? Efficiency is defined as obtaining the maximum economic output for a fixed amount of resources devoted to producing a good or service; that is, the greatest output from a fixed amount of resources, other things being equal. One difficulty arising from this definition of efficiency is that it assumes that policies are neutral and have not distorted the relative cost of inputs. However, take the example of capital subsidies. A government policy allows business low interest rates, fast capital investment write-offs, and similar subsidies which effectively reduce the cost of capital vis-a-vis labour. As a result, less labour is used, creating some unemployment. By the generally accepted definition this is more efficient, since one can substitute subsidized capital for more expensive labour, but in reality there may be a net social cost, since the workers may have to go on the dole and be paid for by society. There are many examples of these types of distortions in manufacturing, agricultural and other sectors of every OECD country.

Another difficulty which arises from using efficiency as a goal is that it says nothing of the distribution of either the resources or the output of the economic system among its members. Hence, another societal goal, and one with which many consumers will agree, is some idea of equity in the distribution of resources and wealth among individuals. Social welfare programs, such as unemployment insurance, old age pensions, medical care, progressive taxation and the like are means of redistributing income and are accepted policies, in greater or lesser degree, in OECD countries.

Finally, natural justice introduces the concept that members of a society -- in our case in their role as consumers -- have certain basic rights, perhaps the strongest in the exchange process being the right to basic information about things they wish to consume and the ability and right to redress when a wrong, intended or not, occurs. Such rights are not amenable to logical arguments nor to proof of being right or wrong. They are outside of the realm of economics, being part of the realm of politics, which is the subject of Chapter 7. However, we should be aware that these basic rights pervade all societies and form the basis for consumer complaints against such things as false and misleading advertising, unfair trade practices and other matters affecting the exchange process. They are rights if a majority of people in the society believe them to be so. And there are many of them which have been called social mores or rules of behaviour. That billions of transactions occur daily, with satisfaction on both sides of the exchange, is proof of their widespread acceptance. The conflict occurs at the margins or when one individual or group violates the rules. That subject will be treated in Chapter 6 on the law.

MARKET THEORY VERSUS REALITY

There is a good deal of truth in the statement that "the consumer movement has been thwarted by its dependence on classical economic theory."[2] This occurs on two fronts. First, the "good" consumer is characterized as budget-minded, rational, relentlessly pushing toward maximizing satisfaction, coldly calculating the expenditure of each penny, or centime, or pfennig, carefully searching out and weighing alternative expenditures. This is not reality. Nor is it but one of the goals of people in societies, such as those in OECD countries, which value consumption as pleasure rather than as toil. Neither is it reality in how most of us spend our money, although in many cases we are as the neo-classical economists would depict us. Second, there are assumptions about the operations of competitive markets which, while useful as analytical tools, too frequently are assumed to be reality.

If honest, competitive markets existed, with undistorted, freely available information, and if every

Table 4-1 Theory and Reality of the Exchange Environment

The Theory	Consumer Reality
1 Markets exist for all goods and services	1 Goods and services will be produced in the private sector of the economy only if they are profitable or subsidized.
2 The firm is assumed to be a price taker in perfectly competitive markets.	2 Perfectly competitive markets are rare and pricing strategy is an important decision area for the vast majority of firms.
3 No consumer or firm possesses any form of market power, therefore there is no incentive to enter into price competition.	3 In addition to (2) above, price competition, or the absence of it, coupled with market power, may result in negative consequences for buyers and sellers.
4 Buyers and sellers remain anonymous; the only information available is price and quality.	4 A great number of exchange transactions occur when buyers and sellers know each other, often over a long time. These relationships influence transactions in indeterminate ways.
5 Products are homogeneous.	5 Relatively few exchange possibilities are perceived as homogeneous by consumers. Within broad product/service categories, exchange possibilities are differentiated on the basis of physical function, price, geographic, seller and informational bases.

(Continued)

Table 4-1 continued

6	Industry is characterised by freedom of entry and exit.	6	Natural and artificial barriers hinder entry of new firms. Existing firms may have absolute cost and scale advantages. Established brand names and advertising create barriers with a corresponding reduction in competition and competitive offerings and a possible reduction in the introduction of new technology.
7	Perfect information - the market is assumed to be an integrated whole and not segmented by limitations on information acquisition and analysis capability.	7	Information is not equally available to all buyers and sellers on all characteristics of exchange items. Conversely, too much information may exist, or it may exist in a fragmented or distorted form unsuitable for optimal consumer decision making. Consumers are differentially endowed with information analyzing capabilities.
8	Instantaneous market equilibrium - markets absorb all inputs and arrive at equilibrium instantly by matching supply with demand.	8	Many markets respond slowly to changes in inputs or outputs. They are frequently out of equilibrium for long periods for reasons which include lack of information, monopolistic elements, regulatory interventions, and political considerations.
9	Transactions are costless.	9	Exchange transactions are almost never costless. They often comprise a significant proportion of the final cost of a good or service.

individual had the capacity to obtain and process limitless information and make faultless decisions, the development of policy for the consumer in the exchange process would not be an issue. However, by studying the world as abstracted in economic models, and then contrasting them to the real-world situations facing consumers, we can begin to understand and explain consumer dissatisfaction and agitation in the marketplace. Much of this dissatisfaction can be seen in the violations of the assumptions commonly used in neo-classical economics. For example, a common assumption is that one should leave the unfettered "free" market alone so that the "guiding hand" of economic forces can solve all consumers' problem. Consumers experience problems precisely because the theory frequently does not coincide with marketplace reality.

Table 4-1 lists the most common areas where theory diverges from reality. On the left side of the table are the theories and assumptions commonly applied to market processes; on the right are generalizations of the realities of many, if not most, marketplaces.

Kuhlmann demonstrated that most economic models tend to assume an "observer-oriented" approach, where the many aspects of the problem are known. This is contrasted to the "consumer-oriented" perspective, where individuals are confronted with situations in which the dimensions of the decision to be made are poorly understood and infrequently encountered, where a major task is simply collecting and organizing information about it. While this is not completely true in all exchange situations, nor does Kuhlmann suggest it is, "..... there is the danger that these models ..... may be over interpreted and used as the basis for practical measures of [consumer] policy."[3]

The task for the balance of the chapter is to determine, in general, when reality and theory coincide, when they generally differ, and how various economic and information theory models help us to analyze consumer interests. Finally, we must determine how this information may be used to formulate consumer policy in the exchange process.

CONSUMER WANTS

The first element in the analytical framework presented in Figure 4-1 is the determination of consumer wants. What does the consumer seek in the marketplace? To begin with, consumers generally have a limited budget and many wants; in effect, a consumer has some money to spend, but wants more than the money available can buy. The budget must be allocated to provide as much satisfaction as possible to the consumer within that budget constraint. Some consumers are better at this allocation process than others.

In the first stage of this rationing process, consumers appear to be able to make a rough ranking of preferred ways to spend their money. A second point is that all goods in the basket are, to an extent, substitutes. The degree of substitutability varies. For example, within the basket will be various "necessities", and there will be little substitution of necessities for other goods (e.g., milk and eggs are only limitedly substitutable for bread, as is food for leisure), although "necessities" will be substitutable, such as peas for corn, or rice for potatoes. In other categories there may be relatively wide latitude for substitutability, such as a tradeoff between home repairs and a holiday.

There are, of course, a variety of questions which this framework leaves unanswered. First, we ignore the process which leads to the definition of the basket of goods, of how consumers develop their wants. Second, and related to the first, we ignore how these wants can be changed and by whom. There are two levels on which consumer concerns in this process tend to be raised. The more commonly voiced concern has to do with the direct role of advertising on a day-to-day basis trying to influence brand purchase. A growing area of concern, however, has to do with the role that advertising plays in changing the broader cultural values and tastes of the consuming society.

Many consumers feel that business, mainly through advertising, has a major impact on values. For example, there is no question that for some consumers the make and model of automobile they own is extremely important. And there are a number of consumers and researchers who believe that this desire was developed, or at least enhanced, by years of advertising. But fashion of all types, for food, or clothing, almost anything we consume -- or do not consume in that portion of society which has been termed the "conserver society" -- may be subject to criticism as being unduly influenced by advertising. Some of the most well known commentators on social patterns and cultural values have been shown to be concerned about the effects of advertising on society.[4] The debate continues, with one side believing that advertising only reflects the values of a culture and the other believing that it has a profound effect on changing and influencing those values. That some governments believe that the influence is significant enough for some concern is documented in Chapter 6, where a discussion of regulation of advertising is proof of that concern.

We shall proceed, accepting that consumers are open to influence and that there is often a wide degree of substitutability possible within consumers' preference patterns.

PRODUCT/SERVICE COMPARISONS

A major task for consumers is to compare product and service offerings. The decision is often conducted in a noisy environment, with limited information and with conflicting points of view. To help understand the problems facing consumers and the policy implications of those problems, this section is divided into two parts. The first discusses the types of products and services which need to be evaluated, the second recognizes that consumers' perceptions of whether or not available choices are sufficiently different affects the amount of search they are willing to entertain in the decision making process.

Types of Products/Services

Some products and services are easier to evaluate than others. The simplest case is that of quality uncertainty which can be eliminated (at a cost) by inspection prior to purchase, for example, looking at fruit and vegetables or grades of lumber. These have been called "search" goods.[5] More difficult are "experience" goods, which have to be consumed before they can be completely evaluated. Buying an "experience" good involves a risk. The risk may be as small as eating a candy bar or drinking a bottle of wine. At the other extreme is the case of buying an expensive appliance or automobile. One is unsure of the quality for a long time after purchase, since longevity and low maintenance costs are a large part of the quality content of such products. Probably even more risky, except that laws have been established to protect consumers from many abuses, would be the case of services, such as insurance or fire warning devices, where lack of performance could be both financially and physically disastrous. There is no way to evaluate them before purchase, except from others' experience or from testing which, for individuals, is usually prohibitively expensive and technically not feasible.

The more heterogeneous the products or services are for the same use, the more difficult and costly is the comparison process and the lower the proportion of informed consumers in a population. As price and other cost components (discussed shortly) are brought into the comparison process, costs for consumers to be informed rise and the proportion of informed shoppers declines further.[6] Conversely, with fewer knowledgeable consumers, the greater the sellers' power and their ability to influence consumers.

The result, in many cases, is that consumers resort to rules of thumb. Some of these rules of thumb are used to help decision making in complex situations; others appear to be simplifications and a substitution of simplicity for thought. While some theoreticians may class the latter case as irrational, the fact is that it is a common occurrence. It may not be as irrational as it at first seems, especially if individuals do not value highly the buying part of consuming which entails toil.[7]

For example, a commonly held assumption is that there is a positive price-quality relationship. The vernacular, "You get what you pay for," implies that the more one pays, the more one receives in value. A number of studies have shown that there is only a weak correlation between price and quality. Using evaluations of *Consumer Reports* over a number of years, the earliest dating back to products tested between 1939 and 1949, relatively low correlations between price and tested quality were found (from -.81 to +.82 in one study and about +.25 for a number of others).[8]

Other rules of thumb include using advertising as an indication of quality. Repeat buying is also taken to indicate quality. However, firms may choose to vary quality, high at one time and low at another, which may invalidate this particular measure. As well, warranties are considered another signal of quality, since the seller assumes some of the risk of poor performance. If honored, warranties may be a useful rule of thumb.[9]

A natural tendency in a world where information is not perfect and processing costs are high is to hedge one's bets. If consumers are not sure how to compare products, they will tend to shop where they expect to encounter the lowest potential dissatisfaction (minimize the maximum loss). There is a wide latitude for sellers to create a perception of quality, which to consumers means low risk, where quality does not exist. One way to do this is by charging higher prices, by advertising more heavily and thereby convincing consumers that the higher prices and advertising mean higher value. Examples of this happen frequently and are documented in every consumer buying magazine.

Evaluating quality in its many dimensions is obviously a difficult problem. The inability to evaluate well, and the mistakes which consumers make, is a source of irritation. This does not mean that sellers are always at the root of the problems because many comparative evaluations are inherently difficult. Further, some consumers do not search as they should nor devote sufficient time to analyzing either their own needs or the data they have collected. This leads to the second part of the evaluation problem, how to know when to search and when not to expend any more effort in the process.

Search: Perception and Reality of Alternatives

Whether or not consumers engage in search and devote time and resources to decision making in the exchange process depends on whether they believe there are differences in products and services which justify the cost of search. In theory, people with high search costs will search less than those with low search costs. And those with high search costs will generally pay higher prices.[10] For example, prices in areas where higher income people live are generally higher than they are in low income areas. However, the amount of search in which people engage is still relative and highly dependent on individuals' perception of the need to evaluate alternatives and prices.

The perception-reality question may be viewed in terms of a 2 x 2 matrix, as shown by Table 4-2. It is easy to see that the least of consumers' problems will be found in Box 1, where consumers perceive products to be homogeneous and, in fact, they are. In this situation, assuming away for the time being seller-induced product differentiation, consumers are at their least risk from not searching. If we take the other extreme, Box 4, where products are heterogeneous and consumers perceive they are different, the complexity of decision making increases dramatically, especially with complex products where, even with perfect information, the processing costs to the average consumer may make informed decisions

Table 4-2 Product/Service and Consumer Perceptions

	Consumer Perception	
	homogenous	heterogeneous
homogeneous	homo/homo 1	hetero/homo 2
Reality		
heterogeneous	homo/hetero 3	hetero/hetero 4

difficult. In Boxes 2 and 3 we expect to find the greatest difficulties for consumers and the source of many consumer concerns in the exchange process. With perception and reality different, not only are consumers unlikely to reach optimal decisions, but they are also at their most vulnerable to less than honest sellers.

Using this framework, we now want to try to understand the environment in which consumers must make decisions. We begin with an ideal world where information is perfect and freely available to all consumers.

Where Perception and Reality Match

Imagine a world as in Box 1, where within a given product class all brands are homogeneous and consumers are aware of this fact. In this case the process is very straightforward. In the absence of any other differentiating factors, price becomes the overriding decision criteria. But there is still an issue for the seller. The product category may be substitutable for other products in the consumer's preference basket, for example, one may wish to substitute beef for fish. Therefore, producers of homogeneous goods may still benefit from advertising or price cutting to sell their products.

At first sight, this may appear to be an unlikely situation, but there certainly are "real-world" examples, primarily in agricultural products, where attempts are made to increase the consumption of homogeneous products. For example, cheddar cheese of a given age is a relatively homogeneous product, and a large proportion of consumers probably view it as such. In Canada, we indeed do see the National Dairy Council advertising to encourage consumption of cheese, as well as individual cheese processors advertising their own brands. The NDC is seeking to differentiate the generic product, cheese, from food alternatives. Of course, the sellers' strategy with this apparently homogeneous product is ultimately to differentiate their brand in the consumer's mind, so that brands of cheese are not perceived as homogeneous.

Moving to the other case where perceptions and realities match -- where both are heterogeneous -- we can see that even with freely available, perfect information, major problems can arise for the most astute and informed consumer. The reason is that even if information is free, the time to process that information to the point where an informed decision can be made is not. Further, in a world where products are increasingly complex, where there are many aspects or factors relevant to the decision, processing costs rise rapidly.

Consider, for example, the purchase of a personal computer, something I and many of my colleagues have done recently. This purchase represents quite nicely the problems of both deciding what one's needs really are and then matching a wide and diverse variety of products and their associated services to those needs. Personal computers may be used for a wide variety of needs ranging from playing a few computerized games, to extensive word processing, to closely substituting for the computational functions of a large, main frame computer. I have observed highly skilled teachers of business analysis grapple with the complex problem of trying to make such decisions. They agree that it takes a good deal of thought and effort to objectively evaluate their needs.

Once they believe they know what they want, they then face the task of matching those needs with the wide variety of offerings available in the marketplace. The final decision usually comes as they readjust their needs to match their budgets. The process is much like purchasing an automobile. In this regard, those who can talk with someone who has already been through the process can take advantage of the learning involved in evaluating needs and matching them to products and services (software).

Consider, from a consumer's point of view, the difficulties in the real world of simply defining the relevant criteria in a purchase decision. If a consumer has the required information available, and knows what particular product attributes are important, one is still left with a tradeoff between processing costs and the potential costs of making a bad decision. However, if the consumer does not have even enough knowledge to know what are the relevant criteria, processing costs are compounded (as in the personal computer example). Even if we assume away biased information and deceit on the side of the seller, and even if we make information freely and easily available, there will still be policy implications arising when complex personal needs and complex, heterogeneous products make decisions difficult.

Taking this a step further, with complex needs and complex products there will be benefits to individual sellers in emphasizing particular aspects of their products or services they offer to differentiate them from others on the market. Now, imagine our consumer, who may or may not know exactly what she or he should be looking for, being presented with information which emphasizes one product over another. And imagine a number of products, each of which have a number of aspects being emphasized by their sellers. Simply in the process of differentiating their products, with no ill intent, producers will emphasize different criteria. The consumer may or may not know which, if any, criteria should be important. This makes the process of evaluating alternative offerings even more difficult. The final extension of this is the potential for deceit by producers who manipulate consumers' naivete by emphasizing what are in fact meaningless qualities, while ignoring their products' deficiencies in areas that will be important to the consumer.

To this point we have outlined the problems which we might expect to arise in situations where perception and reality coincide in the market. Now consider those areas where policy implications are even stronger, and where perception and reality in the marketplace differ.

Mismatches of Perception and Reality

Recalling Table 4-2, perception and reality may be mismatched either because sellers are attempting to differentiate what are essentially homogeneous products, or because they may be trying to equate essentially heterogeneous products as homogeneous in the minds of consumers. In addition, consumers may be uninformed, ignorant or lack experience and deceive themselves. Examples of each will be given below.

The first of these, attempting to differentiate homogeneous products, is exactly what we expect to occur, given the nature of competitive market systems. A classic example of this situation is the ability of the Bayer company to differentiate the Bayer brand "Aspirin" from all other acetylsalicylic acids, when in fact it is not different. Another example is the ability of petroleum producers to successfully differentiate brands of gasoline or petroleum in consumers' minds, although this appears less prevalent following the energy shortages of the 1970s. Through packaging, advertising and product standardization, several U.S. poultry producers have been able to brand and differentiate chickens.

The second situation is the case of sellers who seek to have consumers believe that products which are different are actually the same. The logical explanation for such behaviour is an attempt to deceive. In a world of perfect information, such deception could and would be quickly seen by consumers. In the real world, though, such deception is frequently encountered. For example, I read my *Consumer Reports* article about stereo speakers, go to my local electronics shop and am told by the clerk that the brand he has for sale is identical in performance to the one named in *Consumer Reports*. An independent test proves him wrong. This is an example of what occurs many times each day, and many of us tend to accept it as a fact of life.

Another example of attempting to pass off heterogeneous products as homogeneous are actions of professional groups. Many self-governing professional groups, such as lawyers, doctors, dentists, accountants and the like, act as if they want the public to believe that all their members are equally competent. And, as a result, many consumers believe there is little difference among professionals, a belief held by few professionals. Cases of individual professionals providing less than adequate service and taking advantage of trusting consumers occur daily, as evidenced by professional bodies penalizing their most flagrantly unethical or incompetent members. There is no system that we have been able to discover, in any OECD country, available to consumers, which provides information on the competence of professionals. Indeed, information about an individual's professional competence is almost impossible to obtain.

The classic response to many of the problems of product/service comparison in the past has been *caveat emptor* -- let the buyer beware. In a world where products were not complex, where consumers could understand and compare products side-by-side, where distances between producers and consumers were short or even face-to-face, this was probably sufficient. But as the marketplace has evolved and become more complex, consumers have not been able to maintain their bargaining power in the exchange process. The policy questions which arise in this area of the exchange process have to do with the provision of consumer education to improve their decision making, with requirements for sellers to provide a minimum of information with which consumers may make more informed choices, and the discouraging of providing biased or fraudulent information, mainly through the law.

However, the consumer's task is not finished once product/service comparisons have been completed. The consumer must then try to make a tradeoff between the cost of each of the alternatives and the benefits which they provide.

VALUE

In allocating their incomes, consumers weigh the benefits they perceive they will get from a good or service against its cost to determine its value. Cost is treated separately from other product characteristics in the discussion for two main reasons. First, it is a mainstay of economics, many economic theories having assumed away the problems of product/service differences by treating products or services as being homogeneous. Second, since so much has been written about price it is useful to separate it out for expositional reasons. I am convinced that price is just one of a number of product characteristics consumers bring into their decision making calculus, being a dominant consideration when they feel products and services are homogeneous and of lesser importance in deciding on luxury and high status items. Indeed, many products would have much less status were their prices lower.

Cost is a complex concept in use because it requires consumers to summarize their outlay on an item in terms of its price, the cost of acquisition, how well it performs in use, the costs of service and maintenance and how it is financed. Each of these elements is discussed below.

Price

Price is probably the easiest of the elements to determine because it is usually defined as the money paid in return for the good or service. However, what a quoted price includes is not always apparent. For example, some prices may not include installation. Similarly, one may buy a stereo component and learn later that in order to make it work one must purchase a power supply. People renting apartments have often assumed that the price included appliances which were used only for demonstrating the unit, or they assumed that the rental rate for the unit included heat, electricity and waste disposal, when in truth it did not.

A constant and more serious problem may be that of price discovery. Few products or services have identical prices throughout the same geographical area. That is, some stores charge much more for the same product than do others in the same market area. Determining the prices for items in a market area can often be expensive as well as time consuming. For example, in a recent survey of prices in Vancouver, Canada, prices for the Pentax Super Program single lens reflex camera ranged from $275 to $400, a difference of $125 between highest and lowest price. This level of price dispersion was similar to that reported by Maynes and Assum in several U.S. cities.[11]

The critical matter is whether consumers perceive there to be wide price dispersion which would justify their searching. Maynes and Assum found that consumers generally under-estimated price dispersion.[12] More to the point, recent economic models of the possible effects of consumer price searching indicate that not all consumers have to search for lower prices for their efforts to benefit all consumers in the marketplace.

..... there are two classes of [price] searchers ..... efficient and inefficient ..... [F]our outcomes are possible, depending on the relative information costs of the two classes of consumers. If a sufficient number of consumers have perfect information (i.e., they can acquire information at zero cost), then the outcome will be the competitive price [in the market area]. If costs are sufficiently high for both classes of consumers, then a single monopoly price will emerge. The third possibility is that some firms will charge the competitive price while others charge a higher price ..... Here a group of firms chooses to raise its price above the competitive level; these firms generally attract inefficient searchers but have lower sales than firms charging the competitive price. Finally, there may be no equilibrium: this occurs if it is always profitable for at least one firm to change its price up and down.[13]

The findings reported above add support to the experience of national and local consumer information networks that collection and dissemination of price information puts pressure on all sellers to bring their prices closer to competitive equilibrium levels. In effect, those of us who do not shop around are benefited by those that do by the lower prices which result. Furthermore, the political pressure to restrict the dissemination of price information by business is rational and logical, since firms would rather not have price discovery made easier and less expensive for consumers since it restricts their ability to charge higher prices.

Acquisition Costs

Consumers almost always incur acquisition costs for goods and services. They always pay for the costs of distribution in the price of products. For example, businesses determine the ease of consumer access when selecting retail locations. Indeed, real estate prices or rental costs for retail locations are a function of the location's market drawing power. Market drawing power is a function of the ease of access to the site for consumers, indicating a lower cost of goods or service acquisition. The greater the ease of access -- time and distance -- plus the number of other products available to consumers in the immediate area, the greater the drawing power of a site and the higher its value to both sellers and consumers. The attractiveness of a shopping centre, or the downtown shopping area of large cities, is that the concentration of retail offerings reduces acquisition and search costs to consumers.

Other acquisition costs are the costs of distribution. These costs are included in wholesale and retail markups and reflected in prices. Consumers in isolated areas often pay higher prices because of higher costs of goods to merchants. Merchants may also use their monopoly positions in isolated areas to raise prices. That subject is treated in the next chapter. Here we are referring to real cost increases due to factors such as increased transportation costs and higher operating costs, due both to higher costs in an isolated area as well as lower volumes of sales through an outlet. That consumers recognize these differences is evidenced by the shopping trip. It is common for people in isolated areas to save up purchases and make shopping trips to larger urban areas where costs are lower and selection greater. However, if one chooses to buy in a distant city, one may weigh the possible difficulty and inconvenience of obtaining service and exercising warranty provisions as compared to buying locally. Local merchants frequently cite their proximity and service capability as a counter to the higher purchase cost through them. Mail order purchases may result in lower acquisition costs but with similar risks. Acquisition costs add to the complexity of decision making.

Operating and Maintenance Costs

Operating and maintenance costs are important elements of the cost for a number of products. Frequently these future costs are difficult to evaluate. Automobile manufacturers, especially since the energy crisis of the 1970s, have emphasized fuel consumption as a major selling point. Indeed, governments have set requirements for minimum performance standards to reduce consumption, especially in North America. Maintenance, especially of durable items such as automobiles and appliances, may also be a significant cost item which is difficult, if not impossible, to ascertain at the time of purchase. That is why consumer buying magazines frequently survey their readers and compile cost of repair and maintenance records in the hope that past performance is an indication of future performance. One North American manufacturer of large appliances, Maytag, uses its history of low maintenance costs and long performance as a selling tool. They advertise the Maytag repairman as "The loneliest man in town," because he has so few repair calls, using the advertising campaign to justify prices twenty percent or so above their competitors. However, even this relatively hard data is sometimes difficult to understand and utilize without complex analysis.[14]

Various policy considerations and remedies, such as minimum standards, warranties of service, money back guarantees by the seller (as opposed to the manufacturer's warranty) and the like, imposed by legislation or used as a sales tool, have attempted to reduce some of the risk and uncertainty associated with evaluating operating and maintenance costs.

Financing Costs

While financing purchases may also be considered another service to be purchased, it is treated here as a cost consideration because it is often bound up in an evaluation as a cost. Prices often include financing charges, such as higher weekly or monthly payments offered as an alternative to high down payments or to cash.

Some consumers do not separate financing from the price of goods as the theoreticians do. Knowing this, and having seen the exploitation of a number of consumers through high financing charges, many OECD jurisdictions have implemented legislation to highlight the financing costs to purchasers. For example, in requiring the disclosure of real interest rates, or requiring the stating of the final total cost of a good or service which includes all financing charges, governments have tried to make consumers aware of these costs, hoping that they will include them in evaluating alternatives during the exchange process.

The models and concerns discussed in the preceding section, which outline some of the issues which consumers and sellers must deal with in the application of the concept of value in the exchange process, are useful but not definitive in providing answers for policy makers. Prices may be closer to equilibrium levels when a number of persons or organizations engage in active price search and disclosure. But there is still room in the marketplace for firms to charge higher prices, to engage in a policy of changing prices (which may or may not confuse consumers by providing unreliable signals about prices and quality) to lower previous quality levels or to do a variety of things which complicate the evaluation process. However, the models and other concepts presented above provide an analytical capacity for evaluating policy alternatives much greater than what existed even ten years ago. More importantly, it appears that there is more interest in researching these problems, a boon to consumers and policy makers alike.

THE ROLE OF INFORMATION

It should be clear that information plays a crucial role in the exchange process. Underlying everything discussed thus far in the chapter has been the role of information. This section addresses explicitly why information is central to a discussion of the causes of and solutions to a good deal of consumer dissatisfaction in the exchange process.

Availability and Cost

The first question to ask is the degree to which information is actually available to the consumer, and, if available, at what cost. Often it is assumed in the various academic disciplines -- economics, consumer behaviour, information theory -- that the consumer has the data required to make informed decisions. In fact, the average consumer would tend, from experience, to say otherwise. Indeed, there can be a tremendous cost to gaining even the most basic price information, let alone information on relative quality, performance in use and other characteristics.[15] There is no published source for most of such data: rather, consumers must move from store to store, at significant cost, to collect a sample of prices for even a single brand of coffee. Extending this to the comparison of various brands in different stores, the difficulties faced by consumers are compounded. However, "good consumers" store information on frequently purchased items and reduce their information costs.

The major attraction of consumer groups to the average member, and the source of a majority of the groups' operating funds, is the publication of consumer buying tests and advice. That this type of service is valued by consumers is not a fluke. It demonstrates the collective benefits which can accrue from cooperation in reducing the cost of information collection and analysis.

Timeliness

Clearly, information is only useful if it is obtained in time to be applied to the user's benefit. If a consumer is purchasing a new washing machine and the *Which?* article that evaluates machines is due two months hence, that information is not of much use. Unit pricing of grocery products, required in some OECD jurisdictions, is the process of putting per unit prices of items -- price/litre, for example -- on the grocery shelves where the items are sold. When they are available, consumers may compare products on a per unit basis. This is a good example of timely information, information available at point of sale. New information technology, discussed in Chapters 1 and 9, has the potential of increasing the timeliness of all types of information and its application to consumer needs is being watched with interest.

Bias

Much of the information on which consumers rely comes from producers and sellers of products. An obvious worry is the inherent bias in that information. This issue is not necessarily clear-cut. It is in the interests of the producers of superior products to tell consumers about them. However, those with less than superior products may wish to stretch the truth. There are numerous examples of legislation which deals with deceptive trade practices, misleading advertising, and similar issues -- legislation implemented because of abuses in the marketplace -- discussed in detail in Chapter 6 on the law.

Between the provision of factual, unbiased information by some firms and information which is legally false provided by others, there is still a wide range of latitude. For example, most of us accept the fact that sales people will use "puffery" to make their products look good to the consumer.[16] More than one firm tells us, "Ours is the best product in the world." We have all seen an advertisement which says "The only product to give you XYZ, for greater protection and safety." Or, "New Yeast Pills provide three times the daily normal requirements of vitamin Z." Or "Compare our price with the manufacturer's suggested price of Fr 2,000."[17] While not all of us care about these things, highlighting a particular attribute of a product, or making comparisons which may or may not be true, or which may not be of any value, adds more complexity to an already difficult evaluation process.

Advertisers and their trade organizations obviously do not wish to have limits imposed on their ability to transmit information that is within the bounds of legality nor do they wish the law expanded to curb current practices. The American Association of Advertising Agencies funded a study of consumers' "confusion" level stemming from advertising. The study concludes that consumers have high levels of confusion and that advertising contributes only minimally to this problem.[18] However, other researchers have criticized not only the methodology and the definition of consumer confusion, but also the fact that, while purported to be a scientific, academic investigation, the A.A.A.A. will not allow the data which were used for the study to be released to other investigators for independent analysis.[19]

What policy-makers may want to ask is whether providing consumers with an alternative, counterbalancing source of information, less prone to bias, might be a better alternative than more legislation and regulation of seller provided information. A number of years ago, Professor Maynes suggested a small tax on all advertising expenditures to counteract seller biased sources on information and to support consumer controlled sources of information.[20] This suggestion has not been received enthusiastically by advertisers, however.

Processing Capability

Even if consumers have available to them adequate, timely and relatively unbiased information, the quality of their decisions is highly dependent on their ability to process that information. Some individuals are better analysts than others, for a variety of reasons which include education, experience, innate intelligence, and motivation.[21] The examples used previously in the chapter have indicated how complex the task of processing information can be. Indeed, in situations where there are many brands in a product class, or many close substitutes for a product class, simply listing all available choices can be difficult. Following that, attempting to compare alternatives on even two or three criteria requires highly sophisticated processing.[22] The types, forms and availability of information and differences among consumers in how and what information they use is not well understood.[23] Yet consumers do these tasks, sometimes not as well as they would like, on a daily basis. They make mistakes and less than optimal choices, in part because of poor processing skills but also because of the lack of and bias in information.

As in the collection of information, there appear to be scale economies in hiring people who can develop the technical skills to do some of this processing for us. This is what the consumer testing magazines do. Governments often evaluate commercial products for their own use in a similar manner. However, they have almost always refused to release the results of their evaluations to citizens who, in the final analysis, have paid for them. The pressure from business groups against such release is too powerful.

Since many persons benefit from cooperative decision processing, and since social welfare is most likely increased through widespread analysis and dissemination of this information, the policy question of whether governments should pay for at least a portion of such information processing activities is raised. It has been estimated that in the United States, savings to consumers from some form of comprehensive local and national information system would be one hundred billion dollars annually.[24] Projected to the OECD countries, these savings would be quite a bit more than double that amount, given inflation since the time those estimates were made. Governments subsidize or pay for testing in countries such as Sweden, Denmark and France. Furthermore, such a subsidy would seem to be a logical extension of the conclusions from market models and consumer protection discussed previously.

CONSUMER INFORMATION AND EDUCATION POLICY

It seems quite clear that consumers' major interests in exchange transactions involve information and education; information in terms of amount, timeliness, truthfulness, and the like plus the education and experience to be able to use it effectively in deciding how to optimize one's consumption possibilities. The policy issues which arise include some sort of system to identify the magnitude of problems which are discovered in the exchange process, an information system which consumers of various levels of intelligence, age, experience and education may avail themselves to help in decision making, a funding mechanism for the system and, perhaps, rules, standards, or guarantees which provide some confidence in the information which is being purveyed to consumers.[25]

Problem Identification

The occurrence and magnitude of consumer problems in the exchange process obviously points to a system which informs policy makers of where consumers are having problems.[26] There are vestiges of consumer information networks set up in some countries. For example, some government agencies keep records of complaints about malfunctioning products in order to take action where consumer safety is concerned. Consumer organizations in the European Communities have a Consumer Interpol system where national consumer organizations, the IOCU and BEUC inform each other when they discover consumer problems.[27] In general, however, we were not able to discover formally designed systems which inform consumer policy makers of problem areas in decision making, information or other consumer concerns. This general problem is addressed in Chapter 8.

Information System Components

Each time one studies consumer interest in the exchange process attention is continually refocussed on the problems consumers have with information. It is recognized by many consumer researchers that this is the major difficulty problem which consumers face in the marketplace.[28] There are many things which we do not know about the design and operation of such systems but the one thing on which most consumer advocates will agree is that in general, consumers do not have enough information and much of the information they have is often highly biased.[29] There has been a relatively long running academic discussion about consumer information overload, where a number of researchers have contended that public policy that provides more information will tend to overload consumers and reduce the quality of decisions.[30] However, other researchers, either re-analyzing this previous work or from additional research, have shown that more information is better.[31] And while it is true that in many situations consumers do not have enough information, there are also cases where a great deal of information is available but knowledge of its availability is limited and access to it is expensive. So, while opponents of increased information may use information buried in hard to get places as support against the possible expansion of information and its wider dissemination, the cost of access and the economics of information acquisition remain a prime consideration in any program to assist consumers.[32]

The information presented previously in the chapter has led to the development of Table 4-3 which sets out the major components and policy considerations in a consumer information system. Each one of these components is discussed in turn.

Products/Service - The first column in the table contains policy areas with consumer interest implications, such as accommodation, energy, food, and safety as outlined in Table 1-1. Obviously some consumers will be more expert and have more need for information in one area than in others.

General Class Buying Considerations - The first type of information consumers need is a general overview of what they should be considering in making a buying decision. That is, they need a way in which they can determine their needs and which criteria and the amount of weight which should be

Table 4-3 Information System Components and Policy Considerations

Product/Service	General Class Buying Considerations	Specific Item Characteristics	Item Analysis	Price Historical To Real Time	Firm Information Historical to Real Time
	Which?		Individual	Collection	Collection
Transportation					
	Consumer Reports	National		Dissemination	Dissemination
				Newspapers	
Accommodation	Govt. Brochures		Consumer Organizations	Telephone	
				Television	
Leisure	Telephones Cassettes	Regional	Financial Times	Magazines	
	Auto Magazines		Business Organizations	National	Analysis
				Regional	
				Local	
(See Table 1-1 for expanded listing of consumer concerns)	Brokerage Firms	Local			
	Professional Organizations		Govt. Bodies	Electronic Buying Services	Legal Considerations

put on each criteria when evaluating various types of items or services they wish to purchase.

There numerous ways ways in which this information is transmitted. Consumer buying magazines in all countries provide such type of general overviews in many of their articles. There are government brochures, for example, some distributed by departments of agriculture or health which provide information on purchasing food or drugs. Some years ago a jurisdiction in Florida had a telephone system whereby consumers called and listened to a cassette tape on how to buy items such as washing machines, mattresses, etc. Such a service was tested in Vancouver, British Columbia by Consumer and Corporate Affairs Canada several years ago. Purchasers of automobiles may avail themselves of informative articles in automotive magazines. A number of security brokerage firms provide very informative and unbiased advice on the buying of securities. And some professional organizations have distributed information on "how to pick your accountant" and the like. Many trade organizations have similar types of publications.

However, this information is often dispersed and difficult to locate, when it is available, and since even some diligent consumers have difficulty finding them, there is a basic problem of collection, analysis and dissemination. While the payoffs from providing a central source of this type of information may be high in the aggregate, funding for maintaining a data bank is critical, as we shall see is the case for many of the other components of consumer information systems. Furthermore, the needs and value of information varies among individual consumers. Systems need to be designed to satisfy, as effectively as possible, the various levels of consumer needs.[33]

Specific Item Characteristics - Information on specific characteristics of items or services are usually available to consumers if they choose to collect and analyze it. Of course, the problem is that it is not cost effective for consumers to do this in all situations. For large ticket items, such as homes and automobiles, consumers often see it in their individual self interest to engage in information collection, search and analysis. Even here, with complex products such as automobiles and even homes, there are a variety of cost savings which cooperative information collection and dissemination may bring about.

Another dimension of the problem is the geographic coverage of product information. For example, consumer organizations publish mainly national, less frequently regional and almost never local information on individual item characteristics. They publish information on only a few services, such as life insurance. Again, this a problem of the economics of information problem, since most organizations do not have the economic support to provide information on products which are only distributed locally. While there have been some tests of local information systems in North America and England, and while several have run effectively for a number of years, for example one in Washington, D.C., and while I have been told there is some information of this type on a few cable television and information networks, local consumer information systems are not well developed. While a good deal of some valuable local and regional information is from many, it is seldom catalogued in a systematic and useful form. Some of it is transitory if it is broadcast electronically or not readily accessible in the case of newspapers. However, until one has an inventory of information available it is almost impossible to estimate the magnitude of the resources necessary to fill any gaps. Perhaps, if such an inventory were accomplished, we would find that there is more information available than we now think. Of course, the opposite could be true. The French experiment with a national information network and the possibility of nodes for local access, described in Chapter 9, is a large scale experiment which has many possibilities. Indeed, the Institute National de la Consommation (INC) now offers its product and service information to consumers.[34]

Item Analysis - Item analysis is the decision making process where consumers match specific goods and services to their own needs. Historically, this analysis has been done by individuals for themselves and friends. But, as products and services have become more numerous and complex, consumer buying magazines have entered into the analysis by setting out alternatives and rating items on various characteristics. They have often gone further than this and designate "Best Buys," which connote a particularly good combination of product characteristics and price. These best buys only occur where products/services are relatively homogeneous and substitutable. Nonetheless, consumers still must rank their alternatives according to their particular needs.

Some of the policy considerations in this area will be how much analysis is possible and in what form it is presented to consumers. With the wide range of different consumers and their needs, specific recommendations of all products and services is probably unrealistic, at least in the short run. However, ranking of the most frequently bought and most difficult to compare products and services on their efficacy in different uses, format of information presentation and similar matters need to be evaluated for their potential costs and benefits. As with many of these other information questions, there is much we have yet to discover about what is useful for consumers and requisite policy alternatives to analyze.

Price: Historical to Real Time - One of the major evaluation characteristics in the exchange process is price. The scale economies to collective assembling and analysis of real time price are probably great. Historical prices on the one hand are useful for rank ordering products in a general way, while in the decision making process and purchase act real time price within the relevant market area is critical since prices may vary widely.

Consumers generally have a wide range of sources and techniques available to obtain price information. Newspapers, telephoning sellers, electronic media and store visits are all potential information sources. With the expansion of electronic information transmittal capabilities and a decline in its real cost, a number of buying services have evolved whereby consumers have access to buying at low prices over a large geographic area. However, there are few comparative, real time price information sources readily available to consumers on a local or regional basis.

Firm: Historical to Real Time - Similarly, information on the performance of firms selling products and services may have a positive effect, both in helping consumers make better decisions and in the public effect of increasing competition in services. Consumers, even if they have information on nationally produced and sold products, need information on the performance of local sellers of those products, especially for those where service and maintenance is an important component of the purchase. Consumers have great difficulty in obtaining such information to help in evaluating services. It is in this area of information about service where consumers, at least in Canada, considered information most difficult to come by.[35]

Better Business Bureaux would contend that they provide this type of information to consumers. However, given that they are funded by business and given their modus operandi, consumers who have attempted to use this source of information to evaluate firm performance have been frequently disappointed. Few adequate information sources of this nature exist.

Funding - Funding is a critical part of any public policy decision and one of the major drawbacks to expanded consumer information systems. One of the most contentious issues in consumer information programs is the assertion by consumer advocates that consumer information programs are public goods and should be funded, at least partially, through tax revenues. It is hard to deny that some elements of consumer information programs are not public goods. They benefit a wide range of people and the returns from taxes spent in this manner are large. Dunn and Ray estimated that at least 100 billion dollars annually would be saved in the United States if a consumer information program of the type described earlier were implemented. Savings to OECD members were estimated to be at least double that. Indeed, governments in Scandinavia and France subsidize consumer testing and information programs.

Ideology about the function of government obviously has acted as a deterrent to increased government support of consumer information programs. Government research and dissemination of information to industries such as agriculture, business and foreign trade are widely accepted in the OECD countries. However, for some reason, government funding of consumer programs in the same countries is not acceptable. As previously discussed, there have been long ranging efforts in both Canada and the United States to have data on products purchased for government use released, but these have been steadfastly refused as an invasion on the rights of business. However, that debate will not be continued here. It is submitted that this is a political question and the power of producers is generally greater than that of consumers. The result is that the information remains suppressed.

The amount of funding necessary to significantly improve what is now available is probably not great. Professor Maynes has suggested a one or two percent tax on advertising expenditures as a source of revenues for countervailing information for consumers.[36] Discussions with people operating consumer magazines suggested that the amount of funds needed to do an acceptable job is not great. However, serious policy questions arise. How should this type of aid be allocated among consumer organizations, present and future? Would governments take over the functions of existing consumer and private testing organizations? How would information be distributed? Would combinations of private and public testing and information dissemination programs be acceptable?

Education

Consumer education is a general matter, not restricted to information processing nor to the exchange situation. However, we do know that the more highly educated members of the population are those most capable of making good decisions and that education plays a role in this capability. In fact, it is only as people attempt to make better buying decisions that they become aware of the lack of information with which to do so. This awareness is at the root of many calls for improved information systems.

Rules, Standards and Guarantees

The simple expansion of consumer information systems, in and of itself, is probably not as efficient nor effective a proposal for improving consumers' interest in the exchange process as is a combination of information and prescribed rules of behaviour, standards and guarantees.[37] For example, rules regarding the type and amount of information to be provided to consumers on packaged food products, the requirement of information dissemination on conditional sales contracts, limitations on the amount of puffing and on false and misleading advertising, and a wide variety of other rules are probably much more effective than simply providing more information. The rationales for using various policy instruments is discussed in Chapter 8.

SUMMARY AND CONCLUSIONS

Needs for consumer policy in the exchange process stem from the fact that consumers have difficulties deciding what they really want and then matching their wants to the many complex products available to them. With complex and conflicting alternatives this is frequently a difficult, costly process. Consumers function in an imperfect information environment where information is seldom free, where it is often distorted, is frequently not readily nor widely available and it is often costly and difficult to process, leading to a number of possible problems and their attendant policy considerations.

A framework was provided to structure the analysis and evaluate consumer policy in the exchange process. A more general consumer policy framework is presented in Chapter 8.

NOTES

1 Bagozzi, R. P. (1974) "Marketing as an Organized Behavioral System of Exchange," *Journal of Marketing*, 38 (Oct.), pp. 77-81.

2 Creighton, Lucy Black (1976) *Pretenders to the Throne.* Lexington, MA: D.C. Heath and Company, p. 85. The discussion which follows uses and expands on her analysis.

3 Kuhlmann, Eberhard (1983) "On the Economic Analysis of the Information-Seeking Behaviour of Consumer," *Journal of Consumer Policy*, 6, pp. 236-237.

4 Pollay, R. W. (1986) "The Distorted Mirror: Reflections on the Unintended Consequences of Advertising," *Journal of Marketing*, 50:2 (April), pp. 18-36.

5 Nelson, P. (1970) "Information and Consumer Behavior," *Journal of Political Economy*, 78, pp. 311-399.

6 Cave, Martin (1985) "Market Models and Consumer Protection," *Journal of Consumer Policy*, 8, p. 340.

7 Using the term "consumer behaviour" as we do here and as is common practice in the marketing profession is really deceptive in many respects. Actually, very little research has been done on consuming behaviour as opposed to buying behaviour, the main thrust of marketing research. Behaviour which has been called irrational may be nothing more than consumers wanting to consume and not wishing to work at the buying process. However, research in this area of consuming behaviour is in its infancy, as has been pointed out by Russell Belk, President of the Association for Consumer Research (Seminar, Faculty of Commerce and Business Administration, University of British Columbia, Vancouver, March 1986).

8 Alberta Consumer and Corporate Affairs (1979) "What Price Quality?" *Market Spotlight*, (March); Friedman, Monroe (1967) "Quality and Price Considerations in Rational Consumer Decision Making," *Journal of Consumer Affairs*, 1 (Summer), pp. 13-23; Gardner, David (1970) "An Experimental Investigation of the Price/Quality Relation," *Journal of Retailing*, (Fall), pp. 25-41; Morris, Ruby, and Bronson, Claire (1969) "The Chaos in Competition Indicated by *Consumer Reports*," *Journal of Marketing*, (July), pp. 26-34; Oxenfeldt, Alfred (1950) "Consumer Knowledge: Its Measurement and Extent," *Review of Economics and Statistics*, 32, pp. 300-316;

Riesz, Peter (1978) "Price versus Quality in the Marketplace, 1961-1975," *Journal of Retailing*, (Winter), pp. 15-27; Ross, Myron H., and Stiles, Donald (1973) "An Exception to the Law of Demand," *Journal of Consumer Affairs*, 7:2 (Winter), pp. 128-144; Sproles, George (1977) "New Evidence on Price and Product Quality," *Journal of Consumer Affairs*, 11 (Summer), pp. 63-77.
9 Cave 1985, pp. 343-345.
10 Cave 1985, p. 337.
11 Maynes, E. Scott, and Assum, Terje (1982) "Informationally Imperfect Markets: Empirical Findings and Policy Implications," *Journal of Consumer Affairs*, (Summer), pp. 62-87; Forbes, J. D. (1987) "Price Dispersion in Consumer Markets: Theory, Empirical Evidence and Policy Implications," in Paul A. Anderson and Melanie Wallendorf, eds., *Advances in Consumer Research, Vol. XIV*. Association for Consumer Research, forthcoming.
12 Maynes and Assum 1982, pp. 77-83.
13 Cave 1985, p. 337.
14 Friedman, Monroe (1987) "Predicting Frequency of Problems Experienced by Owners of Used Cars: A Statistical Analysis of Six Years of *Consumer Reports* Survey Data for 1979 Model Cars," in Paul A. Anderson and Melanie Wallendorf, eds., *Advances in Consumer Research Vol. XIV*. Association for Consumer Research, forthcoming.
15 Wilde, Louis L. (1980) "The Economics of Consumer Information Acquisition," *Journal of Business*, 53:3:2, pp. S143-S158.
16 See Preston, Ivan L. (1975) *The Great American Blow-Up: Puffery in Advertising and Selling*. Madison, WI: University of Wisconsin Press, which presents an insightful discussion of puffery in the United States. Healy, Maurice (1978) "Advertising: what the consumer wants," in Jeremy Mitchell, ed., *Marketing and the Consumer Movement*. London: McGraw-Hill Book Company (UK) Limited, pp. 179-189, discusses the puffing situation in the U.K.
17 Leifeld, John, and Heslop, Louise A. (1984) "Reference Prices and Deception in Newspaper Advertising." Guelph, Ontario: Department of Consumer Studies, University of Guelph, (May).
18 Jacoby, Jacob, Hoyer, Wayne D., and Sheluga, David A. (1980) *Miscomprehension of Televised Advertising*. New York: American Association of Advertising Agencies.
19 Preston, Ivan L., and Richards, Jef I. (1986) "The Relationship of Miscomprehension to Deceptiveness in FTC Cases," in Richard J. Lutz, ed., *Advances in Consumer Research*, 13, Provo: UT: Association for Consumer Research, pp. 138-142; and discussion between Ivan Preston and Jacob Jacoby, Las Vegas, Nevada, October 18, 1985.
20 Maynes, E. Scott (1973) "Consumerism: Origin and Research Implications," in Eleanor B. Sheldon, ed. *Family Economic Behavior: Problems and Prospects*. Philadelphia: Lippincott, pp. 290-291.
21 See Bettman, J. R. (1979) *An Information Processing Theory of Consumer Choice*. Reading, MA: Addison-Wesley Publishing Co.; and Crosby, Lawrence A., and Taylor, James R. (1981)

"Effects of Consumer Information and Education on Cognition and Choice," *Journal of Consumer Research*, 8 (June), pp. 43-56.

22 Johnson, Michael D. (1984) "Consumer Choice Strategies for Comparing Noncomparable Alternatives," *Journal of Consumer Research*, 11 (Dec.), pp. 741-753.

23 Biehal, Gabriel, and Chakravarti, Dipankar (1986) "Consumers' Use of Memory and External Information in Choice: Macro and Micro Perspectives," *Journal of Consumer Research*, 12 (Mar.), pp. 382-405.

24 Dunn, Donald A., and Ray, Michael L. (1980) "A Plan for Consumer Information System Development, Implementation and Evaluation," in J. C. Olson, ed., *Advances in Consumer Research, Vol. VIII*. University Park, PA: Association for Consumer Research.

25 Capon, Noel, and Lutz, Richard J. (1979) "A Model and Methodology for the Development of Consumer Information Programs," *Journal of Marketing*, 43 (Jan.), pp. 58-67.

26 Andreasen, Alan R., and Manning, Jean (1980) "Information Needs For Consumer Protection Planning," *Journal of Consumer Policy*, 4:2, pp. 115-125.

27 Domzalski, Yves (1984) *The Interpols of the Consumer Associations*. Brussels: Bureau Europeen des Unions de Consommateurs, May 17-18.

28 Beales, Howard, Mazis, Michael B., Salop, Steven C., and Staelin, Richard (1981) "Consumer Search in Public Policy," *Journal of Consumer Research*, 8:1 (June), pp. 11-22; and Sarel, Dan (1983) "A Comment on Capon and Lutz's Model and Methodology for the Development of Consumer Information Programs," *Journal of Marketing*, 47:3 (Summer), pp. 103-107.

29 Warneryd, Carl-Erik (1980) "The Limits of Public Consumer Information," *Journal of Consumer Policy*, 4:2, pp. 127-141.

30 Jacoby, Jacob, Speller, Donald E., and Berning, Carol Kohn (1974) "Brand Choice Behavior as a Function of Information Load: Replication and Extension," *Journal of Consumer Research*, 1 (June), pp. 33-42, Scammon, Debra L. (1977) "'Information Load' and Consumers," *Journal of Consumer Research*, 4:3 (Dec.), pp. 148-155; and Malhotra, Naresh K. (1982) "Information Load and Consumer Decision Making," *Journal of Consumer Research*, 8:4 (March), pp. 419-430.

31 Russo, J. Edward (1974) "More Information is Better: A Reevaluation of Jacoby, Speller and Kohn," *Journal of Consumer Research*, (Dec.), pp. 68-72; Rudd, Joel (1983) "The Consumer Information Overload Controversy and Public Policy," *Policy Studies Review*, 2:3 (Feb.), pp. 465-473; and Sarel 1983.

32 Ratchford, Brian T. (1980) "The Value of Information for Selected Appliances," *Journal of Marketing Research*, 17 (Feb.), pp. 14-25; and Wilde, Louis L. (1980) "The Economics of Consumer Information Acquisition," *Journal of Business*, 53:3:2, pp. S143-S158.

33 Kiel, Geoffrey C., and Layton, Roger A. (1981) "Dimensions of Consumer Information Seeking Behavior," *Journal of Marketing Research*, 18 (May), pp. 233-239; Claxton, John D., Fry, Joseph N., and Portis, Bernard (1974) "A Taxonomy of Prepurchase Information Gathering Patterns,"

Journal of Consumer Research, 1 (Dec.), pp. 35-42; and Ratchford 1980.

34 Mayer, Robert N. (1986) *Videotex in France: The Other French Revolution.* Salt Lake City, UT: Family and Consumer Studies, University of Utah (September), pp. 36-38.

35 Claxton, John D., and Ritchie, J. R. Brent (1981) "Consumers' Perceptions of Prepurchase Shopping Problems and Solutions: Major Findings and Directions for Action." Ottawa: Consumer Research and Evaluation Branch, Consumer and Corporate Affairs Canada, RG23-56/1980e; and Claxton, John D., and Ritchie, J. R. Brent (1979) Consumer Prepurchase Shopping Problems: A Focus on the Retailing Component," *Journal of Retailing*, 53:3 (Fall), pp. 24-43.

36 Personal discussions.

37 Cave 1985, p. 345; and Courville, Leon, and Hausman, Warren H. (1979) "Warranty Scope and Reliability under Imperfect Information and Alternative Market Structures," *Journal of Business*, 52:3, pp. 361-378; Priest, George L. (1981) "A Theory of the Consumer Product Warranty," *Yale Law Review*, 90:6 (May), pp. 1297-1352.

5. INDUSTRIAL ORGANIZATION

Whereas the previous chapter discussed the influence of the micro elements of the exchange process, this chapter discusses the more general aspects of market structure, governments and industrial organization and the consumer interest.

As was pointed out at the end of Chapter 2, policy in any jurisdiction develops within a specific the cultural, political and legal environment more or less unique to that jurisdiction. Furthermore, too often, especially when dealing with policy matters in a single jurisdiction, one may take values and norms as given. However, since this study encompasses policy evolution in many countries, looking beyond a single country or political jurisdiction, such implicit factors must be made explicit. Indeed, as the interaction and interdependence of nations becomes greater -- with the European Economic Community's cross-cultural policy being the most obvious example -- social and cultural factors will become increasingly the major constraint on policy cooperation.

For our purposes, although much has been written on the subject, we need only point out the importance of the plethora of concepts and ideas about what is appropriate in a given culture in the evolution of policy. That is, the concrete and abstract symbols, institutions -- legal, political, social and economic -- and the norms by which a society operates and the values which are held by its members, have a bearing on the economic, legal and political environment within which policy develops in a given jurisdiction. The importance of cultural values and their impact on consumer and other policy must be kept in mind during the discussion of industrial organization which follows.

INDUSTRIAL ORGANIZATION

This section first discusses the traditional concepts of market structure used in industrial organization. Industrial organization is the study of the way in which an economy and its various segments are organized and interact with each other. Next, a model of industrial organization is discussed and adapted to the consumer interest. Third, the implications of the three general market structures, pure competition, oligopoly and monopoly, are studied using the model. Finally, the focus is put on the difficulties of developing policy for oligopoly situations.

The Traditional Economic View

Before we can apply the economist's models to the consumer policy field we need to briefly review two key points about economic theory surrounding industrial organization. It is not by neglect that so much of the successful theory and modelling in the area focusses on the two extremes of the market structure spectrum, perfect competition and monopoly. They are relatively clear cut cases and the action of competitors can be pretty well specified. That is, in purely competitive or monopolistically competitive markets, sellers have little control over pricing and earn only "normal" profits; on the other side of the coin, in a monopoly situation, a rational firm will produce less than the "correct" amount and, as a result, will price higher and earn "abnormally high" profits.[1]

But, most facing consumers in OECD countries are neither of the extremes. Rather, most important markets are oligopolistic in nature. That is, a relatively small number of firms share a large proportion of the business volume as is documented in Tables 5-1 and 5-2. Examples of oligopolistic markets include the automobile industry, petroleum companies, food manufacturing and retailing, department store chains, and financial institutions. Indeed, most products we buy and many of our services are produced or sold in oligopolistic markets. Modelers of oligopolistic behaviour have much more difficult problems than on the two extremes described above because they are unable to provide definitive answers to how firms act in oligopoly situations. This occurs because a firm's actions are dynamic, depending on what their competitors do, and neither economists nor psychologists have been able to predict human behaviour well. In other words, in oligopoly situations, not only do the economics of the situation enter into the decision, but the reactions of people in competing firms -- or more importantly, the estimates of these reactions by competitors -- greatly influence decisions which business people make. As a result, there is a large grey area of theory in industrial organization. There is little consensus on how to approach the selection of appropriate policies and there is no cohesive theory to predict economic unit behaviour such as that which exists for the extremes of pure competition and monopoly.

Second, in general, economic analysis uses efficiency as the criterion for rating the performance and operation of the marketplace. There are actually three different efficiencies which can be used -- allocative, technical or productive, and dynamic efficiency. Allocative efficiency seeks *pareto optimality* as the goal. *Pareto optimality* is the concept that if an economy is allocatively efficient, then at a given point in time no person can gain anything more from the use, given resource endowments, without causing someone else to be worse off. Technical efficiency looks for the lowest cost production such that all firms operate at the lowest point of their long-run average cost curves. Dynamic efficiency, on the other hand, focusses on growth by building on the current productive base to push the productive capacity of the economy upward.

According to many economists, these efficiency criteria are the goals we set for our economy. The problem, of course, is that these goals say nothing about distribution of the outputs of the economy. Such distributional questions are the difficult ones. They are

Table 5-1 Comparative Concentration Ratios, OECD Countries, Market Share of "n" Largest Firms

Nation -	Canada	France	Ireland	Japan	Sweden	UK	US
Year -	72	69	68	70	70	73	72
#Firms -	CR4	CR4	CR4	CR5	CR4	CR5	CR4
Method -	Emp	T/O	Emp	Pdn	Pdn	Emp	Shpd

CR-prcnt							
90-100	5	44	0	45	283	10	12
80-89.9	6	25	2	23	54	15	10
70-79.9	10		4	21	46	13	22
60-69.9	7	26	1	21	52	11	29
50-59.9	6		6	17	36	20	54
40-49.9	11	51	4	21	28	26	60
30-39.9	11		6	12	16	27	67
20-29.9	5	76	10	5	12	14	95
10-19.9	8		5	4	2	14	66
0- 9.9	2	16	0	1	1	2	14
Totals	71	238	38	170	530	152	429

SOURCE: Organisation for Economic Co-operation and Development, Committee of Experts on Restrictive Trade Practices (1979) "Concentration and Competition Policy." Paris: OECD.

NOTES:

- Year = year study conducted in country.
- #Firms = number of largest firms in industry on which concentration ratio calculated, e.g., CR4 means four largest firms.
- Method used in study (Emp = industry employment; T/O = Industrial turnover; Pdn = Value of production; Shpd = Value of factor shipments).
- Numbers in the table represent the number of industries or industry sectors out of the total sample for that country who had the precentage concentration listed on the left column of the table, e.g., 10 of 71 industry sectors in Canada had four firm concentraton ratios between 70.0 and 79.9 percent of the market.

the ones faced by politicians. As an aid to assisting decisions, a model which states only that resources are distributed efficiently, but fails to address what to do if it turns out that the efficient distribution puts all the returns in the hands of owners of non-labour factors of production at the expense of labour, and hence out of the reach of the vast majority of

Table 5-2 Comparative Industrial Concentration in OECD Countries -- Percentage of Industry Sectors in Each Concentration Classification

Nation -	Canada	France	Ireland	Japan	Sweden	UK	US
Year -	72	69	68	70	70	73	72
#Firms -	CR4	CR4	CR4	CR5	CR4	CR5	CR4
Method -	Emp	T/O	Emp	Pdn	Pdn	Emp	Shpd

CR-prcnt

90-100	7.0	18.5	0.0	26.5	53.4	6.6	2.8
70-89.9	22.5	10.5	15.8	25.9	18.9	18.4	7.5
50-69.9	18.3	10.9	18.4	22.4	16.6	20.4	19.3
30-49.9	31.0	21.4	26.3	19.4	8.3	34.9	29.6
10-29.9	18.3	31.9	39.5	5.3	2.6	18.5	37.5
0- 9.9	2.8	6.7	0.0	.6	.2	1.3	3.3

SOURCE: Adapted from Table 5-1.

NOTES: May not add to 100 percent due to rounding.
- See notes to Table 5-1 which explain how to read this table.

consumers, is of little use in helping politicians with their decisions. Or if any other group suffers at the (invisible) hand of the market, then so be it. Economists leave the normative decision of distribution to the political arena.

While there are problems with some of the assumptions discussed in this section, the economic theories provide a good point of departure from which to evaluate consumer policy in industrial organization.

A Model of Market Structure

A paradigm commonly used in the industrial organization was adapted for use in the consumer policy field and is presented in Figure 5-1. The model asserts that there exist basic conditions in the environment which lead to a particular market structure. Structure, in turn, will strongly influence the behaviour and conduct of firms in the industry. This conduct, in turn, affects the performance of those firms. Each of these stages in turn feeds back to the basic conditions, leading to either a status quo or an evolution over time. The model was modified by adding the explicit basic values and attitudes section which was discussed at the beginning of the chapter. Each of its components is discussed in the following sections.

Policy Environment -- Values and Attitudes - The major adaptation of the model from its common form is the explicit inclusion of cultural values and attitudes as a separate element. As discussed at the outset of the Chapter, from nation to nation and between subcultural and geographically distinct groups within a nation, it is uncommon not to find variations in values and attitudes about public policy, political activity and behaviour within the society and, generally, what the function of government and laws should be.

The Basic Conditions - The basic conditions are divided into those on the supply and those on the demand side of the market. On the supply side are those factors which affect a firm's ability to produce, such as costs, availability of raw materials, the type and evolution of technology used, the labour environment, product durability and perishability, and value to weight (transport-related) ratio. Simply put, the supply side conditions are economic factors affecting the production and distribution of goods and services.

The other half of the basic conditions are the demand factors which in large measure determine the type of market which is likely to evolve. These conditions are driven from the consuming rather than producing side of the market. Among them are the level of purchasing power in the economy, the price elasticity of demand for the good in question, the availability and closeness of substitute products, the rate of growth, seasonality and cyclicality of the market, the manner of purchase -- whether the good is a consumer or an industrial product -- and the type of marketing activities employed to generate or alter demand.

Figure 5-1 Consumer Interest/Industrial Organization Paradigm

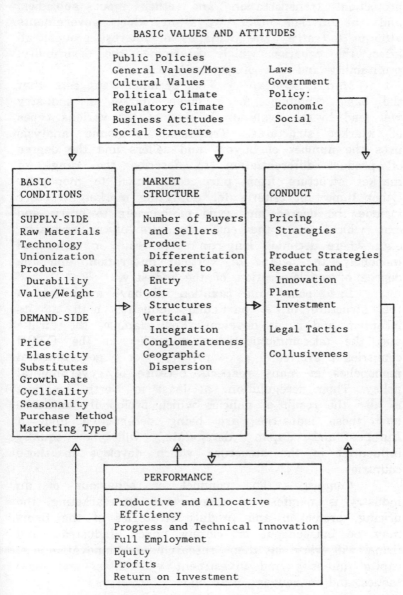

```
┌─────────────────────────────────────────────────┐
│              BASIC VALUES AND ATTITUDES           │
│                                                   │
│   Public Policies                                 │
│   General Values/Mores        Laws                │
│   Cultural Values             Government          │
│   Political Climate           Policy:             │
│   Regulatory Climate            Economic          │
│   Business Attitudes            Social            │
│   Social Structure                                │
└─────────────────────────────────────────────────┘
```

BASIC CONDITIONS	MARKET STRUCTURE	CONDUCT
SUPPLY-SIDE Raw Materials Technology Unionization Product Durability Value/Weight DEMAND-SIDE Price Elasticity Substitutes Growth Rate Cyclicality Seasonality Purchase Method Marketing Type	Number of Buyers and Sellers Product Differentiation Barriers to Entry Cost Structures Vertical Integration Conglomerateness Geographic Dispersion	Pricing Strategies Product Strategies Research and Innovation Plant Investment Legal Tactics Collusiveness

```
┌─────────────────────────────────────────────────┐
│                   PERFORMANCE                     │
│                                                   │
│   Productive and Allocative                       │
│    Efficiency                                     │
│   Progress and Technical Innovation               │
│   Full Employment                                 │
│   Equity                                          │
│   Profits                                         │
│   Return on Investment                            │
└─────────────────────────────────────────────────┘
```

Policies which alter the values of these inputs, such as subsidization of capital, tax holidays, tariff protection, transportation and other input subsidies, and the myriad other ways in which governments attempt to satisfy the demands of interest groups, all affect the equation which determines the desirability, profitability and risk of production.

Market Structure - The paradigm suggests that the basic conditions in a given market or industry will lead to the evolution of one of the various types of market structures. Traditional economic analysis uses the number of buyers and sellers and the degree of product differentiation to describe the range of market structure from pure competition to monopoly. Other important criteria for analyzing market structure include the degree and type of barriers to entry and exit which exist, the cost structure of an industry, e.g., where declining long-run costs result in a natural monopoly, the degree of vertical integration, and the degree of conglomeration of the industry.

Law, policy and taxation all have an effect on the structure of a particular industry, both at its inception and as it develops. For example, the airline and the telecommunications industries in the OECD countries evolved as private or governmental monopolies in many respects because of governmental policy. Their deregulation, at least in North America, is also the result of policies which profoundly influence how those industries are being deregulated and, if Europe and Japan deregulate, will be equally influential in the structure which develops in those countries.

Conduct - The conduct or behaviour of an industry is manifest in many ways. In marketing, the pricing, promotion and product strategies of the firms may be independent or closely linked. Industries and firms will vary in their research and innovativeness, capital intensity and investment will differ, and legal tactics and maneuvers may vary.

From a consumer interest policy perspective, we can focus more closely on the types of conduct which would generally be discouraged or banned on the one hand, and encouraged on the other. Among the former are such behaviours as collusion, which may restrict both competition and the assortment of products and services available to consumers, predatory marketing practices, such as overcharging consumers in areas where firms have market power to allow them to charge lower prices in areas where markets are competitive, deceptive advertising and the like. Behaviours which might encourage or facilitate the consumer interest include cooperation among firms to provide industry wide consumer information and decision making assistance, freer entry and exit, prohibition of concentration where benefits do not accrue to consumers, and the promotion of activities which promote healthy competition. In those industries where natural monopolies appear desirable or where the competitive model is deemed inappropriate -- medical and health services, for example -- an effective regulatory system is needed. What must be remembered is that policy need not always be reactive in nature -- preventing consumer problems from occurring is the preferred approach and will be discussed in Chapter 8.

Performance - In the final analysis, a firm's performance is influenced by their competitive behaviour, or lack of it. On the economic side, this includes questions of productive and allocative efficiency across an industry, the amount of technological progress which occurs, the degree to which full employment is realized, and the allocation of resources. At the national level, citizens will be interested in how well the resources and productive capacity of the economy are utilized. The result of this utilization affects the total output of the economy and what is available for consumption by members of the society. From the consumer policy point of view, consumers generally are perceived to want more rather than less.

From both the firm and especially the industry level, policy makers will be concerned with profits, return on investment, excess capacity and other criteria which are affected by how firms manage their resources and technology. To use monopoly as an example, it would be expected that a monopoly market structure would lead to underproduction and higher prices -- conduct which in turn would cause inflated profits and slowly rising costs -- the X-inefficiency phenomenon which results from lack of competitive pressure[2], and finally to lower efficiency. Clearly, while there will be inefficient firms in any economy, too many of these types of economic units will affect the overall economic performance of the country, will result in less total output, and will not be in the best interests of consumers. These costs have been estimated to be in the area of six percent of the national income in the United States.[3] Such types of estimates must, by their nature, include a good margin for error. Nonetheless, the welfare losses due to monopoly may be high and are of obvious concern to consumers, since these losses reduce consumers' income. We have not researched losses due to monopoly in other OECD countries only because of a lack of resources. However, they are an obvious source of consumer interest in industrial organization.

A PARADIGM FOR THE CONSUMER INTEREST

The paradigm in Figure 5-1 indicates that in generating industrial policy we can focus on any of the paradigm's stages as criteria in evaluating that policy from the consumer interest viewpoint. For example, suppose that we are concerned about monopoly and its (potential) evils. We could evaluate the market structure of a particular industry and, finding that a monopoly exists, act to disband it -- a recent example of such an approach is the American Telephone and Telegraph breakup in the United States. Alternatively, we could determine that while a monopoly exists, it is not evil *per se*, and so choose to focus instead on its behaviour. Finally, we could focus on performance, studying firms' profits, capacity and other criteria in a comparative context to decide whether they are in the consumer interest.

This is the role of the paradigm in its original form; to study the options and potential problems in regulating industry, with the questions of who and why to regulate answered in the standard economic analysis. With our modifications the model becomes a tool for studying that same area from the consumers' point of view.

There are still problems in applying the model, the largest being that of trying to define the goals of consumers in the economic realm since the goals of individuals as consumers are not always separable from the goals of individuals as factors of production. For example, a given individual may seek from consumer policy a greater degree of product safety than currently exists in the market. Such a desire would arise from his or her experiences as a consumer. But the policy solution chosen may well have a negative impact on the level of employment, which conflicts with that same individual's role as labour. A problem in the consumer policy field is that individuals, not surprisingly, tend to put their economic concerns ahead of their consumer interests.

What we want to do, though, is to bring into the model those factors which facilitate analyzing consumer interests and which are less business-oriented and more consumer-oriented; that is, more balance in the policy process.

The Market Structure Spectrum

Many of the important consumer concerns can be identified by evaluating markets in terms of their structures and the consumer policy focus which this seems to imply. Figure 5-2 summarizes the major policy implications which the paradigm suggests for the different market structures.

Pure or Monopolistic Competition

In pure or monopolistically competitive markets there are a large number of small sellers operating in what might be called a rivalrous environment. In this

Figure 5-2 Consumer Policy Implications of Market Structure

	Pure Competition	Oligopoly	Monopoly
Structure	Many Small Firms	A Few Large Firms	Only One Firm
Conduct	Problems lie in deceptive trade practices, fraud	May be competitive or collusive; not predictable	Rationally, to raise price and lower quantity
Performance	Competition leads to "normal" profits	Depends on conduct, and so is unpredictable	Excessive profits and returns
Policy Focus	On individual firm behaviour via trade practices law, information, price discovery	On reducing forces which lead to collusive and anti-competitive behavior	On regulating pricing, profits at fair levels with acceptable service levels

situation most of the consumer policy concerns focus on conduct or behaviour, particularly with respect to fraud or deceptive practices on the part of individual sellers. It is precisely the large number of sellers and the low barriers to exit and entry which act as a natural check on firms in the industry. In turn, the close competition keeps profits and growth in check, since no firm has the power to earn "abnormal" profits.

Small retailers in various product areas, including clothing, specialty housewares, home entertainment and specialty foods are good examples of this structure. Pricing, and hence profits, are kept in check by the ease with which consumers can compare across stores. The better the service and the more helpful the information they offer consumers, the more successful a retailer is likely to be. And even in the absence of laws and regulations directed at deceptive retailers, in the long run it is expected that word will get around if a retailer is less than honest with its customers and potential customers will take their business to one of the many competitors.

The market itself will tend to regulate those involved. The policy areas of concern are largely to effectively deal with fraud and deception. This is as close as our markets tend to come to those idealized in the purely competitive "free market" models. The overriding policy measures here are to maintain the freedom of entry and exit which leads to rivalrous competition, to discourage collusion, and to enhance prohibitions against deception and fraud.

Monopoly

At the opposite end of the scale, monopoly similarly presents few problems in the identification of policy needs, although the actual tools used in response to those needs tend to be somewhat more controversial. The point here is that where a firm has monopoly power it will, if rational, tend to increase its price above what would normally -- under a competitive structure -- occur in the market. The result will be somewhat lower levels of output and extra profits to the firm at the expense of consumers.

There are a wide variety of circumstances where monopolies might surface, the most familiar of which include so-called natural monopolies such as telephone, gas and electrical utilities, government provided services and, especially for a group of consumers, geographic monopolies. In many of these cases a regulatory environment of some form has evolved which attempts to balance profit and return on investment for the firm and the provision of goods of sufficient quality and quantity at a reasonable price for the consumer.

But there are still many problems which develop in the regulation of monopolies. First, one wants to be able to evaluate whether or not regulation is effective. Included in this are the not so easy to answer questions of: on what bases do we evaluate regulation; in whose interest is it intended to be; in whose interest does it actually turn out to be; and what are the relevant criteria on which to regulate?

Second, it may be that we should be less concerned about the highly visible monopolies than we should about those which are *de facto* monopolies but perfectly legal. Using our earlier example, in a large city the number of retail clothing stores which exist may represent as close to pure competition as the retail goods sector gets. But in a smaller isolated town, a store may constitute a virtual monopoly, especially for consumers with limited mobility. Indeed, even within a large city we can think of, for example, a small pharmacist who recognizes that his clientele, composed of pensioners and other less-mobile people, are "captive" and so acts accordingly as a monopolist -- on a limited geographic basis. Similarly, zoning regulations which restrict entry frequently provide existing retailers with *de facto* geographic monopolies. Whether or not any individual case is of sufficient importance to require policy intervention must be decided on its merits.

In the case of monopoly, then, there are still many difficulties in identifying the problem firms and in choosing specific regulatory tools. But from a general perspective, the need for regulation of one form or another is generally called for. From the consumerist's point of view, the main concern is seeing that the interests of consumers are put forward as vigorously as possible and in the face of generally greater resources available for lobbying on the part of the firms being regulated.

The Grey Area of Oligopoly

Oligopolies account for a significant proportion of the markets in OECD nations, although their importance varies by country as shown in Tables 5-1 and 5-2.

The reason that oligopoly presents problems from a policy standpoint is that, unlike the cases of pure competition and monopoly, market structure and behaviour interact so as to make the actions of firms unpredictable. On the one hand, they may be fiercely competitive. On the other, there may not be sufficient competitive forces to induce the economically preferred levels of output and prices that would occur in purely or monopolistically competitive markets. However, it is probably not in the best interests of either consumers or business to assume that regulation is better than no regulation. The point is that with oligopoly, firms behaving in their own best interests may or may not be in the consumer or public interest. That question will depend on the circumstances it faces and the attitudes of the country within which it is operating. If regulation or control is imposed prematurely, more harm than good may result. More about this question in Chapter 8.

Regulation, or lack of it, in air fares and routings provides an excellent example of oligopolies in action where competitive forces appear to be able to produce the desired competitive results in one instance while remaining highly uncompetitive in another. There has been a dramatic decline in prices and significantly increased competition in air fares in North America, especially the United States, since deregulation. Savings to air travellers in the U.S. have been estimated to be at least $6 billion (in 1977 dollars) annually.[4] Although the pace has been slower in Canada, pushed by deregulation south of the border and some internal deregulation, fares have also come down. In specific cases, such as charter fares, this has also been the case in the U.K. And economic efficiency has improved.[5] However, the collusive behaviour, indeed the near monopoly behaviour of other European airlines, although highly regulated, has hardly been in the consumers' interests in those countries.[6] There are many reasons and examples of collusive behaviour. As far back as 1776, as the insightful Scottish Professor, Adam Smith, pointed out, business persons in industries whose structure lend themselves to collusive behaviour will do so, unless restrained.

Methods of Oligopoly Co-ordination - It is the possibility of the collusion among firms in an oligopoly into a *de facto* monopoly which presents the greatest threat from an oligopolistic market structure. Obviously, if the firms in an industry can come to an agreement on the way in which to divide the spoils of their actions, there can be a tremendous benefit to organizing and monopolizing a market. There are five ways in which firms are generally seen to accomplish this.

The first method is through explicit covert or overt agreement. Such agreement may take many forms, but each has at the basic level the goal of either reducing or limiting the output of the industry so as to raise prices, or setting standard prices above the normal equilibrium in conjunction with sharing of the market among firms. Among the methods used to accomplish these goals are quota or market share agreements. Another tool is industry-standardized unit prices or margins over cost which are agreed to through meetings of the firms concerned. These agreements have often arranged via "industry associations" or other bodies whose declared purpose appears to be pro-consumer but whose real purpose is to administer the agreement. Also, we can include in this group legally sanctioned organizations of firms, such as the European cartels, agricultural marketing boards in Canada and agricultural marketing orders in the United States. Although organized under the auspices of the government and the law, the desired end is the same -- to gain sufficient market power to be able to control price, restrict output and raise profits.

A more subtle form of oligopoly coordination is through a mechanism known as price leadership. In this situation there is a single firm, which may change over time in the industry, whose price changes tend to be matched by the other firms. Indeed, the economist will tell you that this is simply rational behaviour on the part of the firms -- the last thing oligopolies want is a price war, so they naturally tend to price very close to each other. Price leadership may be the result of one firm tending to dominate the others in size or market power, it may be closer to a subtle form of tacit collusion, or it may be the natural result of similar cost structures. As with oligopolies in general, it is unclear what the source of pricing similarities is, so the required reaction to them is similarly unclear.

A still looser form of coordination is the use of rules of thumb, such as standard profit margins. Often, these rules develop historically without any ill-intent on the part of the firms involved, but their effect is similar to any other tool which might act to raise prices. Rules of thumb do this by ignoring to some extent the demand side of the market.

Factors Limiting Oligopoly Co-ordination - Despite the many ways in which firms in an oligopoly may coordinate their actions to collude, there are a variety of factors which tend to limit either their ability to coordinate or the effectiveness of such coordination. First, as the number of firms involved increases so does both the difficulty in maintaining solidarity among participants and the potential benefits to any one member from breaking the agreement. The more firms, the greater the competitive pressure and the greater the danger, particularly where illegal collusive activities are concerned, that the activities will be visible to the relevant authorities.

Similarly, the greater the product heterogeneity, including differences in firm location with varying transport costs, and the greater the rate of product perishability or physical or technological change, the harder it is to coordinate the action of firms. The greater the differences between competing products, the more difficult it is for the firms to come to an agreement on what constitutes a "fair" price for the relevant products. If some firms have products which are demonstrably superior and which are so viewed by consumers, it usually is not in their interest to collude because they have a competitive edge over other industry members.

Sometimes the realities of the production or the buying process inhibits coordination. For example, the greater the fixed costs in an industry, the greater the likelihood that an agreement will break down, particularly in difficult economic times, as firms scramble to meet their break-even points. On the buying side, where orders tend to be large or "lumpy" in nature, making every order relatively important, firms will be encouraged to try to sidestep the agreement in the hope of making a sale.

Finally, the social structure of an industry has an important bearing on the effectiveness of coordination. First, the easier it is for a given producer or seller to maintain secrecy between itself and a buyer with whom it is dealing outside of a collusive agreement, the more likely a breaking of the ranks will occur. Conversely, if shipment amounts and destinations are easily seen by competitors who participate in the scheme, then such a breaking of the ranks would be bound to elicit retribution from the other firms, and so would not be as likely to be undertaken. Second, the social structure of the people in the various firms is important. The more that they are friends and the less that they are simply competitive business people, the more likely that the opportunity will arise to develop collusive agreements.

The general point is that the greater the extent to which normal competitive forces exist in an industry, the less likely that oligopolies can coordinate to the detriment of the consuming public. The reasons why oligopolies might come into existence in the first place are varied. It might be small markets, high fixed costs, government infant industry protection, or any of a number of other factors in combination. But we can look at the factors which encourage or limit oligopoly coordination as independent of the initial reasons for why the oligopolies exist.

This is the important lesson for the policy field -- that the potential remedies to the problem of oligopoly do not necessarily lie in the initial causes of the oligopoly. If an oligopoly exists because of abuse and dominance of the market by a few firms, then the policy action should probably be directed at these firms. But, because some oligopolies result from natural market forces, policy must, in those cases, be directed not specifically at the firms, but rather at the market in general in an attempt to foster those forces which limit coordination while, hopefully, creating sufficient legal barriers to inhibit firms from engaging in collusive behaviour.

GOVERNMENTS AND THEIR CORPORATIONS

The largest monopolists in the OECD are the governments. And their involvement in their respective economies, with one exception -- Switzerland -- has increased over the past decade, as shown in Table 5-3. When crown or government corporations are included in these numbers, the involvement is even higher. The involvement is ubiquitous, ranging from provision of basic safety and fire protection, the military, to housing, health services, education, food, welfare, justice and many other concerns which vary from country to country.

This is not necessarily bad for consumers, since many of the areas of involvement result in income redistribution and greater equity. Of course, this value judgement is highly specific to individual preferences and depends on whether one gets or one gives up.

The policy concern for consumers is how to control and influence how much involvement the government has in the provision of goods and services and the way in which these services are provided. Market mechanisms are replaced by political and other mechanisms in the control and direction of the operation of government-provided services. The ease with which influence and controls are implemented and the effectiveness of efforts to represent consumers in government-provided goods and services is highly influenced by the form of government and attitudes about how much citizens should be involved in it. As is discussed in depth in Chapter 7, having consumer representatives in sufficient numbers being put on the

Table 5-3 Government Expenditures as a Percentage of Gross Domestic Product in Selected OECD Countries, 1973-1983

Country	Currency		Government Final Consumption Expenditures	Gross Domestic Product	Percent	Percent Change
Canada	C$mil	73	23037	123560	18.6	+2.9
		83	84104	390340	21.5	
United States	U$bil	73	270.4	1326.4	20.4	+0.3
		83	685.5	3304.8	20.7	
Japan	Ybil	73	9336	112441	8.3	+1.9
		83	27997	274639	10.2	
Australia	A$mil	73	6133	47394	12.9	+4.8
		83	30413	171898	17.7	
Austria	Scmil	73	81913	543458	15.1	+3.6
		83	226026	1205808	18.7	
Finland	Mkmil	73	10694	71364	15.0	+4.4
		83	53208	274941	19.4	
France	Frbil	73	149.8	1114.2	13.4	+5.6
		83	654.2	3439.9	19.0	
Germany	DMmil	73	163160	918900	17.8	+2.2
		83	334150	1671600	20.0	
Italy	Lbil	73	14345	89746	16.0	+4.0
		83	107380	535904	20.0	
Sweden	Kmil	73	120782	464456	26.0	+3.5
		83	159425	541038	29.5	
Switzer-land	Frmil	73	14815	130060	14.4	-0.7
		83	27900	203860	13.7	
United Kingdom	Pdmil	73	13429	73997	18.1	+3.8
		83	65955	300993	21.9	

SOURCE: OECD (1984) "Quarterly National Accounts." Paris: Department of Economics and Statistics, No. 4.

regulatory and administrative tribunals or advisory bodies to the institutions providing these services, developing communication paths to the bureaucrats who are responsible for the services, fostering good relationships with the politicians involved, implementing an effective information program and relationship with the mass media, and a variety of other methods are used to try to influence government. While the ballot box is often touted as the way to influence governments, this method is probably the least effective since national elections take place on broader issues. And, once in power, governments are subject to most of the same pressures as were their predecessors. Furthermore, the small but cumulative day-to-day interactions and decisions which are necessary to influence the provision of goods and services are lost in the larger concerns of an election. While important, elections are infrequent and only a partial answer.

The consumer concerns we have outlined previously -- efficiency, equity and justice -- hold for government services as they do for private firms. Government intervention is said to be justified to counter market failures and to improve efficiency. Indeed, such things as medical care and education, while private in some instances or existing along with publicly financed services, frequently have been taken over by government because of citizen demand. And it is not always inefficient, as ideologues for "free enterprise" would have people believe. The highly skewed and expensive private medical care system in the United States, where the affluent get excellent care and the less affluent a much lower level of service, when compared to the publicly insured or financed medical systems in other OECD countries, is not a good example of economic efficiency and illustrates the distributional inequities of market systems. My French friends and visitors to that country have complained bitterly about the bureaucracy and power of local magistrates and the individual's feeling of helplessness when being subjected to the whims of the power of these bureaucrats to limit the freedom of those they are supposed to serve.

It would appear to be part of the consumer interest if consumers had a role in molding government, but more importantly bureaucracies, to the wishes of consumers. These matters become normative questions of whether the distribution and use of power is just and equitable. Is it what was intended? The correcting mechanisms of the market place, when they work, may need to be supplemented by other mechanisms when governments provide goods and services. The framework for consumer policy presented in Chapter 8 will help structure some of these types of problems and suggest some solutions which may help in these matters.

MACROECONOMIC POLICY

Who questions the relevance of consumers' interests in the level of economic activity, in questions of fiscal policy, in the level of tariffs and protection afforded industry, in levels of military spending, in all manner of macroeconomic decisions affecting people in their consuming roles? As discussed in Chapter 1, government's role is to balance the interests of consumers, business and labour in the economy. And there are many conflicts among these groups. High interest rates reduce the number of jobs but benefit saving consumers and reduces inflation, which erodes the buying power of consumers on fixed incomes. In such situations it is difficult to determine what is in the consumers' interest. However, there are other issues for which it is less difficult to determine a clear cut consumer interest. Until recently most consumer groups only infrequently questioned these types of decisions from the point of view of their constituencies. As Lucy Black Creighton maintained, consumer groups have neglected this critical area of their interests probably more than any other.[7]

However, that is changing. Consumer groups over the past decade or so in the European Economic Community, both at their country level and at the Community level, through the coordination efforts of BEUC, have produced a series of position papers and engaged in lobbying efforts on a wide range of industrial organization *cum* macroeconomic issues. One example is the *Report on Air Fares*, cited earlier. Many of the policies of the Common Agricultural Policy, by far the most costly of EEC programs and a consumer of a lion's share of its budget, has been questioned by consumer groups. However, the current policy document of the International Organization of Consumers' Unions contains only passing recognition of macroeconomic concerns.[8] This may be justified on the grounds that so many microeconomic and safety problems exist in developing countries, where the organization has chosen to devote its efforts, that macro policy is a luxury their limited resources cannot afford to deal with yet.

In Canada, the Consumers' Association of Canada has established policies on many macroeconomic issues over the last decade and regularly makes comments on government policy in these areas.[9] In the United States, the Consumers' Union has established advocacy offices in four regional locations and has made comments about economic policy to a degree. But, because of their tax free status, which allows no lobbying, they must be careful in what they say. Nonetheless, a number of other public interest groups and the Consumers Federation of America have commented increasingly on such policy issues.

Given the complexity of macroeconomic policy and consumers, there is only space here to point out that it is an area of great importance to consumers. However, because these issues are often complex and frequently affect groups of consumers differently, consumer advocates will have to pick the issues on which they choose to comment. Further, since most countries have consumer ministries at the cabinet level, these ministries should, in the normal course of their mandate, represent consumers in such high level policy decisions. Since such a ministry does not exist in the United States, consumers there may feel less well represented and the need for other methods for influence may be greater. However, that subject is outside the scope of this book.

SUMMARY

Consumer policy in industrial organization is shown to logically focus on the structure -- competitive, oligopoly or monopoly -- and on the conduct and performance of firms in an economy. The goal of such focus is the fostering of an efficient economy which produces maximum output. As governments become an increasing factor in the provision of goods and services, consumers need ways in which to counter the lack of market mechanisms to help influence the activities of these non-market driven institutions. Further, the current level of representation of consumer interests in macroeconomic policy decisions frequently fails to adequately reflect the interest of citizens in that policy.

NOTES

1 Baumol, William J., Panzar, John C., and Willig, Robert D. (1982) *Contestable Markets and the Theory of Industry Structure*. New York: Harcourt Brace Jovanovich, Inc., provides a summary of recent thought in this area as well as their recent contributions which expand on traditional views.
2 Leibenstein, Harvey (1966) "Allocative Efficiency vs. X-Efficiency," *American Economic Review*, 56 (June), pp. 392-415.
3 Kamerschen, David R., and Wallace, Richard L. (1972) "The Costs of Monopoly," *Antitrust Bulletin*, 17:1 (Summer), pp. 485-496.
4 Morrison, Steven, and Winston, Clifford (1986) *The Economic Effects of Airline Deregulation*. Washington, DC: The Brookings Institution, p. 1.
5 Caves, Douglas W., Christensen, Laurits R., Tretheway, Michael W., and Windle, Robert J. (1985) "An Assessment of the Efficiency Effects of U.S. Airline Deregulation Via an International Comparison." Madison, WI: Wisconsin Economic Research Institute, University of Wisconsin, (Dec. 1), mimeo.
6 BEUC (1985) *Report on Air Fares*. Brussels: Bureau Europeen des Unions de Consommateurs, July 11.
7 Creighton, Lucy Black (1976) *Pretenders to the Throne: The Consumer Movement in the United States*. Lexington, MA: D.C. Heath and Co., pp. 91-92.
8 IOCU (ca1984) *IOCU: Giving a Voice to the World's Consumers*. The Hague: International Organization of Consumers' Unions.
9 *Canadian Consumer*, almost any issue in the last decade will contain an example.

6. CONSUMERS AND THE LAW

Laws regarding consumers and their relations with manufacturers and sellers have evolved rapidly over the past several decades. The rate of technological change in the market place has, in many respects, invalidated the principle of *caveat emptor* -- let the buyer beware. In addition, the growth in government pointed out in Chapter 5 has been accompanied with a growth in regulation, with the result that consumers have voiced the need for access to and protection from regulatory institutions and governments.[1]

Unique geographic, cultural, economic, political, legal, and administrative systems have made it inevitable that the concept of consumer protection has been observed from different perspectives and has developed at varying speeds in the OECD countries. And yet, this chapter will point out that, despite the many differences in legal systems, institutions and processes, there are many similarities in the solutions found to problems common to consumers in all countries.[2]

The purpose of this chapter is to expose the reader to the philosophy of the law, to show some practical examples of how that philosophy is applied and affects consumers, and to look at where the law seems to be heading in each of the areas addressed. It makes no claim to be a comprehensive overview or comparative analysis of consumer law in the OECD countries. That task was beyond our resources. Having said that, it frequently compares the situation in several countries to clarify concepts and illustrate difficulties. In this regard we have been selective and have had to bypass legal detail which, while important to lawyers, need not concern us here.

No one has made a comprehensive collection or analysis of consumer law in OECD countries, although several studies cited here cover portions of that whole.[3] Indeed, without these efforts I would not have been able to have as complete a chapter.

The first part of the chapter presents a number of definitions and some basic philosophical problems in making and using laws to deal with consumer problems. Secondly, the major legal concerns of consumers are discussed under the headings of prices, information, advertising, deceptive practices, product safety, liability, credit, contract, regulation and redress.

DEFINITIONS AND BACKGROUND

The law is the most formal and most precisely stated set of rules, institutions and processes for prescribing and administering a society's accepted rules of behaviour. It also prescribes penalties to be imposed for unacceptable behaviour. Because of this function of the law in society, members of the legal profession have been in the forefront of many developments in the consumerism movement, both in using remedies in the law to redress inequities in the marketplace as well as in advocating and designing new law for areas in which the existing law has been found inadequate for consumers.

The law in each OECD country has a legal system based on one or a combination of two basic legal systems, **civil or common law**.

Civil law developed in a large majority of those countries which were once included in the domain of the Western Roman Empire. The main features of civil law systems include the existence of codes covering large areas of the law and setting down the rights and duties of persons in fairly general terms, a less strict regard for judicial precedents than the common law, and a great reliance on the influence of academic lawyers to systemize, criticize and develop the law in their books and writings.[4]

Common law is the body of principles and rules of law developed and stated by judges in opinions on particular disputes or claims, or derived inductively from examinations of various opinions in various relevant cases.[5] Derived from the common law of England, the common law system is the basic legal framework of the United Kingdom, Canada, Australia, New Zealand, Ireland, Wales, and the United States. Although legislation is playing a much greater part, and in some areas a predominant role, under the common law judicial precedent is still regarded as binding or persuasive on deciding a particular legal case. Case law is built up over time as courts make decisions, either interpreting legislation or setting precedents where legislation does not exist. As one author describes the difference between these two systems, "Common law systems are more adversarial or accusatorial than the inquisitorial civil law systems."[6]

Statute law refers to the body of principles and rules of law laid down in statutes and statutory instruments passed by government legislatures. Where statutes exist, the judge is obliged to adhere to the rights and remedies as specified. Statute law is superior to common law in that it may amend, overrule, or abolish inconsistent principles or existing judicial practices. This flows from the political concept of parliamentary supremacy, held in check by some form of constitution.

New statutes are introduced by the legislature involved when common law does not evolve rapidly enough or when a particular government deems the present direction of the law to be undesirable. However, statute law does not exist by itself, but over time is interpreted by the courts in the evaluation of common law surrounding and interpreting a statute. In effect, the civil law system is a system of statutes with relatively less judicial interpretive latitude than is found in common law systems.

Civil vs. Criminal vs. Administrative Law differentiate types of laws which are distinct from the legal systems (civil or common law). They can be differentiated according to the courts in which each is enforced, the procedures used for enforcement, and the sanctions which may be levied for their contravention.

From a consumer's perspective, **civil law** proceedings are the means by which they may maintain and defend their private rights as set out by common or statute law against any other individual or business. The plaintiff in a civil suit is the private consumer and it is she or he who must initiate the proceedings as well as be responsible for financing the action. If the suit is lost, the plaintiff must also pay the defendant's court costs. The cost, complexity, and time required to complete the proceedings often discourage consumers from initiating civil actions. Only the most confident individual plaintiffs with relatively large potential settlements pursue their civil rights through the courts because the costs of lawyers and case preparation necessitate large potential damages to justify the risks involved.

The plaintiff in a **criminal** action is a prosecutor who acts on behalf of the state. A criminal charge is brought against the defendant by the police or a public official. The preparation, presentation, and costs are the responsibility of the state. It is, therefore, the existence of the state in criminal law which differentiates it from civil law. Though it is possible for a private individual to initiate a criminal action, the legal and practical considerations make this an unlikely route. However, a consumer or consumer group may lobby for and assist the state in the initiation of a criminal action.

Administrative law is concerned with the rules, mainly statute laws, governing the function and powers of governmental agencies whose responsibility it is to develop, implement and administer government policy. Their functions and areas of intervention seem ubiquitous. In the area of consumer protectionism, administrative law might give specific government agencies the power to: require private persons to do or to refrain from certain conduct; to investigate; to require information, statistics, returns, etc. from individuals or business; to license; to grant or refuse permission for the carrying on of particular kinds of business or trades; and to tax.[7]

The application and interpretation of administrative law can be challenged and modified both in the courts as well as by the individuals who are chosen to administer it by the government(s) involved. For example, the complex Common Agricultural Policy of the European Economic Community is based on administrative law and a wide and complex arrangement of administrative bodies.[8] In many cases, consumers have found it difficult to be heard by administrative tribunals whose bureaucrats may become almost a law unto themselves. The discussion and examples of regulation presented in this chapter and elsewhere in the book are evidence of this phenomenon. A good deal of consumer advocacy effort has been spent trying to ensure access to these bodies and to develop a process through which consumers' interests are routinely considered in the development and application of administrative law.

Modern consumer legislation usually combines each of these three law types, but the specifics vary widely among countries. It is not uncommon, therefore, for one country to classify a specific consumer right as a civil matter while its neighbor classifies it as criminal or administrative. For example, the truthfulness doctrine underlying most advertising legislation is a criminal matter in France, but a civil matter in Germany.[9]

Philosophical Conflicts in the Law

In the development and application of laws there are philosophical conflicts on matters of freedom, equity and efficiency: *freedom*, in that as soon as a law is imposed freedoms are restricted; *equity*, in that all individuals or groups in a society usually are not affected equally by a particular law; and *efficiency*, in that laws vary in their effectiveness in accomplishing their purpose.

Over the last 200 years the moral philosophy of utilitarianism has been the basis for developments of laws and justice in the Western World.[10] The general concept underlying this philosophy is that governments should work to provide for the greatest good of the greatest number of individuals. The corollary to this is the frequent erosion of individuals' rights for the greater collective good. It is all too easy under this philosophy to violate minority rights with a resultant despotism by the majority. In general, any "bill of individual rights" is open to erosion under utilitarianism and courts and legislatures constantly face problems of balancing the two.

Another conflict is that of *equity*, in that the imposition of a law almost never falls equally on each individual in a society. A classic example of the unequal effects of legislation on consumers is the case of sales taxes on basic necessities. Because such taxes are a flat percentage of a purchase, the relative impact of sales taxes is greater on the less affluent consumers who spend a greater proportion of their income on necessities than more affluent consumers. Of course, this example assumes that equality in income distribution is a policy objective of the particular jurisdiction imposing the law.

The third conflict is a question of how to *efficiently* impose a particular policy. While individual freedoms may be abridged by a law, and while its effects may be unequally distributed within society, on balance, the decision maker may decide that efficiency and ease of imposition and administration indicate that a tradeoff among these considerations is appropriate. Such is often the case with sales taxes, import quotas and similar laws.

The final philosophical dilemma facing the consumer is that the law lies in the "social contract" philosophy which implies a "bill of rights" for individuals which is guaranteed and which may not be abridged. Basic to the "social contract" is the requirement that, "Each person is to have an equal right to the most extensive basic liberty compatible with similar liberty for other."[11] In question here are some rights which are basic to individuals and not subject to erosion for whatever reason. In most societies the right to life holds such a position, but even here, for the unborn and the terminally ill, there is a continuing debate.

Who is the Consumer?

A clear and concise definition of the person to be protected is needed in order to create new and update existing consumer legislation. No existing legislation has such a definition but four ways have been suggested for viewing the problem.[12] The more traditional point of view is defining the consumer as a subject of certain protective measures. A narrow definition could include only private persons using goods and services for private ends. However, a consumer may be identified by means of objective criteria such as being considered a consumer if he or she engages in certain activities. For example, having certain types of credit up to a certain limit or taking correspondence courses or making travel contracts. A third approach excludes as a consumer activity individuals engaged in professional transactions, such as a doctor who, despite being an individual, is not considered a consumer while at the work place. Lastly, the consumer may be regarded as being more than one person. In the area of collective consumer interests, and where law permits, the consumer may be an entity whose members have a common interest.

The Commission of the European Communities acknowledged the problem of defining the consumer when they stated, "The consumer is no longer seen merely as a purchaser and user of goods and services for personal, family, or group purposes but also as a person concerned with the various facets of society which affect him either directly or indirectly as a consumer."[13]

Federalism - Jurisdictional Problems

All the OECD countries have multiple levels of government which affect consumer legislation in greater or lesser degree. Members of the European Communities have imposed upon them a supra-national set of laws. Further, all the OECD countries are members of the United Nations. That organization also attempts to influence consumer policy and is another potential level of jurisdictional influence. This short section briefly outlines some of the major concerns and effects of jurisdictional problems in consumer law. A detailed examination of jurisdictional questions in consumer law for the United States and for the European Communities is the subject of a recent and most welcome addition to the consumer law literature. [14]

The effects of differing jurisdictions on consumers range from minor inconveniences to potentially serious health and safety problems and reduced effectiveness of consumer policy. For example, information labelling requirements are frequently different between jurisdictions and consumers must search for the information they may normally expect on a package. Weights and measures have frequently been different. For example, the United States is the only OECD country where metric measurements are not standard. It is not uncommon to see products being produced in a jurisdiction where their sale is prohibited and being sold in another jurisdiction where their sale is legal. [15] An example of this is pharmaceutical products and pesticides. This kind of difference has resulted, for example, in a firm moving from a jurisdiction where regulation is more stringent to one where restrictions are fewer. Indeed, national governments, states, provinces, counties, and municipalities have often used less stringent laws and taxation provisions, including consumer laws, to attract business and investment. Like disease, fraudulent practices do not respect geographic or political boundaries.

Therefore, there is good reason even within a nation to champion federal or centralized consumer law. In addition, centralizing consumer law jurisdiction in the senior governments, at least in Canada and the United States, would probably result in more funds being available, less duplication of effort, and greater detection of violations and ease of enforcement.

However, if the central government is less than enthusiastic about consumer protection, as the Reagan government has been in the United States, then centralized law might not be enforced nor expanded as it would under a more proactive, albeit less senior, jurisdiction.

These examples of jurisdictional problems are but a few of many which affect consumer law and add to the difficulty of designing legislation. Having said that, through cooperation between jurisdictions, through developing model legislation, through colloquia of Attorneys General, consumer lawyers and similar experts who have experience in designing and implementing laws for consumers which work, a wide range of legislation has been developed to help consumers have a fairer deal with respect to other interests in the market place and in the political/regulatory environment.

PRICES

Perhaps the highest profile and most immediate concern of consumers is the price of goods and services. Price is the most visible of the economic indicators; it is the backbone of economic theory and price levels are of ongoing concern to consumers and producers alike. It is not surprising, therefore, that there is a body of consumer law relating to price. Some of the price related laws covered in this section could have been treated in the section on information, which follows, but are discussed here because of the importance that price itself has in the economic process. It is this process which the laws in this section are designed to help function more efficiently and effectively.

A class of laws has developed which are aimed at making price more visible, with the goal of helping consumers make faster and better comparisons among competing goods and services. They also attempt to ensure that quoted prices are not misleading. These laws recognize that price is considered a good indicator of relative value and attempt to maximize the value of price information. Another class of laws has attempted to use price to solve social problems, such as to control inflation or redistribute income. For these problems price legislation is a very ineffective policy tool to attain these goals and, except in the short run, are generally counterproductive. The first part of this section discusses those laws which attempt to use price in its most informational form.

Price Display

Price displays are required in a variety of situations where consumers might otherwise be misled. The rationale behind this law is that a number of consumers are apparently embarrassed to ask the price of goods and, if they want a product and ask for its price, they do not return the good or will not refuse to buy it if the price is higher than they wish to pay. In the United Kingdom, for example, petrol stations are required to display the prices of at least two grades of petrol and the price for parts of gallons if it differs from the ordinary price, the argument being that once someone has driven up to the pump and has to ask for the price, he or she would be unlikely to drive away if it was thought that the price was too high.[16] Extending this idea, one must ask whether or not sellers should be required to post a price for all goods offered for sale.

The policy question is, of course, how much price information should be required of sellers and what are the implications of allowing goods and services to be offered for sale without visible price quotations. Since the decision to withhold price information rests with the seller, we might question the motivation for doing so. The only apparent motivation is that not quoting a price, particularly a high one, helps the seller to identify potential buyers (through their inquiries) in a direct contact situation, allowing them to persuade the prospect that the price is justified or affordable. Implicit in this is their belief that displaying price would discourage such consumers from any inquiry at all. Clearly, this is not only a legal question, but one of ethics and morality which is best solved in the political arena, the subject of the next chapter.

Unit Pricing

Unit pricing is the requirement for sellers to display the price of comparable products in a standard price per unit. For example, all tomato sauces may be required to be quoted as a price per 100 ml. This is usually required at point of sale, for example, on the grocery shelf where the product is being sold. Unit pricing is designed to assist consumers to compare prices. It arose from some classic experiments in Sacramento, California, where a number of highly educated ladies were asked to buy the least expensive cost per unit shopping basket. Because of the wide proliferation of sizes it was found that the task was difficult. For example, which can of coffee offers better unit value -- the 2.15 lb. tin selling for $4.95 or the .98 lb. tin selling for $2.15? Many products, such as meat, fish, cheese, vegetables, and fruit have been offered on a unit price basis (7 francs per kilogram or $2.99 per pound) for years. (Give up on the example? The $2.15 package costs $2.30/lb. while the smaller package sells for $2.19/lb.)

Unit pricing laws may also help where there has been a proliferation of sizes and packaging forms. For example, several years ago a class of mine looked at the liquid detergents offered in a large supermarket and found that the package sizes varied from 16 ounces to 14 3/4 ounces. It appeared that the only reason the smaller packages had been offered was to disguise the fact that their prices were more per unit than the standard 16 ounce size. Similarly, some glass bottle packages of similar types of merchandise were made hour glass shaped, i.e., narrow in the centre and large on the top and bottom. It was contended that this was to make consumers believe they were getting more, since such bottle shapes appear larger than straight round forms because they are taller and often have tops and bottoms of greater circumference. Almost invariably, this shape of bottle held less than standard packages and cost more per unit. I hasten to point out, however, that this bottle design for slippery liquid vegetable oils was a great improvement over their straight sided predecessors. Similar concerns occur with underfilled packages, such as detergents, whose large format and underfilling are probably due to two reasons, obtaining larger exposure for advertising on the grocery shelf and for consumer deception.

Another way to facilitate comparison is to permit only standard sizes. However, in choosing this latter route one may end up restricting unduly the need for experimentation with different packages which may be to the benefit of consumers. Nonetheless, some jurisdictions have enacted standardized package sizes of products as well as unit pricing.[17]

There have been several studies which purport to show that consumers do not use unit-pricing information in their decisions. However, there is a great deal of evidence that some consumers use unit pricing as one of a number of ways to evaluate price. It appears that the jury is still out on the question of legislated unit-pricing's effectiveness in increasing price discovery and transparency.

Comparative/Regular/List Prices

There are a wide variety of situations where claims about prices, often compared to "regular" or to competitors' prices, are misleading or patently false, and where laws have been passed in an attempt to reduce the frequency of misleading or patently false price claims. A Canadian example provides some insight into how subtle these price comparison problems can be. In Burnaby, B.C., a drug store chain (Shoppers Drug Mart) distributed a flyer to local homes claiming "the best possible dollar value and saving on every item, every day, whether drugs, vitamins, prescriptions or toiletries." One recipient of the flyer thought the claim would be "really marvelous if it were true", but "also thought they were promising the moon", and so decided to do an actual price comparison on a prescription drug. When she discovered that Shoppers Drug Mart's prices were, in fact, significantly higher than their competitors' she filed a complaint to the responsible federal agency. An investigation resulted in a charge being laid, a conviction and the drug store chain being fined $10,000.[18] The case is interesting for two reasons. First, it points out that price claims need not be quantified in order to be misleading or false under the law. Second, it shows how a consumer's concern or complaint can prompt authorities -- who otherwise would likely not have investigated the store's claim -- into investigation and the laying of charges.

Another widespread deceptive practice involves comparing a sale price to some "normal" price. In Canada, it is illegal to advertise a price and compare it to a "normal" price if substantial sales have not been made at the "normal" price in a reasonable period preceding the ad.[19]

But a related practice which seems to help skirt this law involves using the "manufacturer's suggested list price", or MSLP, rather than some "normal" price. MSLP's are the retail prices that manufacturers put on their products, with standard wholesale and retail markups included. These prices may be the actual price at which the merchandise sells, but are often only a starting price from which bargaining takes place to determine the real selling price in the market. While MSLP may be generally adhered to in some companies or industries, in others it may bear no resemblance to the actual market price, which can be substantially lower. The difficulty with outlawing MSLP is that it and related practices, such as pre-priced packages, have legitimate uses and benefits for members of the distribution channel, particularly in saving on the costs of pricing merchandise when it enters stores.

The deceptive use of these techniques occurs when MSLP or pre-packaged prices are deliberately set so high that advertised discounts or savings relative to the MSLP are not really what the consumer saves, given the real market price. What is a saving of $4.00 on a MSLP of $10 if the "normal" store price is $7.00? It is for exactly this reason that in its 1979 Report on Bargain Prices and Similar Marketing Practices, the OECD Committee on Consumer Policy stated:

> The incidence for sales below recommended retail prices is such that the Committee believes on balance the use of recommended retail prices for price comparison purposes should be subject to regulation.

The differences in the way different countries deal with "recommended prices" show that it is problematic in policy formation. Although there appear to be no blanket bans on their use, almost every OECD country has at least some form of control available. In France, a government order can stop their use, while Germany and the UK go further, stating that recommended prices may be banned where they are used to deceive or create confusion in consumers. Denmark, on the other hand, seems to have no explicit controls on their use.[20] The policy question, again, is one of honesty and truthfulness in a practice prevalent in many of the OECD countries. Limiting comparative prices to those in the marketplace would limit the use of a usually legitimate tool to avoid prosecution under laws against quoting as "normal" prices above those prevailing in the market. Indeed, in Canada the use of MSLPs or "recommended" prices is addressed exactly as any other price comparison used in advertising -- the quoted price must have been generally used by the vendor within a reasonable period preceding the ad, especially where an inference of savings over the quoted price is made.[21]

Resale Price Maintenance

Resale price maintenance (RPM) is the practice of a manufacturer prescribing a retail price for merchandise and refusing to supply or otherwise (losing orders, late orders) disciplining retailers who cut prices. RPM is only effective for highly visible and strongly demanded branded merchandise because those retailers discounting merchandise depend on competing retailers to maintain the standard price and thereby make the discount price a bargain. The attractiveness of RPM can be seen when you consider that manufacturers incur much conflict with those retailers who carry large stocks of the manufacturer's merchandise, advertise the brand strongly, and maintain an attractive store with competent personnel, if a few of their competitors cut price and take advantage of the merchandising efforts for the brand by fellow retailers. The consumer concern is a lack of price competition at the retail level. This concern is relatively small if there are many competing brands in the market.

RPM laws vary widely in the OECD countries. For example, while there are no RPM laws in Belgium and Italy, the practice is completely banned in Germany, France, and Luxembourg. In the UK there is a ban on RPM against third parties, and Denmark bans it except in special circumstances.[22] In the United States the law is determined on a state-by-state basis, while in Canada there are federal laws banning it. The experience in Canada and the United States is not only that laws are needed, but that enforcement is critical since strong forces encourage the existence of RPM where a manufacturer has the economic power to enforce compliance. Further, one researcher has stated that businesses would be economically irrational not to break laws, such as those against RPM, because the penalties handed down by the courts are so low as make them irrelevant.[23] This area will continue to be a controversial one in consumer law.

Price Increase Clauses in Contracts

Contracts containing clauses about price increases are most important when two parties enter into long-term agreements. Not unreasonably, the vendor will usually attempt to provide for unilateral price increases in the good or service to keep up with either inflation or production costs. There are two types of price increase clauses of interest to the consumer.

The first type is the index clause which allows the vendor to keep prices in line with the general rate of inflation. France, West Germany, and Belgium, for example, do not allow an index clause because it would be counter-productive to their general economic policies.

Of more concern to consumers is a clause providing for the unilateral right to raise prices without changing the context (validity) of the contract and which bars the consumer from opposing the increase or access to arbitration on the increase. Most legislation prohibits such clauses. Where they are allowed, for example in West Germany, France, the Netherlands and Denmark, the law usually provides for government intervention and/or gives the consumer the right to withdraw from the contract.[24]

Inflation

In recent years, the desire to control general price level increases has led governments to place more emphasis on controlling prices directly. This has been done by establishing specific and general price codes. Which type of code is chosen depends primarily on the economic and philosophical viewpoint of the government in power. For example, in the United States before Reagan was elected President in 1980, price controls were used to attempt to thwart inflation. Under the Reagan administration, deregulation and tight monetary policy were chosen over the former direct controls. Direct intervention to control prices has been evident in Italy, Belgium, and the Netherlands, while both direct and indirect controls, such as tight fiscal and monetary policy, have been seen in France, Canada and the UK. This changes over time and with governments. Although an analysis of the effectiveness of each policy is beyond the scope of this book, several of the problems that might result are worth noting.

Typical price control legislation usually permits the government to issue orders controlling prices of some or all goods and services. Market regulation must be imposed by administrative means rather than by the pricing mechanism. For example, Belgian inflation legislation set maximum prices, monitored profits, made price increases subject to application to a commission, allowed commodity groups to design agreements (stability pacts) to control price increases on an industry wide basis and allowed the government to control price index clauses in contracts.[25]

The administrative control that results from the use of price legislation as a tool to protect consumers is fraught with ideological problems and its effectiveness is highly questionable when viewed in the cold light of hindsight. However, since price is such a visible thing, because the general public and politicians like "quick fixes", and because of their immediate short term effects, laws which affect prices are frequently resorted to in times of inflation and similar problem situations. The problem is that price controls attack only a symptom or outcome of inflation and income inequality, not the source of the problems. The result of using price control mechanisms to these ends is the need for yet more stringent, bureaucratic counter measures to control their side effects. Almost without fail, one ends up with situations which defeat the original intent of the legislation.

Classic examples are legion in food and housing policy. Poland has had recurrent crises of food shortages caused by prices fixed at low levels to both consumers and farmers. Farm output continues at low levels, food shortages are rampant and a black market in food exists. The government meets violent resistance each time they attempt to raise prices to more realistic levels. The European Community have fixed prices at artificially high prices to farmers and use a large proportion of the Community budget to subsidize prices to both consumers and farmers. Excessive farm output results in the classic butter mountains, wine lakes and the subsidized dumping of excess farm production on the world market creating low and distorted world prices and production decisions. Many countries have fixed rental prices for housing at unrealistically low levels. The result has been under investment in housing by private investors. Governments have either had to embark on large public housing programs or have had to face the political pressures of un-fixing prices. Under stringent financial controls of recent years, with very limited government resources, those countries with large public housing programs have seen increasing shortages. A variety of black market subterfuges to circumvent and take advantage of the abnormally low levels of rent are reported in the press with regularity.

The examples in this section are evidence that price is a good indicator of relative value, but not an efficient way of redistributing income. The problems and their symptoms are merely delayed to a future date or transferred to another group in society, such as taxpayers, or landlords, or farmers. Of course, this may indeed be a satisfactory solution to some, but in a policy treatise such as this book, one should point out the implications of these anomalies.

CONSUMER INFORMATION

The history of the development of the common law regarding truthfulness and the need for accurate information is stark evidence that the courts, for many years, have recognized that sellers have frequently manipulated or suppressed information which would have helped consumers make better decisions. In Chapter 4 the theoretical and practical importance of accurate, timely, unbiased, properly analyzed, and generally useful information was dealt with at some length. It seems a logical development that laws have been passed requiring sellers to provide consumers with basic information about products and services. Some of the most ancient consumer information laws were requirements to accurately weigh and measure food products. Butchers putting their thumb on the scale is notorious in consumer folklore.

Many countries have introduced laws ensuring that at least a basic amount of information is provided consumers and that that information is displayed in a manner which makes it easy for consumers to find and comprehend. The international symbols of a skull and crossbones to denote poison and a stylized explosion for danger from incineration are well known. The next section discusses seller-provided information, other than advertising. The section following it will then turn specifically to the concerns with advertising as a source of consumer information.[26]

Labelling, Weights, and Measures

Labelling, legalistically, denotes a "legal system aimed at providing objective product or service information either attached to the product itself or accompanying the service by means of a written statement."[27] It is the producer or retailer who is normally obligated to provide the label in conformity with the legislation.

The number of goods and services available and their differences in technical construction, chemical composition, and performance, has made it virtually impossible to provide comprehensive labelling legislation. Therefore, countries have developed a system of laws to provide a general framework for designing information to be provided to consumers. The finer details are left in the hands of administrative regulators to create, monitor, and enforce. The amount and enthusiasm of enforcement depends on the jurisdiction.

Countries such as Belgium, Denmark, the UK, Ireland, Canada and France have given their administrative regulators rather broad powers. This is in contrast to West Germany, Italy, and the Netherlands where the regulators are restricted to specifically authorized products. However, the substance of the two types of legislative frameworks is fairly similar.[28]

Labels are selling tools as well as consumer information sources. Over-exuberance and the desire of sellers to deceive consumers has led to laws which specify how, where, and in what size of print type and a variety of other information which must appear on labels. I still remember labels without specification of the amount of contents, warning labels for poison almost hidden on the backs of packages and the like. I also remember the uproar in Canada when package goods producers reacted to the introduction of the current packaging laws which require readable labels.[29] Danger warning signs were required to be on the front of packages, print had to be of readable size and so on. Packagers assured the public that prices would be higher, that some firms would go out of business, and similar dire consequences would result, all due to the fact that sellers had to provide buyers with minimal information about the products they were selling. A decade later, none of the predicted effects of this labelling legislation had come about, except that consumers now have laws which ensure some basic information.

The expansion of international trade and the creation of the European Communities has highlighted the need for greater standardization of weights, lengths, quality, description, and packaging of products across countries. Pre-packaged foods in many countries must now have a label stating the ingredients in descending order of volume or weight as they occur in the product.[30] The name and address of the packer is usually required by the importing country if the exporting country's domestic laws do not require it for their home consumers. Weights and measures regulations, requiring the disclosure of quantity of specified foodstuffs, fuels and other miscellaneous goods are now common. An interesting situation is provided by Smith and Swann.[31] The U.K. Weights and Measure Act 1963 (amended 1976) specifies, "The greater quantity in which alcohol is served in public houses -- beer must be sold in quantities of 1/3 pint,

1/2 pint, or multiples thereof, and gin, rum, whisky, and vodka must be sold in multiples of 1/4, 1/5, or 1/6 of a gill." New regulations have been enacted to further protect the consumer by requiring that a pint of beer be served in a glass where the pint mark is visible and below the rim of the glass so as to allow for the head, which is not included for measurement purposes. This is a good example of legislators recognizing the weak position of the consumer (in this case, perhaps, in a reduced state of decision making capability). The UK alcohol example also shows that there are some types of measures which governments just cannot bring themselves to change, even though a pint of English bitter beer is surely no less nor more refreshing than 568.5 mls. of the same tonic. And only the English would care to know how much a gill is.[32]

Probably the oldest and most widely accepted types of laws protecting consumers are those which require sellers to accurately provide buyers with specified amounts (by weight and/or volume) of products and which also provide an enforcement mechanism to periodically calibrate such measuring devices. These laws are frequently highly specific and have come about in many areas through years of application and revision. Automatic packaging operations require laws which specify ranges of tolerance, e.g., 500 ml. plus or minus 3 ml. with an average fill of 500 ml. There is a large industry built around measurement in the processing and packaging of goods, and as far as we could determine, all OECD countries have government agencies which administer and enforce weights and measure legislation.

Still, different languages and systems of measurement have maintained artificial trade barriers between countries. In the future, it appears the use of general symbols will be more widely accepted as will more standardized weights and quantities. Once the United States completely accepts metric measures, at least the standard of measure will be common for OECD countries.

Collective Information Systems

In addition to information required by law in all OECD countries, businesses may provide consumers with information they consider appropriate for promoting their products and firms. Of course, this information must fall within the scope of the truthfulness doctrine discussed elsewhere in this chapter, and, subject to restrictive practices legislation, businesses may organize a collective information system whereby they supply product and service information in areas such as product performance and quality, reliability, provision of certain services, and origin of products. Some of this information is commonly provided in the form of distinctive labels, trademarks, seals of approval, or certificates of quality. The medieval guild seals for gold and silver makers and other trades were among the first information sources to provide consumers with this type of assurance of quality. The goal, from the producer's point of view, is to show evidence of third party objective assessment of the quality of his or her products.

There has been a trend toward collective information systems championed by state authorities and agencies. Such systems enjoy voluntary support of the business community who join to promote their products. These information systems include standards setting organizations, trade associations, professional and technical organizations. Trubek, Trubek and Stingl report that the Federal Trade Commission identified over 400 of these groups in the United States alone.[33] These voluntary providers of information and standards are not generally legal entities required to provide information to consumers. However, although they do often lead to standardization in the presentation of information for consumers, only infrequently do consumers have input to the design of the standards and information reporting formats. It is also interesting to note that when consumers and consumer policy makers do want revisions to legal requirements to provide information, producers point to the voluntary provision of such information as proof that mandatory requirements are not needed. However, as self-regulation in advertising discussed in the next section will show, when such requirements are not legal some firms choose not to report information, and consumers are less able to make good choices than if more information were provided in a comparable framework.

Having said that, much of the information provided is quite useful to consumers. In addition, one association, the French *Association francaise pour l'etiquetage d'information* (AFEI), allows for a 50-50 representation of suppliers and consumers on the panel that decides what information will be presented about products, the design of their labels and so on. Their labels do not merely describe the product but indicate the performance as compared with a standard model. As an example, the AFEI label for a vacuum cleaner lists the following:

- type of construction
- voltage
- weight
- power
- flex
- dust sack
- "full" sign
- dust capacity
- effectiveness on hard surfaces
- effectiveness on carpet.[34]

Private Institution/State Agency Information

The question of the liability of private consumer testing institutions in reporting the results of their tests and making comparisons among products of different manufacturers is of interest here. The right to freedom of the press and to information permits a consumer association or state agency to publish its results in a comparative form. As long as the institute is independent of business, works in an objective and scientific manner, and the information is accurate and true, the testing organization will probably be excluded from the strict regulations of comparative advertising. "However, the question of civil liability of a testing institution may arise if, in consequence of negative test results, a producer is criticised or, all the more, if consumers are discouraged from buying a certain product."[35]

Only in Denmark is there a special act (Danish Act of 1974) governing civil liability of a comparative testing institution. In countries with codified law, the rules developed by the courts seem to be quite similar. Fault or negligence must be found before a testing institute is liable for prosecution. In common law countries, the principles of defamation apply. Current laws governing comparative testing appear sufficiently permissive to allow critical testing as long as due care is exercised. This is evidenced by the numerous consumer reports being published in many OECD countries.

ADVERTISING

The media, and television in particular, perform a key role in consumer protection, but they do not always observe the same high standards as they rightly expect from business.[36]

The largest source of consumer information is advertising. To the extent that advertising provides consumers with information about prices and the potential performance of goods and services, it contributes to their protection. However, when it deceives, confuses, unduly distorts, or otherwise acts negatively on the information used by consumers, it can be deemed to be against the consumer interest. Clearly, there is a trade-off between the businesses' right to sell products and services and the consumer's right to complete, truthful and fully disclosed information. Advertising legislation attempts to reconcile these rights by placing the producer (advertiser) and consumer on more equal grounds by setting standards and limits for deception in information transmittal through advertising.

Before we go on to look at specific issues in advertising, it is useful to look at an example of a legal reaction to an advertising problem. The various restrictions put on advertising by the law appear to act in the consumer interest, at least to the extent that what is transmitted in advertisements is true. However, the truth says nothing of what is omitted from them. But even with this type of law in place, the informational content of an ad, in and of itself true, may be misleading when viewed in its total context. An example is shown in Figure 6-1, where adjacent to the misleading advertisement is the same information presented in a less deceptive manner. The reason this example is interesting is that it comes from a book published by a government ministry (The British Columbia Ministry of Consumer Services) providing guidelines for advertisers to help them understand what is and is not considered false and misleading advertising under the law. In general, the sanctions provided by the legislative system are by way of injunction or penalty. Preventative control, pre-screening of advertising, and the training of advertisers about the law, as in the example in Figure 6-1, are becoming more popular as complements to existing civil or criminal remedies. It is useful to keep this trend in mind as we turn to how the various OECD countries deal with advertising legislation.

Truthfulness Principle in Advertising

The concept of the truthfulness doctrine is basic to all countries, regardless of their legal system. However, there are institutional and ideological differences in the interpretation of what is and is not truth and how each country deals with the problem. The matter is extremely technical and out of the range of consideration here, except for some generalizations which help the reader to understand the problem.

Figure 6-1 Examples of Misleading and Non-Misleading Advertising

SOURCE: British Columbia (1976) *General Advertising Guidelines*. Victoria, B.C.: Ministry of Consumer Services, p. 5-5.

From a policy perspective the goal, of course, is to have information presented in as true and undistorted fashion as possible, recognizing that defining truth is a difficult task.

Generally speaking, France and Great Britain are governed by a system of criminal law in advertising. West Germany, Belgium, Italy, the Netherlands, and Luxembourg employ civil law, and Denmark and Ireland rely mostly on administrative law.[37] The United States, Canada, and Australia are countries which use combinations of the three basic systems. In fact, no country relies exclusively on one means and, depending on the severity of the infraction, will employ one or more remedies.[38]

One of the largest obstacles in all countries for persons wishing to bring an action for false advertising is to prove the advertisement was a false representation or distortion of fact, yet deceit does not necessarily have to lie in lack of specific factual information, as the example in Figure 6-1 shows.[39] Indeed, the commonplace use of puffery -- "Jones' super-duper liver pills are the solution to all your morning problems," and similar statements -- is considered to be an expression of opinion and therefore not sanctionable by criminal or civil law in some jurisdictions. In others, business can only puff so much before they are subject to sanctions.

Puffery makes an interesting example of how lightly the courts can apply the truthfulness principle. The reason it is interesting is that the law on puffery states, in a nutshell, that although puffing is composed of outwardly false statements about a product or service, such puffing will not be punishable unless deceitful.[40] On the one hand, this interpretation makes some sense when we look at examples like the *Chicago Tribune's* claim that it is the "World's greatest newspaper", a claim which, I would think, would be unsupported by any objective bystander. Such statements are the heart of salesmanship, and often are phrased to invite the customer to investigate and decide for her or himself. Hence, the courts, in general, consider them to be not deceitful. But what about less clear claims than that of the Tribune, cases where the claim may be deceiving to some segment of the population? This is the area where rules and laws are difficult to formulate, with consumerists on one side and business and the advertising industry clearly on the opposite.

The actual borderlines can be extremely nebulous as the following example from the United Kingdom illustrates:

But when in *Robertson v. Diciccio*, 1972, a salesman described a car as "beautiful", the court said this word referred not only to its appearance but to its "fitness" and "performance" . . . and since it was in poor working order, he was found guilty. Beauty should evidently be more than skin deep![41]

So, also, it is evident that puffing does not necessarily always work to the seller's advantage.

Still, if an advertisement does turn out to be judged false or misleading by the courts, we are not aware of consumers being able to obtain damages, except in rare cases (such as the English one shown above, which was the result of a private suit). What about those who purchased a certain dish washing detergent whose manufacturer was convicted of false and misleading advertising for gluing dirt on a plate to be dipped in a competitor's wash water, but using non-glued dirt on the plate going into its own brand -- not surprisingly showing its own brand's superior cleaning power? As we will see, in the U.S., firms have been required to publish corrective advertising when information in their ads was deemed misleading, but as general policy it comes down to judicial judgment and interpretation to put value on the benefits which may have accrued to a firm through its misleading ads. Perhaps in the future more of those windfall gains will be returned to the consumer.

Information Standards in Advertising

The truthfulness doctrine has been deemed not sufficient, by itself, in protecting the consumer. Most acts based on the principle are concerned with false statements but they have not addressed the issues of ambiguous statements, half-truths, and puffery. Consumers are demanding that advertising fulfill minimum information requirements as well as being acceptable within the morals of the jurisdiction.

The International Chamber of Commerce states that advertising:

..... should help to promote health, should not induce people to use articles that may be harmful to them, should protect young people and minorities, should not discriminate against women or any other part of the population, should be directed towards peace and understanding, and should help preserve national resources.[42]

Perhaps this is a rather idealistic statement in light of the fact that businesses use advertising as a marketing tool and not for the betterment of society. On the other hand, a recent directive by the EEC which incorporated some of these notions has attracted the attention of many European legislators and prompted new standards of information and objectivity in advertising.[43]

Comparative Advertising

Complete prohibition of comparative advertising would certainly not be in the best interest of the consumer. On the other hand, unregulated comparative advertising may prove to be misleading or provide useless information. Presently, most of continental Europe prohibits, or at least severely restricts, any form of product comparison in advertising. The common law countries appear more receptive to this type of advertising and will only disallow comparative advertising if it is defamatory. One would think that if consumers were better informed about differences among products that they would make better decisions. Indeed, that is what all consumer testing magazines do, compare and contrast goods and services in a manner which is structured and conducive to helping consumers choose those products which best suit their needs. The concern is that allowing competitors to use the power of mass media to contrast their products to others may mislead. Again, judicial interpretation and experience is going to be needed to set the parameters of this selling tool and to balance its use in the consumers' interests.

Legislation concerned with advertising on radio and television has not been influenced as much by consumer needs as it has from a perspective of general public policy regarding advertising. Media policy, influenced by concerns over the financing of radio and television and competition with newspapers, is the main governmental concern which has determined what the consumer sees and hears. These policies have developed over the years and are really the outcome of the interaction of pressure groups and public attitudes. In turn, public attitudes appear to have been influenced by activities of the pressure groups who have not wanted advertising to be carried on particular media.

There are numerous available examples of how these government and public attitudes are translated into different information policies in the OECD countries. Belgium and Denmark, on the one extreme, strictly prohibit advertising on radio and television. State run broadcasting stations in the UK and Germany also prohibit advertising, but permit it on privately owned and operated stations. Most other European and common law nations are, however, more lenient in this regard. There are other, more specific restrictions possible as well. For example, cigarette and alcohol beverage advertising is highly restricted in all countries. Most prohibit cigarette advertising on radio and television, and where it is permitted the message must include a health warning to the effect that smoking may be harmful to one's health. Greater restrictions exist for high proof alcohol than for low proof ones such as beer and wine.

Regulating Advertising

It is clear that advertising regulation is of concern to policy makers in the OECD countries.[44] However, because the consumer interest in advertising is not clear cut and depends on a variety of situations, the law in this area reflects this unsureness and lacks cohesiveness. The critical matter in regulating advertising is the prevention of unacceptable material from appearing in the first place. However, if it does appear, the regulators want to be able to swiftly remove it from the media. If objectionable material remains in the media while a long court battle ensues over its legality little is gained from laws restricting improper use of this marketing tool.

To tackle this problem, systems have been developed which view advertisements before their use, provide for quick, injunctive relief by the courts to stop ads which appear to be seriously questionable under the law, and punish or sanction firms convicted of violating the law. Some countries have portions of all of these means of control while others have few if any of them. We have found no summary analysis of how these activities work in all OECD countries.

No country attempts to control advertising by one means only. It is common for a country to have at its disposal sanctions in at least two and possibly three of the civil, criminal, and administrative law, and many also use some means of self-regulation by the advertising industry. Countries which control advertising with criminal law usually impose penalties such as fines or imprisonment for gross infringements of the law.

One country which has an interesting division of criminal, civil and administrative responsibilities, plus industry self-regulation, is Canada. The federal government's ability to control advertising is derived principally from criminal law, although it also has tremendous regulatory powers in the broadcast media via the licensing of broadcasters.[45] Canadian provinces have the power to legislate civil rights, including the ability to restrict certain advertisements on television within the province. Most provincial advertising laws grant the relevant ministry the power to terminate false, misleading, or deceptive advertising without having to go to the courts. Overall, the effectiveness of these legal powers might be judged by the short time in which authorities can stop an objectionable ad -- often within days of a complaint. Further, any broadcast advertiser of foods, drugs or cosmetics must have their advertisements pre-cleared by a government agency before broadcast.[46] The criteria for acceptance include its content, the depicted composition, and claims about the efficacy of the product.

Finally, extensive industry-developed codes and guidelines and a system of self-regulation exists. For example, guidelines exist in such areas as the use of comparative advertising and depictions of sex-role stereotyping. In the case of feminine hygiene products and children's ads, the industry has gone further by creating mandatory pre-clearance by a panel of industry and non-industry members. The province of Quebec has prohibited advertising to children for a number of years but in 1986 that law was overturned and is under appeal. All media firms, print and broadcast, retain the right to reject an ad for either legal or taste-related reasons.

The system in Canada represents one of the most comprehensive levels of advertising regulation in the world. In particular, the degree to which, through industry self-regulation with non-industry representation, it also takes into account not only issues of deception, but also the "soft" issues of taste, public opinion, and public decency.[47]

Because criminal and civil legislation only provide sanctions for offenses already committed, some governments have adopted a system of administrative controls to prevent false and misleading advertising from entering the media. These systems usually include negotiation among state authorities, business and consumer organizations to map out the rules to be followed and to direct their implementation. Denmark and the UK have both adopted an administrative system to complement the existing criminal legislation.

While the traditional remedy for advertising infractions is the injunction "go forth and sin no more," the sanctions rarely have matched the monetary gains which firms may have obtained from using false and misleading ads. Fines for the infraction have seldom been large. Furthermore, they do not seem to fit the crime of distorting information and deceiving consumers. Because of this, a number of countries are now considering corrective advertising to act as a deterrent and to wash away the lingering impressions of the misleading ad left in consumers' minds. A recent case in the United States may serve as a precedent for future advertising violations. However, there are indications that the effect of such sanctions may not be those desired.

..... an FTC administrative judge found that Warner-Lambert falsely advertised that Listerine prevents, treats and cures colds and sore throats. He not only ordered that Listerine cease and desist from making any such claims but also ordered that the following disclosure be made in any Listerine advertisements for two years: "Contrary to prior advertising, Listerine will not prevent or cure colds or sore throats, and Listerine will not be beneficial in the treatment of cold symptoms or sore throats."[48]

A system of self-regulation in advertising has been used in conjunction with other more traditional control methods in many OECD countries. Self-regulation usually developed from public concern about advertising, at times given impetus from the threat of regulation. The industry concerned often organized self-regulatory groups which had little power to enforce possible sanctions, except refusing publication and moral suasion. In the beginning, only industry members were on the regulatory boards, but in recent years the trend has been to include "independent" outside members. France, Canada, the United States, the United Kingdom and most other major countries have non-industry representation, such as members of consumer groups, on the councils. One of the few that does not is Belgium, but it is anticipated that changes will be made to include independents in the near future.[49] As can be seen, this area of law, or quasi-law depending on the jurisdiction, is in flux and developing almost daily.

DECEPTIVE MARKETING PRACTICES

While most businesses operate within the bounds of acceptable behaviour most of the time, both legally and morally, and while most OECD countries have relatively free market economies with the ideology that a business may implement marketing strategies which will best serve their interests in making a profit, some marketing practices are considered deceptive *per se* and are legally excluded from the marketer's tool kit. Further, in every country we have investigated there are examples of a few firms whose success and *modus operandi* depend on deceptive practices. In these cases, consumers and honest competitors are frequently the victims of deceptive marketing practices employed by the discreditable few.

Jacob Ziegel, Professor of Law at the University of Toronto and expert in consumer protection, summarizes the concern of unscrupulous marketing behaviour as follows:

A perusal of the many schemes ..... cannot help but leave one with a feeling of admiration for the ingenuity and inventiveness of some of the performing artists -- and also with a strong sense of misgiving about our failure to come to grips with them much faster than in fact we do. Some of the schemes are so transparently fraudulent (bogus invoices for unsolicited advertisements, switch and bait offers, and "free" gift promotions are cases in point) that it is surprising that they were ever allowed to obtain a foothold at all. And even after the more sophisticated schemes have been exposed, officialdom appears in some cases to have approached them with unduly indulgent eyes. Referral sales and franchise promotions are conspicuous examples.[50]

Deceptive practices have thrived for many years in many countries, primarily due to the lack of consumer protection agencies and the absence of comprehensive and enforceable legislation. Legislation in the area of trade practices has two identifiable goals. First, prescriptively, it provides sanctions for those who violate the various acts. Second, proscriptively, it informs businesses of what is and is not acceptable behaviour. Trade practices laws have evolved because courts, in the past, would only prosecute the most flagrant violation of acceptable business behaviour, and because a great number of the public felt that many types of behaviour preyed on their own lack of sophistication. As the law evolves, and prosecutions and resultant court decisions occur, both goals of the legislation are fulfilled. However, in an increasingly complex market, we again see the law having difficulty keeping stride with business practice.

Indeed, a major problem with trade practices legislation is that the requirements for a criminal action are ponderous and time-consuming, and the practice often continues, to the detriment of the consuming public, until the court case is adjudicated. Since the legislation is enforced by the state, under times of budgetary constraint the level of enforcement may decline as funds are taken from the enforcement agencies. The most significant areas of deceptive practices and how various countries have dealt with them are described below.

Door-to-Door Sales

The rationale for legislation on doorstep selling is that consumers frequently find themselves in a position where they feel coerced to enter into a contract. By the very fact that the sales are made at the customer's residence they are unable to make product comparisons. More importantly, many of these questionable sales are made by persons with highly developed persuasive powers who use techniques that, in the cool light of reason a day or two later, cause the consumer to reconsider. To top things off, it is often difficult to trace the seller, who frequently has a legally binding contract, often for large sums of money, sometimes in excess of $1,000 (6-7,000 French francs).

Examples of questionable door-to-door sales infractions include home repair soliciting with high finance charges or hidden costs, a *free* inspection of a part of one's home (a furnace for example) which

leads to the consumer paying for a repair that was
not needed, *free* home demonstrations of vacuum
cleaners resulting in a sale at a price double or more
than a comparable machine in a local department
store, persons claiming to be survey takers who then
make sales pitches, or persons stating they represent
charities who often persuade the consumer to buy
something not really needed.[51]

A variety of methods have been designed to
provide consumers with greater power in their
doorstep selling purchases. In Denmark the method is
complete prohibition of door-to-door sales. Other
countries require prior registration of persons selling
door-to-door, while some require salespersons to provide
the consumer with the terms of the sale in writing.
Sometimes a cooling off period (such as 7 days) is
available at which time the consumer may revoke the
decision to enter into the contract. Afterwards, the
contract is legally binding and the consumer cannot
legally rescind.[52]

Referral Selling

Referral selling is the practice of the salesman
obtaining a list of potential clients from the buyer --
usually friends or relatives -- in exchange for an
alleged refund or similar inducement on the purchased
item.

The net benefits accruing to the consumer are,
generally, small or non-existent. The possible loss of
the person's friends and the high initial cost of the
product *vis-a-vis* the cost of a similar product in a
store make referral sales a consumer nightmare.

According to a recent U.S. survey of referral sales
of a vacuum cleaner outfit, only 10% of the
customers received more than $75.00 from three
bonuses (refunds) each. This represented a
relatively small amount towards the cost of a
$282 vacuum cleaner which had a wholesale price
of $60.00.[53]

Corrective legislation for referral selling ranges from outright prohibition in Canada to no restrictions in other countries.[54]

Pyramid Schemes

In pyramid selling, the purpose of the scheme is to recruit new "distributors" to whom the product, in the form of "inventories", can be sold in large quantities. There is little attempt to sell the product to the ultimate consumer. "Sell costume jewelry to your friends and neighbors. Initial inventory only $2,500. Recruit new distributors and double your profits." The person who initiates the scheme induces others to buy into the business and become distributors also, often with a significant entry fee. The new distributors are then permitted to recruit others and receive payment. All schemes finally fail as the initiators run out of "marks" (the tricksters' name for individuals who fall for their schemes). They then develop a new scheme and are off again. As I wrote this piece, in late 1985, a pyramid scheme involving home produced yogurt had just been evicted from the province of British Columbia. However, others will appear in another form, as they have throughout history.

Countries such as France, West Germany and Belgium regard pyramid selling as a form of fraud and deem them criminal offences. Denmark has guidelines under the Ombudsman which prohibit the schemes. The United States and the Commonwealth countries generally attack the problem with both civil and criminal legislation.[55]

Bait and Switch

In the bait and switch scheme, an item is advertised at a very low price as "bait" to the consumer. At the store, however, the salesperson will attempt to "switch" the customer from the advertised item to another product -- usually of "higher" quality and for "just a few dollars more." Most consumers are not aware the technique has even been used on them.

However, disenchanted sales people in the organizations concerned have frequently reported that they are fired or otherwise disciplined if they sell the "bait" merchandise rather than the "switch" merchandise. Government investigators to whom I have spoken over the years say that in some instances people almost have to fight to purchase the advertised merchandise, so determined are the sales people not to sell it. Honest merchants, whose business is hurt by their competitors' use of bait and switch, are frequently the ones who inform enforcement agencies of the use of the technique.

The U.S. Federal Trade Commission (FTC) has outlined six practices which can be used as guidelines for identifying bait and switch offenses:

- Refusal to show the advertised item.
- Disparagement (to discredit) of the advertised product.
- Failure to have the advertised item available in reasonable quantities.
- Refusal to promise delivery of the advertised item within a reasonable time.
- Failure to deliver the advertised item within a reasonable time.
- Discouraging sales personnel from selling advertised products.[56]

A recent case in the United States serves as a good example:

..... in *Tashof v. FTC*, the FTC did not have any direct evidence of salespeople switching customers from $7.50 glasses to more expensive ones; rather FTC relied on the fact that out of 1400 pairs of eyeglasses sold, less than 10 were sold for $7.50 (in proving) "bait" advertising![57]

Civil sanctions are the most common for the bait and switch offenses although most countries also have criminal sanctions for flagrant cases.

Unsolicited Goods

Also known as inertia sales, marketing unsolicited goods is the practice of sending the consumer merchandise which has not been ordered. The book, phonograph record, or small household appliance is usually accompanied with a note stating to either pay for the item or return it. Another version of the accompanying note might read "If you don't want more, send a card saying so ... if you would like more, do nothing." Some consumers feel obligated to pay the money, keep the merchandise and maintain these shysters in business.

Some of the major countries in Europe consider infractions of unsolicited goods legislation to be a criminal offence (France, U.K.), while others deem it a civil matter (Netherlands, Belgium, Denmark, West Germany). One Commonwealth country has only civil means of control (Canada), while another has criminal and civil control (Australia). A common denominator to most legislation is a provision -- derived from the rule of contract law that nobody can be a party to a contract to which he or she has not given approval -- that the consumer is neither obligated to return nor to pay for unsolicited goods.[58]

It is worthwhile at this point to note also that the postal system and direct marketing to consumers in general is a widely abused area in most countries. The United States provides an excellent example of one approach to limiting the abuse of this form of selling. The *Mail Order Consumer Protection Amendment* of 1983 allows the Post Office to issue cease and desist orders against a person or business who violates mail order laws. Schemes which fall under this act include chain letters, coupon redemptions, misrepresented merchandise, and travel plan schemes. Between April-September 1983, one hundred and seventy-nine complaints were filed, with one hundred cease and desist orders being issued. Interestingly, no charges or penalties were levied, since the Post Office will forego proceedings if the suspected abuser agrees to certain terms. These terms might include returning money to those who responded to the ad or scheme, altering the advertisements or promotional material to the satisfaction of the Post Office, and agreeing that future violations will result in the withholding of all mailing privileges (not just those pertaining to the scheme in question). The consensus seems to be that the approach is successful in reducing fraud in the mail.[59] In spite of this law and its enforcement, *Consumer Reports* provides convincing evidence that there are firms that have used the mails to defraud consumers and misrepresent goods and services for years. Indeed, they present their "mailorder rogues' gallery" of firms, one of which dates back to 1963 and still active in 1986, who have generated numerous complaints from their fraudulent activities over the years.[60]

Gifts, Games, and Premiums

Many types of products and techniques have been devised to differentiate products and services of one seller over others and much legislation has developed around such schemes. For example, glassware, toys, dishware and many other items have been given to purchasers of gasoline. Trading stamps, redeemable for merchandise in catalogues or for products during the next visit to the store, created much controversy in North American markets during the 1960s and 1970s. There are many contests and games of chance played every day to ..."Win a free trip to Majorca (or Florida, or Hawaii) by purchasing our product and receiving the chance to play 'Super Football' -- or some other game." The problem is that such techniques are deceptive when, for example, prizes are offered but never given, or prices are raised to pay for the premiums so that the contests are not really free. A further concern is that firms which do not take advantage of using such techniques are at a competitive disadvantage, particularly in the case of small merchants who cannot afford to mount such campaigns.

A wide variety of approaches to regulating these activities can be seen in OECD countries. Legislation regarding bonuses or premiums is quite old, but is oriented towards general business legislation protecting competitors rather than specifically protecting consumers. Laws regulating trading stamps in Denmark, Luxembourg and England exemplify this approach.[61] With the proliferation of gifts and games unrelated to a specific purchase -- such as free samples delivered to homes or games which do not require purchases -- increased regulation has recently been enacted in several countries, the fear being that such gimmicks will both increase the possibility of irrational purchases and distort competition. France, Germany and the Netherlands are notable in their reaction in this area.[62] As an example of the specifics such laws might contain, Canadian laws require the disclosure of the chances of winning a particular contest, no undue delay in distributing prizes, and the disclosure of the names and addresses of winners to any interested parties.[63]

A number of other deceptive practices have been identified and laws passed to regulate their use. They include schemes such as double ticketing merchandise and billing the higher price, the publication of testimonials about products without the consent of the testifiers, and selling above advertised price during the period of a sales campaign and others not mentioned here.

What has evolved in many countries is a dialogue and the development of systems to control the use of such practices. These include a negotiating approach, the specification of individual rights of consumers through laws as illustrated above, voluntary codes, and the development of sanctions for those who violate the law. No law, unless defined in very broad terms, can change as quickly as trade practices, so systems which do not require legislative change on a continuing basis appear most effective in controlling deceptive practices. Systems, such as those operating in the UK and Denmark, where guidelines or codes of practice are worked out with sellers, appear to be reasonably successful. Again, the ways to control these problems is currently evolving.

PRODUCT SAFETY

Product safety laws are implemented under the general philosophy that while sellers of products and services are granted the opportunity to sell into a market that they have a responsibility to ensure their wares, if properly used, are not harmful to the public. The reader will recall that the start of consumerism and the major impetus behind the first consumer legislation evolved out of the exposing by Upton Sinclair of the filth and harmful products emanating from the meat packing plants of Chicago in the early 1900s.[64] Since then, many product safety laws have evolved. A complete listing of them is not needed for our purposes. Indeed, complete books have been written about the subject. We can only describe and discuss the basic structure of laws in the most relevant product areas and provide the interested reader direction to more specific treatments of the problems. The field is changing rapidly as evidenced by the recent acceptance of the European Communities of a general product liability policy to harmonize laws in the Community in this area.[65]

The general, perhaps ideal and theoretical, approach to product safety includes a system of safety testing/approval before products are released to the public, a means of monitoring safety during use, procedures to correct safety problems if found during use (which includes, among other things, a product recall procedure), and laws which justly make sellers liable for damages to consumers injured by using unsafe products.

There are two important practical and philosophical problems to address in the development and implementation of safety and health programs. First, how long to test? One may test so much and so long that consumers never get a chance to use a product, or the testing procedures may be so costly that manufacturers will not entertain new product developments. On the other hand, such as the case of drugs, less stringent testing requirements could provide benefits earlier but at some risk. What constitutes sufficient testing is obviously a question of judgement. Critics of stringent testing laws are justified in stating that one only measures the costs of being wrong, for example, some people suffer the side effects of a drug. The analyses rarely calculate the benefits foregone from early usage from the use of a drug. There are legitimate arguments on both sides.

A second major question is concerned with liability. What is justifiable liability? If a seller takes reasonable precautions in testing and producing a product should it then be liable for product failure in normal use? Should sellers be liable for injury or other product related losses when consumers misuse products or use them for purposes for which they were not intended? What about liability to ignorant consumers or children misusing products?

Examples of Food, Cosmetics and Drugs

Examples are the only way we can see to provide an overview of the very complex systems of safety laws. These areas of food, cosmetics and drugs are those which have received attention for the longest time and have the most complete system of controls and have had the most experience in their implementation and operation.

For example, legislators have attempted to set standards for the composition, transport and storage of foodstuffs and cosmetics. They have also prohibited or limited the use of various additives. However, legislation has not gone so far as to require manufacturers of foodstuffs and cosmetics to prove their products are safe for consumption. It is felt imposing such a requirement may be in the consumer's interest but that the number and types of products to be supervised make such a move administratively and economically impossible. While some countries use a policy which requires the listing of additives which are unacceptable for use in these products (Britain, West Germany), other countries go the alternate route by listing those which are acceptable (France, Italy). Denmark does both, listing positive and prohibited substances.[66]

Further, control of additives in foodstuffs is not the only preventive means available. Manufacturers of foodstuffs must meet standards of health in manufacture, inspection, storage, packing, maintenance and filing of records, personnel health restrictions, quality, and hygiene. Whereas in most countries the government ministries have the final say in quality and safety standards, some of these requirements are set by national trade associations, with little consumer representation in the decisions. The Netherlands, as an example, leaves this up to the relevant trade associations where the requirements concerning additives are binding on association members. The effect of this type of lack of consumer representation has not been widely researched.[67]

Mandatory inspection of food and of manufacturing, storage, transportation and selling facilities by health officials is common to all countries. The establishment, operation and frequent use of scientific laboratories, both private and public, to analyze foodstuffs, cosmetics, and drugs have greatly benefited the consumer and provided regulators with scientific means to develop and implement safety laws. Manufacturers have been forced to adopt scientific health and safety techniques if they had not already done so. Administrative and criminal sanctions are provided for in all countries. Products can be ordered off the shelves, prohibited from further sale, and recalled. Criminal sanctions mainly involve fines although prison terms have been levied in severe cases. Until recently there were no civil law remedies for violation of food and drug acts because there is an absence of a contractual agreement; recent years, however, have seen the rise of contraction leading to civil liability (see the product liability discussion later in this section).

Protection against harmful drugs has generally been considered to require the most stringent measures, probably due to feelings that they cause potentially more serious problems. Recent examples of such problems with drugs and devices include Thalidomide -- which caused limb deformities in the newborn[68] and the Dalkon Shield -- an interuterine birth control device which caused damage, infertility and some deaths.[69]

Four systems of control for drugs are currently being utilized. Harmful drugs are being prohibited. For example, the British Sale of Food and Drugs Act of 1875, the precursor to the current 1955 legislation, states that "no person shall sell to the prejudice of the purchaser any article of food or drug which is not of the nature, substance, and quality of the article demanded by such purchaser."[70] Prosecution of the manufacturer for contravention is possible without proof of actual injury. Licensing of manufacturers' products is required in many countries. The extent of information provided varies from simple registration to supplying the composition, desired effect, and side effects. Registration with documentation is required in Belgium and Luxembourg. Belgian law requires the results of analytical, pharmacological, toxicological, and clinical investigation to prove the harmlessness of a drug. In Luxembourg, proving the harmlessness is not mandatory. Similar rules apply in the U.S. and Canada. Proof of effectiveness is the strongest legal requirement and exists in countries such as France and West Germany. Before the drug is allowed on the market, it must go through all the tests mentioned above to prove harmlessness in addition to having to prove its effectiveness for the purpose intended. Denmark has one extra requirement on the introduction of a new drug: it must offer something new, from a health point of view, which does not exist currently on the market. It is not surprising that Danish drug stores carry only a fraction of the number of drugs which most other European drug stores do.[71]

Other Consumer Products

Safety legislation for products, other than food, cosmetics, and drugs, is wide and varied. In some areas it has been traditionally left to the industry to design and adhere to many of their own standards, but governments have also developed safety standards to supplement industry requirements, especially in response to unfortunate incidents that have arisen over time. For example, in the 1920s and 1930s the chemical industry introduced man-made fibre cloth which was made into clothing. One product, rayon, was so unresistant to fire that a spark could cause a fire that was almost explosive (because of the fine fuzz on the main fabric strands which was highly flammable). The United States subsequently introduced legislation which requires specific levels of flammability resistance for fabrics.[72] Today, most nations have extensive, specific regulations with respect to flammability of textiles. For example, the U.S. and Canada have different tests for flammability for sleepwear, bedding, mattresses and carpets and rugs.[73]

Often, safety regulations or standards are set by industry itself. In many cases, though, the consumer is not afforded much protection, because the manufacturers are not bound in principle by their own product standards. An exception is in Denmark where poisons, explosives, and certain chemicals must comply with comprehensive legislative standards. Other products, such as appliances, have only minimal government standards, the responsibility traditionally being with the industry concerned. Most legislation is aimed towards the standardization of products, and more pressure is being put on industry to allow state and consumer organizations to participate in the standard development process. This is being accomplished today by subjecting more products to safety requirements, formulating new framework legislation, and assigning responsibility to the relevant ministries.

Unfortunately, such drives to protect the consumer do not always work for the better, as a recent example in the U.S. shows. In the early 1970s, stringent regulations were imposed by the U.S. government regarding the flammability of children's sleepwear. Because most of the commonly used fabrics could not pass the tests, manufacturers searched for a flame retardant they could put on the fabrics, finding a suitable one in TRIS phosphate. TRIS passed short-term toxicity tests and was subsequently widely used; however, by March 1976 extensive scientific research suggested TRIS was in fact carcinogenic in the longer run and, in 1977, it was banned. The costs of this problem were vast: consumers paid higher prices for a less durable, unsafe product; manufacturers of both the textiles and the sleepwear faced multi-million dollar sales and inventory losses and lawsuits; retailers spent millions in refunds to purchasers; and the government spent extra funds on health care.[74] The obvious question is, to what extent can unilateral imposition of safety regulations take place before greater dangers are introduced to consumers. On the other hand, if safety problems do arise, should governments do nothing in fear of creating another TRIS? There are obviously a number of tradeoffs to questions of this type.

LIABILITY

Product liability is a legal term which is used to describe the law surrounding liability for personal loss or damage caused by the purchase and/or use of a product or service. Two types of damages can be distinguished:

- loss or damage suffered by the purchaser because he or she does not receive exactly what he or she is entitled to under the contract with the supplier (loss on bargain).
- loss or damage suffered by the purchaser or third person because the product causes personal injury or property damage.[75]

The law on liability is complex and technical. As well, its application to consumer problems is developing at a rapid rate. To help in the exposition of this complex area, the next section is divided into three parts; defining who is at fault; reducing the directness of relationship between buyer and seller for liability; and determining the intent and, therefore, the amount of damages.

Who Is Liable?

Common to all OECD countries is the obligation on the manufacturer to provide products which do not endanger the consumer. To determine whether a product is dangerous and whether the danger is attributable to the manufacturer, a basis for liability is required. All countries use a "duty of care" standard in one form or another and incorporate a system of classification which is used as a benchmark in determining fault. Any person injured by a dangerous product is entitled to a claim on one or more of the members of the chain of distribution of the product. In other words, it is quite possible that the manufacturer and supplier are jointly and severally liable if it can be proven that both were negligent.[76]

However, a manufacturer or supplier is not automatically liable for injuries caused by its products. It must be established that the danger from use of the product was due to the manufacturer's fault, not as a consequence of the consumer's incorrect or hazardous handling of the product. However, failure of the manufacturer or supplier to take adequate precautions gives rise to liability.

The concept of duty of care obligates the manufacturer to produce goods which do not pose a safety hazard to the consumer. It is up to the manufacturer, and government in an increasing number of cases, to decide if and to what extent the product should be accompanied by warnings and operating instructions. Naturally, this decision depends on the type of product involved, how it is to be used, who will use it, where it will be used, and when it is to be used.

The employees of the manufacturer are the main determinants of whether adequate care in manufacturing is being maintained. To restrict the possibility of the manufacturer avoiding liability by blaming an employee for a dangerous product, legislators in most countries have placed extensive liability on the manufacturer for fault or negligence by its employees.

When companies are producing "state of the art" products, products which use the latest and often relatively untried technology, they may be absolved of some liability since they claim that they did all that they could but that the technology's newness was such that they could not have predicted an outcome which injured a purchaser. Their case would be strengthened for using a "state of the art defense" if they had made every reasonable effort to inform the buyer of the newness and possible danger in the technology.

As an example of determining who is liable, English law uses five general criteria as a benchmark for determining liability for fault: (i) the likelihood of accident; (ii) the gravity of such accident; (iii) the obviousness of risk; (iv) the cost of prevention or reduction of risk, and; (v) the inherent risk attached to the goods in question.[77] But other countries do not use a specific classification system. They attempt to answer the question of whether the product was unfit for its designated purpose. If the product is found unfit for its designated purpose, then the product would be defective and the manufacturer held liable.

In most countries, excluding the United States, the onus is on the victim of the defective product to provide proof that the manufacturer was at fault. The main problem associated with this is apparent: the complexities of the manufacturing process are so technical that it is difficult, if not impossible, for the victim to be able to provide enough evidence for conviction, both due to the technical requirements and to the economic costs associated with providing proof, given most person's personal wealth as compared to a company with relatively greater resources and their reputation at stake. There is little national legislation providing specific rules for establishing fault. However, the courts have been coming to the aid of consumers. In English, French, Belgian, and Luxembourg law the victim is not required to identify the exact cause of the defect or act of negligence. West Germany, the Netherlands, Denmark, New Zealand, Australia and others are shifting the burden of proof from the victim to the manufacturers. Negligence on the part of the manufacturer is presumed unless proof to the contrary can be furnished.

The development of product liability under the new law in the European Communities is being watched with interest. Passed in July 1985, its usefulness in providing consumers with assists in product liability cases is held to be minimal and provides wide scope for member governments to limit compensation.[78] While there may be pessimism and doubts about the efficacy of the new regulations, given how long and difficult is the process of law-making in the Community, the directive still appears to be a step in the right direction.

The most interesting recent developments in product liability have been in the United States where injured parties have been awarded damages in "delayed manifestation" cases. These are cases, such as cancer caused by asbestos exposure, long term exposure to environmental pollution, and the like, where often, only many years after exposure, is the damage apparent. "..... hundreds of delayed manifestation suits [are being filed] monthly ....."[79] The state-of-the-art defense is not applicable here so that manufacturers are extremely worried about this increase in their liability and have been lobbying for legislative relief in the form of time limits for filing suit and the appropriateness of the state-of-the-art defense.[80]

Another interesting development is a law in Japan which provides for an insurance scheme to compensate consumers for physical injuries caused by defective products without the need for court litigation. Manufacturers and importers pay a fee, for safety mark stickers affixed to approved and tested products, which includes within it the cost of the insurance to pay for claims. While the number of claims on the scheme have been small -- 62 in 1985 -- the scheme is innovative and will be watched with interest.[81]

Buyer-Seller Relationship

In contract law, there were historically problems with sellers being responsible only when one could show a contractual relationship with the person(s) injured. For example, a bystander, having been injured by a poorly constructed blade on a lawnmower that was being operated by someone else, could not claim damages from the manufacturer by way of contract. There was no direct link between the manufacturer of a product and the bystander who suffered injury so the injured bystander could not sue the manufacturer. The courts have been slowly stretching the established concepts of contractual liability since there is no doubt that if there was a manufacturing defect, even though the injured bystander was not a party to a contract, the manufacturer was being unfairly absolved of responsibility. To most lay persons this does not appear to be just.

Also, to the relief of the consumer, the courts have been stretching the historical concepts of tortious liability. Previously, fault or negligence had to be proved by the victim. Now, the trend appears to be in the opposite direction, with fault or negligence presumed and the burden of proof resting on the defendant's (manufacturer's) shoulders. This concept is called strict liability.

Strict Liability - The two main ingredients found in strict liability is the presumption of fault or negligence and the shifting of the burden of proof from the victim of the dangerous product to the manufacturer *res ipsa loquitur*. All states in the U.S. have some form of strict liability and it appears many European and Commonwealth countries are following suit. Essentially, strict liability is "liability without negligence, which normally exists if the victim proves that he has been injured by a product in a defective condition unreasonably dangerous when used as anticipated, and the defect existed when the product left the hands of the particular defendant."[82]

One of the first cases which opened the doors to strict liability was *Escola v. Coca-Cola Bottling Co.*[83] The plaintiff, a waitress in a restaurant, was injured when a bottle of Coca-Cola exploded in her hand as she was putting it in a cooler. The plaintiff charged that the defendant had "been negligent in selling bottles containing said beverage which on account of excessive pressure of gas or by reason of some defect in the bottle was dangerous ..... and likely to explode."[84] Coca-Cola attempted to prove it was not negligent by providing detailed evidence concerning procedures under which the bottles were made and marketed. But the court ruled that the fact that it had exploded was sufficient evidence of liability and awarded damages.

While strict and proven liability have improved consumers' protection and ability to recover damages under the law, there still remain problems in many countries. These concerns and developments are described below.

Manufacturer's Contractual Liability - The notion that there is a contractual relationship between a manufacturer and the consumer without an actual contract having been entered into between the two parties, a relationship which is needed if the consumer is to be able to recover damages in an action for a defective product, has not been readily accepted by the United States, Commonwealth Countries, and most European countries. In fact, only France, Belgium, and Luxembourg have successfully introduced such contractual liability. Originally a French manufacturer was liable only if it knew a defect existed when the good was sold. The courts extended this by stating the manufacturer is obligated to know of any defects in goods they sell, and that, therefore, a producer cannot escape liability by proving it was impossible to detect the defect. As a result, a type of contractual liability is formed in the absence of a contract.

Only the "contracting consumer" may claim damages, however. Bystanders are not automatically covered by contractual liability. In this case, the bystander would still have to show that the manufacturer was at fault for producing a defective good and attempt to recover damages in that way. The economics of this type of action are usually prohibitive.

Wholesaler's and Retailer's Liability - In general, wholesaler's and retailer's liability will be found to be less than that of the manufacturer. In most cases, the function of the wholesaler and retailer is to act as a distribution link between the two ends of the chain of distribution, the consumer and the manufacturer. Consequently, goods are infrequently altered from the form in which they left the manufacturer. Distributors and suppliers will only be liable for fault in a small number of cases, such as when they have altered the product or stored it for an excessively long time or with inadequate storage precautions. Thus, the duty of care rests on all shoulders, but the majority of the weight rests on the manufacturer's.[85]

The Amount of Fault

Damages are determined in all countries by the extent of personal injury and damage to property. This includes the direct financial losses incurred such as the cost of medical treatment and wages foregone. If the action is based on tort, pain and suffering are usually included.

There are no specific ceilings on the amount awarded to an injured party, although the courts usually base it on what a current insurance settlement would be. In Canada a limit of $100,000 has been put on non-pecuniary losses.[86]

In the United States, lawyers take damage suits for product liability on a percentage basis so that consumer litigants need worry only about having to pay court costs if they lose a suit (not a negligible amount in many cases). That is, the plaintiff's lawyer receives between 1/3 and 1/2 of the judgment if the award is in favour of the client. This and the ability to sue for punitive damages in the U.S. has resulted in an abnormally large number of cases going to court, with many awards being in the millions of dollars.[87]

Finally, it must be noted that there are a number of limitations to filing suits, such as on the time within which actions and damages may be instituted and sought, parents claiming damages for children and the like. These details are technical and better left to more in-depth treatments.[88] Furthermore, firms which know of possible product problems and fail to take corrective action have been subject to punitive damages, damages designed to punish for inflicting damages on consumers, if they continue to produce and sell a product after they became aware that such a possibility existed. The most celebrated case is that of more than 2.3 billion dollars in claims against the manufacturer of the Dalkon Shield which has caused damage to women using it for birth control. Once the problem was suspected, the company continued to sell the product for a number of years.[89]

Service Liability

As a large and growing percentage of consumer expenditures are for services, it is only to be expected that there is an increasing amount of litigation involving contracts for services not delivered. Increasingly, the courts have recognized that consumers frequently incur costs and suffer inconveniences associated with those contracts not being fulfilled. Whereas in the past consumers were awarded damages only for the contract or portion of it which was not fulfilled, recent case settlements have recognized these other types of losses. The landmark case which appears to be at the start of this trend was that of *Jarvis v. Swan Tours Ltd.*,[90] where an English lawyer was awarded damages when a skiing holiday he had purchased to Switzerland did not provide daily afternoon cakes and tea, as advertised, where the hotel was more distant from the slopes than intimated, where the traditional bar was only open one evening in two weeks, where the tour guide was not in attendance nor were any other guests during his second week of holiday "house party" and so forth. The defendant was awarded the refund of a portion of his tour cost plus damages incurred because he had not been able to enjoy his holiday as he could normally expect from the information given to him by the tour operator.

The precedent set by that case has resulted in a number of settlements for damages in other common law countries. The principle of awarding for inconvenience and similar mental costs has also been extended to other, non-consumer, cases.[91] This area of the law opens another Pandora's Box of possibilities which we do not have the time nor space to explore here. However, it is another example of where consumers, and other litigants, appear to have rights being established for them in the courts.

Insuring Against Product Liability

Several countries have legislation where product liability insurance is mandatory in specific industries. For example, West Germany requires all drug firms to be insured and Italian law stipulates all mail order companies to be insured.[92] In France, Italy, and Luxembourg, product liability insurance is uncommon. On the other hand, firms in the United States, West Germany, the Commonwealth countries, Belgium and the Netherlands appear to favour insuring against product liability rather than facing the consequences of a suit without the benefit of insurance.

Strict liability has been alleged to have had a detrimental effect on many American businesses involved with medium and high risk product lines. In 1975, in what was known as the product liability crisis, product liability insurance became either unobtainable or excessively expensive for companies operating in areas such as pharmaceuticals, sporting goods, medical devices, power lawn mowers, industrial chemicals, and ladders.[93] An example was Wilson Sporting Good's decision to discontinue production of its football helmet line due to, allegedly, the number of large settlements awarded to the injured athletes. Despite "exceeding all recognized quality and safety standards", Wilson acknowledged that the risks were just too high to continue manufacturing."[94] However, football helmets are still being manufactured as are the other products cited by Abbott as not being able to obtain liability insurance. It appears that manufacturers need to take more care. Those that have, have remained in business. There is no hard evidence we could find that the product liability crisis really existed. It appears to be a constant concern for manufacturers.

Future Trends in Product Liability

Except in jurisdictions and situations of strict liability, the injured consumer has to prove the defect, the damage, and the causal link between the two. Technological advances in products have made it necessary for the courts and legislators to shift the burden of proof toward manufacturers and the distribution chain. This has placed the consumer in a more equitable position *vis-a-vis* members of the supply chain, a trend which is expected to continue.

Though many of the OECD countries are leaning towards strict liability, there appears to be some movement towards victim compensation by state social security benefits in Europe. The concept of product liability would lose its significance if this were to become reality. In fact, New Zealand has introduced a system whereby injured parties are compensated by social security payments.[95] Australia, Sweden, Denmark and the Netherlands are all considering doing the same. In the United States, the concept of absolute liability is growing. That concept holds that even if a manufacturer did not know about a potential injurious effect of a product at the time of manufacturing, that it should be held liable for any damages. The state-of-the-art defense does not apply.[96]

Because of the doctrine of absolute liability and of the number of law suits being filed in the U.S., many state governments have passed legislation limiting liability and there is increasing pressure on the federal government to do likewise, thereby extending this legislation to all the states.[97] Whether or not this expansion of liability by the courts and its restriction by the legislatures in the United States will spread to the OECD countries is not clear. If it does, the impact on the cost and use of product liability insurance could be significant.

In any event, consumers, on any measure, are better off regarding product liability than they were a decade or two ago. There is no reason to believe the situation will revert to those times. There are also a number or indications, such as the recent passage of product liability legislation in the European Communities in 1985 and court and legislative activities in the United States, that the situation for consumers will improve further, if slowly.

CONSUMER CREDIT

One of the most striking financial developments after the end of World War II was the rise of installment credit. Businesses and financial institutions made credit easily and rapidly available to consumers, often in the stores at point of sale, rather than at financial institutions where these credit transactions had traditionally been consummated. Credit was now available to a large proportion of the population, a situation significantly different from the pre-war period. In an installment credit transaction, the consumer obtains the item immediately and agrees to pay the shopkeeper or credit institution by installment. The credit is for a specific item and the lender usually retains some form of legal title to the purchased product as security until the loan is repaid.

New forms of credit emerged in the sixties making borrowing even easier for qualified consumers. Two of these important new credit devices were personal loans, which come in a variety of forms, and credit cards. In a personal loan, while the borrower is obligated to repay on an installment basis, the loan is not directly linked to the item purchased. However, some form of security is often demanded. In more recent years, personal lines of credit, secured or unsecured, provide borrowers with access to even greater amounts of credit simply by signing a cheque. This is analogous to bank overdrafts in the United Kingdom, but, for most people, involve relatively larger sums than overdrafts for the average U.K. bank patron. In North America, at least, they have been vigorously marketed by credit institutions. Credit card accounts and open lines of credit associated with credit cards have become extremely popular. The consumer is assigned credit up to a designated limit and is subject to certain terms at the time of purchase. As repayments are made, the consumer's borrowing capacity once again gets larger. No specific security is demanded by the lender. Indeed, credit cards and their successors are the vanguard of the electronic funds transfer systems of the future, discussed in Chapter 1.

While industry and consumers alike benefit from the economies of scale associated with the emergence of convenient credit facilities and instruments, and while more goods and services have probably been offered to the public at a lower prices as a result, expanding credit has also brought with it some problems.

The proliferation of credit cards, and the appearance of financially sophisticated third parties -- the credit institution -- in the exchange transaction have tended to put consumers at a disadvantage *vis-a-vis* lenders and vendors. Inadequate and deceptive credit information enticed some consumers to over-extend themselves; indeed, consumers who should have known better entered into credit transactions without thinking of possible consequences. There are many examples of both sellers, lenders and consumers not exercising due caution, or misusing credit laws to their benefit. The goal of consumer legislation in this area has been to put limits on both sides of the credit transaction in order to bring some balance into the situation.

The remainder of this section discusses credit transactions from three perspectives; before the credit contract is entered; at the time the credit contract is finalized; and after the credit transaction has been completed. This is the format used by the Committee on Consumer Policy and it is appropriate for this discussion.[98]

Before the Credit Contract is Finalized

Three concerns have resulted in laws affecting consumer credit transactions before the contract is finalized; discrimination in granting credit, unfair and deceptive advertising of credit and the collection and dissemination of credit reports.

Discrimination in Granting Consumer Credit - A 1972 survey in the United States revealed widespread discrimination on the basis of sex and marital status. More specifically, a person's sex and marital status were used as the criteria for accepting or rejecting a loan application. Females were required to reapply for loans once they were married while males were not. Newly separated or divorced females were refused credit solely on the basis of marital status. Lending institutions changed the credit rating of individuals as the credit rating of his or her spouse changed. Denying credit facilities on the basis of race, colour, religion, sex, marital status, nationality or ethnic origin has been a widespread problem in almost all member countries. Many jurisdictions have accepted the rule of thumb that rejecting an application should be on financial grounds -- the ability to repay -- and not on the basis of whether a consumer is a member of some group or segment of the market.

The United States (Equal Opportunity Act) and United Kingdom (Consumer Credit Act of 1974) both have legislation which specifically addresses the discrimination problem in granting credit. While most other countries do have provisions against discrimination in connection with the sale of goods or services, they are of a general nature and do not directly address the problems associated with credit. Many consumer advocates believe they are deficient in this regard.[99] What is interesting is that this status quo has existed since the early 1970s, with little headway made since the legislation noted above.[100]

Credit Advertising

Policy makers have been concerned with deceptive and misleading advertising about credit which may tend to lure consumers into disadvantageous credit transactions. The following hypothetical statement is similar to those most of us have heard over the years.

New automobile, instant credit, drive away at only $175, or 300 florins, or 7,500 francs per month.

What the advertisement fails to report is a 18 percent per annum interest rate, payments for five years, with a balloon payment (balance still owing and payable) at the end of five years of $2,000, or 4,000 florins, or 14,000 francs, perhaps more than the resale value of the car at that time. Consumer credit policy in this area is designed to provide more complete and useful information for consumer decision making and to attempt to reduce the number of questionable credit deals entered by consumers.

One of two routes appears to have been taken in the area of information disclosure. Where effective credit costs do not have to be stated (Denmark, Belgium, Australia), legislation demands that cash price, total purchase price including interest and additional charges, amount of down payment, installment amount, the number of installments, and the repayment period be specified.[101] More extensive disclosure requirements are found in the U.K., France, Germany, Canada and the United States where, in addition to the requirements listed above, the effective annual credit cost must be included. For example, a credit union in Vancouver, Canada provided the following information in a brochure announcing the cooperative sale and credit arrangements for used Hertz automobiles.

An example of the credit cost.

- $7,000 initial loan.
- 9.9 percent annual interest rate.
- $576.20 paid in interest over the year.
- Four year term.
- $5,678.37 balance outstanding after one year.[102]

Credit Reports - Problems for consumers arise because of difficulties ensuring individual privacy and the possibility of inaccurate credit reports. Modern computers have the capacity to hold large amounts of personal information which can be retrieved at a moment's notice. Controlling the type of information stored in the data files is necessary to ensure that only information essential in assessing an applicant's creditworthiness is held. Further, there have been instances when damaging and false credit information has been put in a consumer's credit record by a credit grantor when the fault for the particular transaction going bad was that of the seller. Consumers do not have access to their files nor recourse to having false information removed from their files. These are the types of problems legislation in this area attempts to resolve. While both lender and borrower benefit from centralized and easily accessible information by reducing the risk of entering into credit transactions with those debtors possessing a poor track record or excessive indebtedness, their misuses have caused legitimate consumer concerns.

One method suggested for solving some of the problems in several of the OECD countries has been the establishment of a state operated information bureau. However, the U.S., U.K., Canada and Germany are strictly opposed to such an idea. They believe that such a facility would be an intrusion on the personal privacy and freedom of the individual and give the state excessive information. These countries have alternative systems which operate quite well and with minimal abuse.[103] More and more work is going into trying to make such information bases secure from unauthorized use, but daily we are reminded that computer hackers, using their school computers, occasionally break the most sophisticated protection systems. In the end, the results will probably be specific to each country and involve tradeoffs between costs, access and protection of individual consumers.

At the Time the Credit Contract is Finalized

Mandatory Information Disclosure - Consumer law advocates believe that the specifications of the credit contract should be available for consumer perusal before the conclusion of the contract and that the credit contract should be presented in writing, in a clear and concise fashion, in understandable language. Such has often not been the case and consumers were unclear about what commitment was being made and their legal position *vis-a-vis* the creditor.

The Committee on Consumer Policy recommended the following specifications in a consumer credit contract for the acquisition of goods or services:

- Names and addresses of all the parties involved, date of signature, signatures of debtor and creditor, address and, where applicable, licence number of creditor or intermediaries.
- Existence of a link between the seller and the creditor where applicable.
- Description of the goods and services.
- Cash price, and differences in the terms offered to cash customers and credit customers.
- Real cost of the credit.
- Effective annual percentage rate of charge for credit and details of the legal possibility of variations in the interest rate.
- Details of repayment terms (frequency, number

and amount of repayments).
- Statement of the customer's rights as regards terminating the contract or effecting early repayment without penalty if the law provides for it, of any obligation upon him to provide security and of the seller's or the credit institution's right to repossess.
- Clear indication of the cooling-off period where applicable.[104]

No country has legislated this comprehensive list of rules. The relatively loose requirements outlined for some types of consumer credit make it difficult to conduct a worthwhile comparison across countries. For example, for non-money lending transactions -- hire-purchase agreements or conditional sales -- in Australia, the "credit providers may quote no rate or express it as a flat rate, simple rate, reducible rate, compound rate, add-on rate, nominal rate or effective rate."[105] To further complicate matters, the rates may be expressed yearly or monthly if the creditor decides to quote a rate at all. However, many countries have laws which incorporate some, if not many, of the recommended clauses. For instance, limits and rules for changing interest rates for credit card customers have been imposed in some countries. And in the United States, although no retailer is obliged to offer a discount for the use of cash, neither can any credit card nor credit firm legally prevent a retailer from offering such a discount from the credit price.[106] These laws make it clear that consumers are better protected than they were one or two decades ago.

Cooling-Off Periods - Consumers having credit at their immediate disposal, sometimes purchase costly and unnecessary items on the spur of the moment. Furthermore, some firms have successfully used credit unscrupulously and have used pressure tactics and moral suasion to induce purchases of questionable products at excessive prices. In light of these events, a cooling-off period has been suggested to allow the customers an opportunity to rethink a credit (other than credit card) purchase.

There are a variety of arguments against having a cooling-off period for credit sales. First among these says that cooling-off periods could interfere unnecessarily with trade, to the ultimate disadvantage of the consumers; that is, sellers would never be sure a deal had been finalized. Related to this, it is said that the purchaser enters a store under his or .her own free will and should expect that the sales staff will attempt to induce him or her to buy. Therefore, if consumers do not wish to be subjected to that pressure they should not enter into discussions with sales people. There is merit in these types of arguments which point out that any legislation regarding cooling-off periods should consider opposing viewpoints.

One way of doing this is to restrict cooling-off periods to certain types or classes of transactions. Many countries have cooling-off periods for credit sales made outside the seller's premises (see section covering door-to-door sales). The normal length of time is seven days. Luxembourg is one of a few countries which allows for a two day cooling-off period for all installment sales, not just those which have been finalized at the purchaser's doorstep.[107]

Bills of Exchange, Promissory Notes - The bill of exchange and the promissory note are two types of financial instruments which offer less transaction time, a potential source of funds, and greater security as compared to cheque or cash payments. As far as security is concerned, the instruments are unconditional promises to pay a certain sum and are completely separate from the goods transaction. The potential source of funds derives from the ability of the creditor to sell the instruments to a third party (usually a financial institution) for a discounted sum.

Excluding the United States and Canada, the consumer has no legal right to refuse payment of the note in instances where the seller has failed to supply the goods or has provided goods in defective condition. Consumers face the injustice of having to continue to make payments to the payee or bearer of the credit. In North America, legislation exists where the holder of the instrument is responsible for the seller's obligations in the event of the latter's default. A simple Canadian example is given below:

> B agrees to buy a freezer and food from S over a period of time. He signs a conditional sales contract with S, who then sells the contract to F, a finance company. B then finds that he is being grossly overcharged for the freezer, that the food is of poor quality and that some of the food has not been delivered. Therefore B has a number of claims against S for breach of contract and misrepresentation. As a result of the new laws, B can now use these claims against F. F cannot force B to pay the installments. Nor can F seize the freezer until B's rights under the contract are satisfied. In addition, in some cases B may be able to cancel the contract with company.[108]

Another solution being considered by some countries is to prohibit the use of promissory notes and bills of exchange in consumer transactions.[109] This alternative, however, would remove two valuable instruments which in most cases have been useful credit devices. One wonders whether providing recourse, as in Canada and the U.S., might solve the problems without resorting to outlawing the instruments altogether.

Unfair Clauses - Many member countries have no specific legislation relating to the insertion of unfair clauses in credit contracts. They are of the opinion that the consumer should be free to enter into a contract and assume its obligations so long as it remains within the boundaries of public policy. On the other hand, a number of countries do provide for a rescision of the contract if it appears that one party (creditor) has taken advantage of the ignorance or irresponsibility of the other. Misrepresentation and duress are two common examples.

Legislation exists in some countries prohibiting clauses which limit guarantee rights, waive legal rights in the event of a material defect and prohibit the purchaser from terminating a contract if the goods are defective or not delivered on schedule. Credit sales of second-hand vehicles and appliances fall into this category.[110]

The inclusion of penalty clauses in credit contracts are quite common. Endeavoring to reduce risk and financing costs, the creditor has a legitimate reason to insert these clauses for late payment. However, clauses often contain extraordinarily high interest rate charges or unreasonable security provisions which are not designed to compensate the creditors for losses they may reasonably suffer through depreciation of the goods while they were held by the consumer. Rather, these extra charges may be intended for debt collection agencies whose sometimes coercive and deceptive tactics do little to assist justice in consumer-seller relations.

After The Credit Contract Has Been Finalized

The Creditor-Supplier Problem - A consumer may enter into two contracts when electing to purchase a good or service on credit. The first is a contract of sale which involves the seller and the purchaser. The second would be with the credit institution. When a credit sale is made, the rights afforded the buyer under the law governing sales are no longer fully applicable.

If for some reason the goods are defective or not supplied as promised, the consumer remains obligated to continue making payments to the credit institution. Similarly, if a consumer makes a down payment on an item and subsequently discovers the financing cannot be obtained, sometimes they will still be obligated to pay the remaining amount or lose the down payment. Sometimes the seller will attempt to enter into an agency agreement with the financial institution:

> The fact that a supplier is "sponsored" by a finance house often gives him a veneer of respectability in the eyes of the consumer, who might otherwise not be prepared to do business

with him; and an unsound firm, from which the customer will probably have the greatest difficulty in obtaining satisfaction if supplied with defective goods, may, if most of its sales are on credit, be kept going only through the credit facilities provided by the house.[111]

There is legislation in more than half the United States in which the creditor and supplier are jointly liable for defective goods or failure to deliver (in cases where they are affiliated or have a common interest). The rationale is that both parties hope to profit from the sales transaction and therefore both should assume responsibility for the good or service offered. The U.S. draws the line where the creditor is not liable for specific performance or consequential damages resulting from errors or omissions of the seller.[112]

Collection Agencies - Over-zealous collectors of consumer debt, sometimes using extremely coercive and morally repugnant if not illegal methods to collect consumer debt, have caused governments to institute legislation regulating debt collection activities. For example, in Canada all debt collection agencies must be registered, and the fees that they charge are regulated by the federal government. Further, three provinces (Alberta, B.C., and Saskatchewan) have debtor assistance programs which, among other things, provide a degree of counselling in dealing with debt problems, including collection agencies.[113]

Administrative control is used to a large extent to monitor financial institutions. The threat of licence revocation for infractions has been an effective method of preventative control. Criminal penalties and civil sanctions, along with forms of contract annulment capabilities, are available in most countries, although they vary considerably from country to country. Consequently, comparisons are not very useful.[114]

Many countries appear to be prosecuting only flagrant violations of consumer credit legislation. Partially responsible for this has been the piecemeal approach taken by many European legislators.[115] Great

Britain (Consumer Credit Act 1974) and the United States (Consumer Credit Protection Act 1968) have taken a comprehensive approach by consolidating all the relevant legislation into one act. In Canada, credit legislation is dealt with separately by each province in their Consumer Protection Acts. Through extensive consultation by the provincial ministries involved, there has been a good deal of consistency and uniformity in these acts across the provinces such that offenses and punishments are effectively the same on a national basis.[116] It is hoped that in this way greater and quicker access to the ministries and courts will result. However, since much of the legislation requires active enforcement by government agencies, during periods of financial cutbacks the level of resources allocated to enforcement declines. Therefore, the level of actual enforcement varies with the economic climate *and* the political ideology of the government in a particular jurisdiction.

CONTRACT TERMS AND STANDARDIZATION

The average consumer enters into a number of contracts each day without even realizing it. Simple undertakings, such as purchasing groceries, riding the subway, and playing a game of pinball, all constitute a contract in one form or another. Consumer policy in the area of contracts aims at simplifying the language and form of contracts to make them intelligible to the average non-lawyer. It also tries to set out all the important elements of the contract in ways which make them more visible, readable and understandable and to make the terms equitable to consumers and avoid protecting and absolving sellers from all liability through excessively one-sided terms.

Contract legislation is found in most countries' civil law (as opposed to criminal or administrative provisions). Its roots can be traced back to nineteenth century ideas of equal bargaining power between the parties and the maxim of freedom of contract. At that time, government was hesitant to step in and interfere with the workings of the marketplace except in special circumstances.

But, without overtly replacing it, the twentieth century has seen increased intervention by both the judiciary and the legislature on behalf of the consumer in recognition of the fact that in many transactions there is a significant inequality of bargaining power between the buyer and the seller, and it is accordingly unrealistic to ascribe to the buyer a freedom to contract and agree detailed terms when in practice he has little choice but to accept those terms.[117]

Both standard-form and negotiated contracts have unilaterally forced the rights and duties of the contracting parties upon the consumer. Regardless of whether the consumer has a choice between a number of preformulated (standard-form) contracts, he or she still has "no influence on how the subject matter of the contract is designed."[118] Even negotiated contracts favour the supplier, since the average consumer rarely possesses the knowledge, skill and expertise to effectively negotiate a contract. The resulting imbalance of power has forced upon the consumer much of the contractual risk, both prior to and after the purchase. Professor Ramsay suggests that expanded and enforceable warranties be treated as products, that is, they add value to the product or service because consumers are assured of performance and therefore have value. If competition does not result in sufficiently effective warranties then the government could step in and regulate their use using a market failure rationale.[119]

The Standard Form Contract

By no means would it be feasible for each and every consumer transaction to be contracted individually. The lack of knowledge on the part of the consumer and the length of time required to complete negotiations obviously make it impractical and inconvenient. The standard form contract, if created in such a way as to be fair to both parties, serves a useful purpose. However, history has shown that specific legislation is required to ensure that suppliers do not use standardized contracts to escape their obligations.

There are three principal areas where terms of a contract are often discriminatory to the consumer in a standard form contract. These are: (1) offending clauses at the drafting stage of the contract; (2) terms relating to performance; (3) terms regarding non-performance and disputes.[120]

Offending Clauses at the Drafting Stage - The drafting stage is when the price of goods and services are agreed upon but when the agreement has yet to be consummated. Various types of unfair clauses inserted by the supplier often appear. For example, when a tentative offer to purchase has been made by the consumer, the supplier might allow a lengthy period of time within which to make the acceptance decision on the offer. In a "sellers market" this would give the supplier greater time to receive additional and (hopefully) more profitable offers while the consumer is left exposed.

Another clause in the contract might be inserted whereby the supplier is the sole person who decides whether the good(s) conform to the contract or fit the purpose specified by the consumer. For example, the seller might provide a home kitchen appliance with a "one-year warranty", which failed in three months, but still not be liable since he could state that it was used excessively. Consumers' rights to some say in the determination of the quality of that appliance could be void if contract terms allow the supplier complete determination of the product's adequacy for the consumer's purpose. In some jurisdictions such contract terms used to be common.

Along the same lines, a supplier might add a term which states that at the time the contract is signed, the consumer was aware of the condition of the good for sale when, quite often, this is not the case. This term would relieve the supplier of liability when the purchaser returns the next day with the defective item. Used car sales businesses have been notorious for this particular type of behaviour.

Even the price can be altered or presented in such a fashion that there is no accordance or resemblance to the agreement as it was originally thought to be presented. Hidden costs, such as service charges, freight charges, transactions costs, financing costs, and option costs are examples of add-ons which can dramatically affect the final purchase price.

Terms of Performance - Suppliers may include terms, often of a very general nature, which absolve or greatly limit their obligation "to comply with promises made, guarantees given or undertakings entered into by himself, his servant or agent."[121] Included here are instances where the supplier significantly alters a contractual agreement or renders no performance at all, an example being where a tour operator is allowed to "substitute an inferior holiday for the one originally booked" without recourse for the consumer.[122] In a case in Toronto, a working couple sued a tour company because aircraft did not leave on time, portions of trips and nights in hotels were missed, several days of the vacation were spent waiting in airports as a result of the delays, and the original seller of the tour would not take responsibility for the actions of a Greek airline which, apparently, was partly responsible for some of the problems. The couple obviously had not contracted for the inconvenience and loss of vacation time due to flight delays and felt that they had a case to pursue.[123] The legal and policy questions such situations highlight are how much inconvenience and loss of time is normal and at what point should those who sign such types of contracts be subject to liability for non-performance? We have previously discussed the way the courts are moving in this area under the section on service liability.

Terms requiring an exorbitant sum of money to be paid as a deposit before work is commenced is also an example of a quite popular term of performance in a contract which operates against the consumers' interests. Victims of such a clause have often found the work performed to be of very poor quality or no quality at all, e.g., left town, and the chances of getting the deposit back to be slim.

Stated delivery dates and guarantees in respect of hidden vices are also performance related. Delivery dates and limit dates (which state the maximum number of days it might take to deliver) given by the supplier are usually made without consultation with or explanation to the consumer. Where hidden vices exist, suppliers might attempt to limit guarantees to a few specific parts or to terminate guarantees within a short time frame. Also, suppliers might attempt to transfer liability from themselves to manufacturers or other third parties.

Non-Performance and Dispute Terms - Additional terms can be inserted into a contract which severely reduce the rights of the consumer *vis-a-vis* the supplier. Suppliers may demand excessive notice in the event of rescission or may insert a clause which prolongs the contract for an extended period if the consumer does not rescind the contract by a certain time. Memberships to record clubs sometimes contain this type of condition. Just as harmful is a term which permits the supplier to amend or renounce the contract without having to explain the reason.

Another sub-area of offending terms include those which prohibit the consumer from rescinding the contract when the other party fails to carry out its obligation. This includes instances where the supplier fails to perform within a reasonable time limit. If payments owing to the supplier cannot be withheld in such cases, it seems clear that the consumer's rights have been infringed by the contract terms.

If a dispute arises between the two parties, the supplier will have the upper hand when the contract has a provision which forbids the consumer from seeking redress in a common law court or, similarly, provides that the contract be "subject to the jurisdiction of a particular court, so as to make it so cumbersome or costly for the consumer to defend his right."[124]

Warranties are a contractual means by which sellers and buyers can specify conditions of performance and the liability of the seller to the buyer of a good or service. They have also been used as a marketing tool to differentiate products from each other. While warranties may have been honored in the breach in the past through exclusion clauses, there has been an increasing move towards making them understandable, allowing transfers of warranties to second time buyers during periods of warranties, and a number of other positive moves which make them of real value to buyers. At the forefront of developments in consumer products warranties is the Province of Saskatchewan in Canada, whose *Saskatchewan Consumer Products Warranties Act* "provides a consumer with a complex battery of individual rights and remedies including the possibility of punitive damages."[125] This type of standardization of form and terms of contract appears to have a number of possibilities for consumer protection and is developing in a number of jurisdictions.

Judicial Reaction

Too often, legislative reaction to the market problems has been piece-meal. Britain, exemplifying the approach to objectionable clauses in standard form contracts taken by many other countries, "proceed(s) on a purely ad hoc and limited basis, depending on what terms have appeared to cause the greatest hardship and what attracted the most publicity." Lately, however, consumers have been receiving a more sympathetic ear from the courts when faced with unfair and offending terms. When consumers have entered into a contract and subsequently been informed of various exclusion clauses, or a business either intentionally or unintentionally misrepresented the true nature of the exclusion clauses, the courts have deemed either the clause or the whole contract to be invalid because consumers had not received notification "of the true value of an exclusion clause."[126] Business has reacted to this by incorporating widely drawn exclusion clauses in their contracts covering every contingency. Thus, in some jurisdictions the consumer is largely back to the original situation.

Another approach has utilized the doctrine of "fundamental breach". Essentially, this prohibits the business from excluding its liability from breaches of the fundamental obligation of the contract. For example, in *Levison v. Patent Steam Carpet Cleaning Co.*, the plaintiff took action against the cleaning company when it failed to return the plaintiff's rug after it was picked up for cleaning. At the time the rug was picked up, the plaintiff was obligated to sign an agreement which stated the rug was "expressly accepted (by the cleaning co.) at the owner's risk" and the company was liable to a maximum of $40. The English court ruled the exclusion clauses void since the return of the carpet was a fundamental term of the contract.[127]

Many exclusion clauses have been thrown out of modern day contracts, especially those which attempt to severely limit the liability of suppliers when they sell goods and services which are not of merchantable quality nor fit for sale. These are made to be implied conditions, considered to be inherent in every contract. Also, a business cannot by reference to a contract or notice exclude or restrict liability for injury or death due to its negligence.

Current legislation exists in most countries which gives the courts a wide scope in making decisions on the extent of business liability or altered non-performance. Usually it is general in nature and attempts to cover all avenues of offending terms (i.e. imposing conditions affecting remedies, or altering the rules of evidence and procedure).

Attempts are being made in many countries to shift the power in contracts towards a fairer balance for consumers and away from the traditionally more powerful business sector. The real challenge to the legislators is to create contractual legislation which covers all areas of concern in an all encompassing manner, protecting both buyer and seller, but which, at the same time, effectively puts a halt to specific offending terms -- a difficult task to say the least.

CONSUMER REDRESS

Many OECD jurisdictions have a wide and impressive array of protective measures designed to aid the consumer in redressing grievances. However, the complexity of law and regulation design and enforcement, consumer ignorance of their rights and redress procedures, and a poorly researched and not well understood process of how consumers decide how and when to seek redress, often combine to produce little benefit from legislative masterpieces.[128]

> The cost in time and money [to pursue redress] is an effective deterrent to the consumer, who is only too aware that his Phyrric victory would see the bulk of any damages awarded frittered away on legal costs. It is one thing to haul recourse to the courts if the house one has [bought] has serious structural defects, but quite another to do so if one's coffee machine breaks down.[129]

To counter this problem, some legislatures are attempting to construct and implement new non-judicial redress procedures which require only a fraction of the normal cost, time, and formality of using the courts. Most of these procedures have been based on the labour relations arena where plaintiff and defendant meet with an arbitrator. Others establish less costly procedures of evidence and trial, such as small claims courts, to supplement civil and criminal law. A relatively new legal technique, the class action, appears to be developing to overcome other impediments to consumer redress.

Civil Remedies

There appears to be a basic philosophy in OECD countries that consumers who have suffered loss or damage from faulty products or substandard services must seek redress on their own. That is, if products and services are able to get past government and industry laws and agreements screening such entry into the market, or their delivery is less than acceptable after passing these screens, neither governments nor industry have further responsibility to consumers for any losses suffered. On the one hand, there is an obvious contradiction behind this philosophy, since we have described above government enforcement of other types of legislation which protects consumers from dangerous products. Still, one must question whether governments should or can provide redress for all the problems its citizens encounter. Be that as it may, this philosophy results in much of the current consumer legislation being found in private law. This in turn results in a number of barriers which frequently prevent the individual from attaining adequate justice and allow unprincipled business persons to continue in business. Few consumers complain. Of those that do, even fewer win their battle due to a lack of legal knowledge and incentive. Less powerful members of society, for example, the poor, young and aged, are especially vulnerable. They pay higher prices and tend to be exposed to a greater number of unscrupulous suppliers.

In order for the consumer to benefit from private law, he or she must be suitably versed and prepared to pursue a complaint through several possible stages. First, the consumer may, if sufficiently knowledgeable and timely, cancel an unsatisfactory transaction. The example of a door-to-door cooling off period during which a consumer may cancel a contract was mentioned previously. Should the consumer and seller come to conflict, a skilled consumer may be able to negotiate a settlement before court action commences. This facilitates speedy redress, amicable feelings, and with minimal formality and cost. The probability of success at this stage depends largely on the individual's legal knowledge, assertiveness, and on whether the supplier is cooperative.

If all else fails, consumers have to be economically and mentally equipped to enforce their rights in the courts. Only in special circumstances is it possible to have a government authority safeguard that interest. The consequence of private law enforcement amounts to consumers *de facto* being deprived of his or her rights, since business is usually well backed by lawyers, associations, chambers or other organizations.[130] Further, business almost always has greater resources to protect their interests than do individual consumers.

Nevertheless, even though difficult and expensive, consumers do have access to the civil courts if their rights have been violated. Matters involving breach of contract, claims under guarantee, and questions of tort law, where the value of the claim is small, are usually handled by district courts. The legal formalities are far less extensive than the higher courts. Frequently the presence of a solicitor is not mandatory. The Federal Republic of Germany has a system of district courts called Amtsgericht, Canada has a network of Small Claims Courts, and the U.K. has County Courts where "..... ninety percent of all civil proceedings are commenced."[131] "No such system exists in France. There is no simple inexpensive judicial remedy in such matters. Thus the consumer must have recourse to common law procedures, some of which are better geared than others to meet his needs..."[132] Interestingly, France is one country which permits a civil action within a criminal jurisdiction. Where the facts to be pleaded in a civil action are also grounds for criminal prosecution, the consumer has the choice of inserting a demand for civil damages in the context of a criminal action brought by the Director of Public Prosecutions.[133]

Surprisingly, in a large proportion of court cases, it is the supplier who is the plaintiff and the consumer who is the defendant/accused. For example, in the Federal Republic of Germany, 95 per cent of consumer related cases taken to court involve the consumer as defendant.[134] In the U.K. the proportion is 89.2 per cent[135] and in Canada has been measured at from 70 to 75 percent.[136] These statistics make it apparent that suppliers often use the courts as a mechanism of enforcement for their claims because of the less costly procedures and speed of these courts, whose procedures were originally set up as an inexpensive route for consumers to settle small claims. In fact, many lawyers I have spoken to in Canada and elsewhere have stated categorically that the Small Claims Court is a *de facto* inexpensive debt collection court for suppliers, except in those cases where individuals take the time to use it for its planned function as "the poor man's civil court". [137]

There are other considerations which consumers would be well advised to keep in mind before initiating court proceedings. For example, all litigation costs, including the opposing party's legal fees, will have to be paid by the unsuccessful party. If the case goes to a higher court the costs accumulate rapidly, and a consumer may be responsible for litigation costs even if the original case had been won in a lower court but subsequently lost in a higher court on appeal. Finally, in the event that the convicted debtor goes bankrupt, the consumer may not be able to enforce the judgment. [138]

In most jurisdictions, it is not overstating the case to say that there is actually little consumer protection available in current civil legislation when low damage or claims amounts do not justify court proceedings. Until the substance of the law gets altered from its current state, business will continue using the courts as a debt collecting service and the consumer will continue to suffer. On the bright side, there have been developments which do not require the use of courts for redress if the parties to the dispute agree to their use. Two of those considered to have particular promise are class actions and arbitration.

Class Actions - A class action is a legal device which permits individuals to join together to sue for a common grievance. One individual consumer suing the government telephone monopoly or General Motors is a pretty uneven contest. Thirty thousand individuals in the same action greatly reduces the imbalances which usually exist between consumers and business in these types of legal proceedings. The small can fight the large. In addition to the individual litigation for damages, class actions are a vehicle for enforcing public policy. They are useful in situations where one or a combination of the following problems is encountered and where the complaint is common to many individuals: where the proof of fact and damage is difficult, expensive, or both; where the sums at stake are too small to justify an individual action; where a conviction may establish a point of principle or stop an undesirable practice without significant damages being at stake; and where the risks to an individual of losing a private suit, because of the awarding of costs to the defendant, would be financially devastating.

Examples of these types of situations are useful in understanding class actions. The proof of fact and damages often is difficult and expensive. There may be a need for laboratory tests and expert witnesses. Most often an individual owner could not afford the cost of this type of proof nor the determination of damage. For example, one may need an expert metallurgist to testify that premature rusting of an automobile was due to improper treatment of the metal before painting at the factory, and such testimony may require laboratory tests for the expert to verify and support his or her testimony. Such a cost is more than individual consumers can afford. However, if the problem is widespread, this type of expense may be spread among the parties bringing a class action for damages.

There are also deterrent effects of class actions which make them potential vehicles to use the courts to define and protect consumer interests and to redress in some degree the imbalance between consumers and the large, financially strong corporate defendant. In the past, individual suits, even if won in court, would fail to stop a generally objectionable practice because the liability was only binding between the plaintiff and the defendant. Through aggregating numerous separate claims of like nature, class actions secure wider-spread co-operation and compel businesses to "disgorge" profits from improper practices. Although class actions are almost always more complicated and more costly than individual litigation, the deterrent effect of widespread publicity which usually accompanies class actions, as compared to the relatively unnoticed individual suits, makes this device, where applicable, especially useful in consumer law.

Class actions are not without their problems. However, there are some interesting legal developments which should make them a more effective tool to save courts and plaintiffs time and money and to save the courts the embarrassment of contradictory rulings in separate actions on identical issues.

The courts in Canada have had difficulty allowing class actions when the damages to individuals are not identical. For example, in the case of the Firenza automobile, a group tried to bring a class action suit against General Motors who had advertised the car to be "durable" and "tough" and "reliable". They brought the suit asking one thousand dollars damages for each of the members of the class in the action. The court refused to hear the case under a class action since there were many consumers who had not had problems with their particular automobile, others had had damages less than $1,000 while others suffered larger damages. Many Firenza owners had suffered damages but, in reality, had few legal means for effective redress because separate legal actions would easily cost $1,000 or more. In actions of this magnitude, a useful redress mechanism obviously needs to be developed.[139]

Immunity from being assessed costs if an action fails is still not established in the Canadian courts. The effect of a potentially large award of costs for a suit which was not successful, especially in the case where proof is difficult and expensive to develop, is a deterrent to using the law to redress consumer problems. There have been proposals that if the courts are required early in a claim to rule on whether an action is brought in good faith and on whether the claim appears to have merit, two positive benefits can accrue. First, defendants will be protected

from frivolous suits with little merit. Second, those
bringing a suit which appears to have merit would be
granted immunity from the awarding of costs should
the suit fail. Even were such a development to come
about, plaintiffs who eventually lose such cases will
still be required to pay the costs of their own
counsel, almost never an insignificant amount.[140]

In cases where a large number of plaintiffs
cannot be identified, as is often the case, courts have
refused to award damages to other than identifiable
individuals. Many times only a small fraction of real
damages is ever paid by the party found liable in a
class action. However, in the United States, through a
device called "fluid class recovery", when the potential
recipients of damages have not been identified, the
courts have for "prophylactic purposes" -- for wrongs
done to the masses and to discourage "preying on the
public" -- directed that the damages be paid out to
the general class under consideration.[141] As an
example, in *Daar v. Yellow Cab Co.*, the defendant,
the Yellow Cab Co., was directed to reduce future
taxi fares until a past overcharge, as determined
under the class action, was repaid to the taxi-riding
public. This type of recovery has been vociferously
opposed by some members of the legal profession as
giving damages to persons who had not been
damaged. Consumer advocates have been equally
strong in their praise of this technique because, first,
that a windfall occurs to others does not excuse the
original act, and it seems that justice is served and
the rights of the plaintiff in the class action are
vindicated by such actions. Secondly, "A successful
class action for consumers can bring compensation to
the people injured by business malpractice. To compel
the defendant to part with improperly gained fruits of
his endeavors and to deter a repetition of the
wrong-doing are two no less important class action
functions."[142]

The effectiveness of class actions, through
extracting total damages and proscribing future
undesirable actions from the firm found liable, would
be greatly enhanced were the courts to use this and

other devices to prevent unjust enrichment. Still, the acceptance of class actions outside of the United States appears slow in coming. In Europe, several countries allow consumer organizations representation in criminal and/or civil proceedings where a common consumer interest exists, but such representation is not as a claimant for that interest.[143] The previously discussed move to common liability laws in Europe, as announced by the EEC's Consumer Council, has no effect on this absence of class actions.[144] In Canada, laws exist at the provincial level which allow for class actions, but narrow interpretation of the laws has made use of the tool difficult. It appears that for class actions to become effective, specific federal legislation in the area is required. Despite a stated intention to move in that direction in the late 1970s, legislation has not been forthcoming.[145]

Thus, although apparently a useful redress mechanism for consumers, there are a number of technicalities impeding the widespread use of class actions. Perhaps with time these issues will be addressed, because class actions have within them redress techniques which address the major problems of many small claims and the ability to prevent unjust enrichment of those who are guilty of an offence.

Arbitration and Conciliation - These are two relatively new methods of handling consumer complaints, initiated in many countries and in a variety of forms, which appear to have some promise in helping the individuals pursue redress without being subjected to the risk of court fees. By far the most popular is a conciliation board composed of the supplier, the consumer, and a neutral conciliator. As the name implies, the conciliator attempts to get the parties to come to an agreement. If they do not, then they are free to pursue other avenues of redress. Under arbitration, a similar situation exists, except that the parties agree that the arbitrator's decision is final and that there is no further recourse that either party may take should they not like the decision.[146] Indeed, through the New York Convention on

Arbitration, most industrialized countries -- including the U.S., but excluding Canada -- work towards ensuring that arbitration awards will be enforced through the courts.[147]

Where the claim is small, the three principals meet in an informal atmosphere and attempt to resolve the conflict. Strict rules of evidence do not usually apply and expert documentation is not demanded. Legal representation is discouraged by limiting the solicitors' fees to a nominal amount.

Because arbitration is not a trial, there is usually no appeal as such, although a court may overturn a decision if it "finds an error of law on the face of the award or misconduct by the arbitrator."[148] Awards may be enforced as a judgment of the court. More generally, all the mechanisms of the lower courts for enforcement of judgments are available.

In a few countries, even though legally available, arbitration is seldom used in consumer situations. France, for example, has recognized arbitration for many years but "the fear of losing causes manufacturers and traders to rule out the possibility of arbitration from the outset."[149] In some areas in North America Better Business Bureaux -- business associations composed of merchants -- and some automobile dealer associations, sometimes in conjunction with some type of consumer organization, have set up arbitration procedures in an attempt to provide redress to consumers and to save their members legal fees in the courts. While some of these programs are said to be working well, they may not be the panacea for solving redress problems and reducing the cost of redress that may have been expected at their inception.[150] However, both consumers and sellers sometimes refuse to go to arbitration because both parties have to agree that the arbitrator's decision is final. In effect, they sign away their right to further recourse. As with other laws and techniques described here, arbitration and conciliation are relatively new but developing.

Criminal Remedies

The logic of criminal remedies in consumer matters is
to foster an ethical business environment and to help
individuals escape the proceedings and costs associated
with civil actions. The state institutes the suits and
bears the costs of the action. Criminal proceedings are
normally used to prosecute businesses which exploit
the fact that only a small fraction of consumers
resort to the courts. While individual consumers may
have recourse to contract or tortious law, the cost of
attempting to obtain redress discourages a large
majority of complaints. Even though there may be
legislation on the books outlawing production of inferior
goods, enforcement of such laws is notable in many
jurisdictions by its absence. This implicitly creates an
environment which encourages the production of
substandard goods and services, affecting not only
consumers, but the honest business persons who find
themselves having to compete against the
unscrupulous. State-instituted proceedings in the
criminal law is an attempt to deter such activities.

It is infrequent that consumers who have been
damaged by a firm are included as plaintiffs for
damages in criminal proceedings. Such inclusion of
damages for redress is now usually considered a
windfall rather than a right in criminal law.[151] The
extent to which a consumer may seek redress via
criminal proceedings depends largely on the consumer's
jurisdiction. For example, the Federal Republic of
Germany, except in extreme cases, does not permit
consumer related disputes to enter the criminal
courts.[152] Most other countries do not have provisions
for individuals to seek damages in criminal
proceedings. But this is not surprising since these
laws are designed to stop practices generally thought
to be unscrupulous by the state. Consumers'
recompense is nominally the generally improved ethical
standards in the marketplace such prosecutions are
supposed to bring about.

Countries with Anglo-Saxon law tend to offer
criminal remedies for a far greater number of

consumer related violations than those under Civil law systems. As an example, the Acts listed below illustrate use of criminal legislation for consumer matters in the United Kingdom:

- Food and Drugs Act 1955
- The Weights and Measures Act 1963
- The Trade Descriptions Act 1968
- The Fair Trading Act 1973
- The Consumer Credit Act 1974
- The Consumer Safety Act 1978[153]

Despite the consumer being assisted by the state in a criminal action, there remains a number of barriers which militate against conviction. The difficulties relate to the broad statutory standards typically found in consumer related criminal legislation which make it difficult to prosecute all but the most flagrant violations.[154]

Since consumers and businesses often compete for governments' legal resources to enforce laws, businesses often win as they generally carry greater weight in the political process, at least in the short run. Therefore, in some jurisdictions enforcement responsibility has been placed in the hands of specialized agencies whose allegiance lies with the consumer. Most countries have a consumer protection department in one form or another.

Where broad statutory legislation exists, the possibility of an unsuccessful action increases due to the interpretation of the laws by the courts. Hence, there is the temptation for consumer protection agencies not to initiate proceedings unless the violation is blatantly obvious and the probability of success relatively high.

Because criminal legislation is often interpreted very narrowly by the courts, it becomes very awkward to apply broad legislation and narrow interpretations to cases of consumer offenses, because judgment and inconclusive evidence are frequently the rule. Criminal law does not lend itself to evidence based on statistical probability and judgment which is vital to such cases.

Last of all,

..... criminal procedure is inappropriate when applied to intricate consumer offenses. Existing criminal procedure evolved for discovering truth in straight forward crimes like murder or theft, where evidence is relatively simple and is capable of being assessed by ordinary citizens comprising a jury or a bench of lay magistrates. By contrast, some consumer offenses are relatively complex and in some cases can only be understood by experts.[155]

The potential of criminal remedies as a redress mechanism is of heightened interest as strict liability becomes more accepted in the courts. Under strict liability, unintentional or inadvertent breaches of law are no defense. Therefore, the ease with which cases can be brought before the courts and the probability of success increases. The critical legal question becomes whether the elements of the prohibited act have been committed. On the other hand, strict liability makes it difficult to distinguish between the major and minor offenders, and "there is a tendency to impose uniformly low penalties which are not a burden to the former."[156] It seems obvious that the law has some developing to do in this area.

Corporate Criminal Offenses - If a consumer offense has been committed by a corporation, the problem of where to place the liability often arises. Is it the shop assistant whose inadvertant mistake gave rise to the offense? Did the senior executive purposefully use a misleading promotional policy that inevitably led to violation of consumer laws relating to truth in advertising? The courts will increasingly have to address such situations as they do in other areas of the law.

By imposing sanctions on the company, the courts appear to feel that senior officers of the company may monitor their employees more diligently, and public disclosure of a company's practices may deter the company and others from similar activities in the future and that the courts will be able to remove illegally acquired profits more easily. However, there is no reason to believe that less moral outcomes may not also result. For example, specific practices may diffuse the decision making process in a large corporation so that it would be very difficult in the future to pinpoint corporate culprits. A company may or may not punish an offender, and the sacrifice firing of a junior employee may be of little value.

Corporate criminal liability obviously has some positive uses for consumers and provides a tool for officials charged with protecting the consumer. An example provides insight to the court's thinking in a United States situation.

The president and chief executive officer of a large national food chain (Park) was held liable for unsanitary storage conditions in one of the company's warehouses. The enforcement authority had inspected the warehouse, found conditions in violation of food hygiene regulations and notified Park by letter. On receipt of the letter, Park had conferred with his vice-President of legal matters, who informed him that the divisional vice-president would take corrective action. Park argued that he could not have taken more constructive action. The United States Supreme Court disagreed and ruled that Park had responsibility and authority either to prevent violations in the first instance or promptly to take steps to seek out and correct them once they were discovered. Liability was not predicated on position, title, or closeness to the violation, said the Court, but because all officers who have power and authority, regardless of how extended and indirect, to secure compliance with the law have an affirmative duty to do so.[157]

The U.K. courts have interpreted corporate criminal liability differently. Junior employees of a company can be prosecuted directly if they have committed an offense. This is done mostly in cases where the junior employees' actions were not driven by company policy but by individual need.

The concept of corporate criminal liability is a relatively new development in the law. It usually does not provide redress for individual consumers. Rather it is a means of controlling some aspects of corporate behaviour. As the concept and its use expands in OECD countries (assuming it will), it will be watched with interest by all parties in the consumer interest environment.

In summary, redress for consumers has improved over the past several decades. However, there are many laws, procedures and expenses which still make obtaining redress in conflict situations difficult. In addition, many would agree with the observation that if governments would more assiduously enforce existing legislation, consumers would be exploited less than at present, standards of behaviour in the marketplace may improve, and the need for individual redress would probably decline.

Anti-trust Legislation

Certainly it is in the consumer interest to obtain products or services in suitable quantities and at a "fair" market price. The consumer gains when resources (capital, labour, land) are allocated efficiently and the transformation of resources into goods (production) is efficient. The consumers' interests in the operation of a relatively free economic system has been discussed in Chapter 5. This brief section serves to point out the major types of policies which attempt to promote competition in the OECD countries. Their effects are generally thought to be of a broad nature and they were not instituted to solve specific marketplace abuses.

Antitrust legislation is based on the belief that the absence of government regulation would lead to a collapse of the competitive markets and monopolization of a country's economic system. Simply put, if businessmen prefer collusion over competition, then the consumer would have fewer products/services at higher prices. This produces an income transfer away from the consumer to the producer.

Another argument says that while the absence of some form of anti-trust legislation does not necessarily preclude competition and free enterprise, such legislation tends to enhance it. Where there is an opportunity for profits, and entry to an industry is not restricted or monopolized, entrepreneurs will quickly enter and provide goods and services at competitive prices. By ensuring free entry, not only will anti-trust law influence prices by providing for a system of effective competition, but it will also ensure production which satisfies consumer wants. Unfortunately, though, these are only assumptions underlying the rationale for anti-trust legislation. The reality may be quite different in practice, with legislation in fact protecting competitors and restricting entry. While that subject is beyond the scope of this book, it has received much attention by many authors should the reader wish to pursue this fascinating subject. [158]

There are a large number of laws and regulations pertaining to anti-trust activity. The following is a fairly comprehensive list of subject areas where legislation exists to discourage restrictive business practices.

- Horizontal agreements and concerted actions.
- Information agreements.
- Collusive tendering.
- Rationalization and specialization agreements.
- Co-operation between small and medium sized enterprises.
- Export cartels.
- Crisis cartels.
- Agreements relating to industrial and commercial registry.
- Market dominating enterprises or monopolies.
- Mergers and acquisitions.
- Joint ventures.
- Boycotts.
- Discriminatory prices or conditions of sale.
- Refusal to sell.
- Selective selling systems.

- Exclusive dealing agreements.
- Resale price maintenance and conditions of sale.

CONCLUSIONS

It should be clear from this chapter why consumers frequently have problems understanding their rights, let alone being successful in pursuing and protecting them. Consumer law is varied and complex. Because of this, there was space to only briefly introduce the many and varied aspects and philosophical underpinnings of consumer protection and to illustrate how they are applied within OECD countries.

Today's complex, high speed, high technology society has contributed to a number of legal problems to which policy makers have been required to respond. The first group of laws and procedures have been designed to maintain competition between producers and assist consumers to make better decisions in a freely operating market. Examples include legislation on the disclosure and quotation of prices of goods and services, requirements for provision of minimum product information, and legislation which attempts to control monopoly and restrictive trade practices. A second group of laws attempts to legislate standards of information, health, safety, weights and measures, contract and credit terms and other rules of behaviour in exchange transactions to provide consumers with a balance of power in the market place.

A third area of laws and procedures has been designed to help supplement existing methods of redress for consumers who feel they have suffered loss at the hands of suppliers. One aspect of many of these laws is the recognition that consumers have limited resources to pursue redress vis-a-vis the resources of businesses to protect their interests against consumers. This is especially true when damages are of relatively small value. Indeed, without some form of legal intervention, unscrupulous business persons are able to defraud consumers over many years. Because the damage to individual consumers is not sufficient for each to pursue redress, even though the aggregate loss to all consumers is large, forms of collective and governmental consumer redress are being explored and developed. Further, non-judicial procedures of several types, such as conciliation and arbitration, are being tried in some jurisdictions.

While there are great differences in the approaches and legal systems in the OECD countries, it appears that this lack of similarity is more form than substance. A consumer who is victimized by an unscrupulous supplier in France tends to be able to address the courts, although in different form and under different rules than one would in Australia or the United States. However, consumers in some countries still have only minimal protection under the law.

It is becoming increasingly important that consumer legislation be synchronized among countries. Faulty goods and hazardous products know no international boundaries. Dumping dangerous products, restricted in national markets, into other countries, many with limited resources to police their own markets, is morally reprehensible. Expanding world markets and trade have created a need for protective measures without regard to national boundaries. In this way, the crafty producer or exporter will no longer be able to take advantage of diverse laws at the expense of consumers.

The difficult policy questions remain; how much protection is really needed and when is enough, enough? On the one hand, many businesses believe the saturation point was reached some time ago. On the other hand, consumer advocates are convinced that much more is needed. These questions, which are really political, require decisions which democratic, pluralistic governments reach in the rough and tumble of the political arena, are the subject of the next chapter.

NOTES

1 Dan Fraleigh made extensive revisions, additions and conceptual contributions to an earlier draft of this chapter in 1984/85. Scott Fraser made further revisions in 1985, following detailed comments by Professor Norbert Reich, of the University of Bremen, made in the Spring of that year. Professor Reich also made insightful comments on the final draft in the Spring of 1986. Iain Ramsay, of the University of Newcastle-Upon-Tyne, made a number of insightful technical and conceptual comments on a final draft of the text which have been included here and in Chapter 8. These contributions are greatly appreciated and acknowledged.

2 Commission of the European Communities (1977) *Consumer Protection and Information Policy: First Report.* Brussels: Commission of the European Communities.

3 Reich, Norbert, and Micklitz, H. W. (1980) *Consumer Legislation in the EC Countries: A Comparative Analysis.* Berkshire: Van Nostrand Reinhold Company Ltd., was especially useful in preparing this chapter.

4 Walker, David (1980) *The Oxford Companion to Law.* Oxford: Oxford University Press, p. 223.

5 Walker 1980, p. 253.

6 Walker 1980, p. 254.

7 Walker 1980, p. 260.

8 Fennell, Rosemary (1979) *The Common Agricultural Policy of the European Community.* London: Granada.

9 Reich and Micklitz 1980, pp. 41-42.

10 Mill, J. S. *Utilitarianism, Liberty and Representative Government.* Edited by J. B. Acton. London: Dent, 1972.

11 Rawls, John (1971) *A Theory of Justice.* Cambridge, MA: The Belknap Press of Harvard University, p. 60.

12 Reich and Micklitz 1980, p. 11.

13 Commission of the European Communities 1977, p. 12.

14 Bourgoignie, Thierry M., and Trubek, David M. (1984) *Consumer Law, Common Markets and Federalism in Europe and the United States.* Florence: European University Institute, (August).

15 Harland, David (1985) "Legal Aspects of the Export of Hazardous Products," *Journal of Consumer Policy*, 8 (Sept.), pp. 209-238; Chetley, Andrew (1986) "Not Good Enough for Us but Fit for Them -- An Examination of the Chemical and Pharmaceutical Export Trades," *Journal of Consumer Policy*, 9, pp. 155-180; Kaikati, Jack G. (1984) "Domestically Banned Products: For Export Only," *Journal of Public Policy & Marketing*, 3, pp. 125-133.

16 Smith, Peter, and Swan, Dennis (1979) *Protecting the Consumer: An Economic and Legal Analysis.* Oxford: Martin Robertson & Co., Ltd., p. 136.

17 Canada, *Consumer Packaging and Labelling Act*, Sec. 11, for example, allows regulations to be set for individual products based on the impression of size/shape proliferation.

18 Bruce, Marian "Giant-killer tells how", *Vancouver Sun*, Nov. 10, 1972, p. 43.

19 Canada, *Combines Investigation Act*. Section 36.1(d).

20 Reich and Micklitz 1980, pp. 21-23.

21 See Consumer and Corporate Affairs Canada (ca1982) "Retailers' Use of Manufacturer's Suggested List Prices for Comparison Purposes in Advertising", Ottawa: Trade Practices Division, Consumer and Corporate Affairs Canada, mimeo, for an overview of the Canadian stand on the issue.

22 Reich and Micklitz 1980, pp. 21-23.

23 Stanbury, W. T. (1976) "Penalties and Remedies Under the Combines Investigation Act 1889-1976", *Osgoode Hall Law Journal*, 14:3, p. 571.

24 Reich and Micklitz 1980, p. 26.

25 Reich and Micklitz 1980, p. 15.

26 For a comprehensive and insightful discussion of consumer information remedies see Federal Trade Commission (1979) *Consumer Information Remedies - Policy Session*. Washington, DC: U.S. Government Printing Office, (July 1).

27 Reich and Micklitz 1980, p. 29.

28 Reich and Micklitz 1980, pp. 29-30.

29 Canada, *Hazardous Products Act*, Chapter H3; *Consumer Packaging and Labelling Act*, Sec. 10, are examples for which corresponding legislation may be found in other OECD countries.

30 See, for example, Canada, *Consumer Packaging and Labelling Act*, which gives the Governor in Council the authority to implement such regulations.

31 1979, p. 135.

32 As part of the research for this book, I inquired of an English pub keeper and six patrons in a pub in Bedfordshire, on May 24, 1985, how many ounces or millilitres constituted a gill. Not one of them could provide me an answer but they went on drinking all the same. Subsequent assiduous research has ascertained that a gill is 1/4 pint or 118 ml.

33 Trubek, David M., Trubek, Louise G., and Stingl, Denis (1984) "Consumer Law in the American Federal System," in Bourgoignie and Trubek 1984, pp. 145-155.

34 Calais-Auloy, J., et al (1981) *Consumer Legislation in France*. New York: Van Nostrand Reinhold Co., p. 87.

35 Reich and Micklitz 1980, p. 37.

36 Rines, Michael (1977) "The Consumer Watchdogs Need Watching," in Christina Fulop (1977) *The Consumer Movement and the Consumer*. London: The Advertising Association, p. 110.

37 Reich and Micklitz 1980, pp. 41-43.

38 Reich and Micklitz 1980, p. 55.

39 Epstein, David (1976) *Consumer Protection in a Nutshell*. St. Paul, MN: West Publishing Co., p. 22.

40 Preston, Ivan (1975) *The Great American Blow-Up*. Madison, WI: University of Wisconsin Press, p. 9.

41 Whincup, Michael (1979) *Defective Goods*. London: Sweet & Maxwell, p. 65.

42 Reich and Micklitz 1980, p. 49.

43 Commission of the European Communities 1977, p. 15.

44 For a fascinating analysis of the opinions of humanities and social sciences scholars' on the long term cultural effects of advertising, see Pollay, R. W. (1986) "The Distorted Mirror: Reflections on the Unintended Consequences of Advertising,"

222 Consumers and the Law

Journal of Marketing, 50:2 (April), pp. 18-36.

45 Scheffman, David, and Applebaum, Elie (1982) *Social Regulation in Markets for Consumer Goods and Services*. Toronto: University of Toronto Press, p. 105.

46 Canada, *Broadcast Act*, Regulation 11.

47 Boddewyn, J. J. (1984) "Outside Participation in Canadian Advertising Self-Regulation," *Canadian Journal of Administrative Sciences*, 1:2 (December), p. 215.

48 Epstein 1976, p. 28.

49 Boddewyn, J. J. (1983) "Belgian Advertising Self-Regulation and Consumer Organizations: Interaction and Conflict in the Context of the Jury d'Ethique Publicitaire (JEP)," *Journal of Consumer Policy*, 6:3, p. 303; Reich and Micklitz 1980, pp. 61-62; J. J. Boddewyn has studied advertising self-regulation extensively. For further details, see his work as follows: (1985) "Advertising Self-Regulation: Private Government and Agent of Public Policy," *Journal of Public Policy & Marketing*, 4, pp. 129-141; (1984) *Advertising to Children: An International Survey of Its Regulation and Self-Regulation*. New York: International Advertising Association; (1984) "Outside Participation in Advertising Self-Regulation: The Case of the French Bureau de Verification de la Publicite'," *Journal of Consumer Policy*, 7:1, pp. 45-64; (1983) "Outside Participation in Advertising Self-Regulation: Nature, Rationale and Modes." New York: Baruch College, mimeo.; (1983) "Outside Participation in Advertising Self-Regulation: The Case of the Advertising Standards Authority (U.K.)," *Journal of Consumer Policy*, 6:1, pp. 53-70.; (1979) *Decency and Sexism in Advertising: An International Survey of Their Regulation and Self-Regulation*. New York: International Advertising Association.

50 Rowell, Frederick (1970) *An Examination of Deceptive and Unethical Selling Practices In Canada*. Toronto: Canadian Consumer Council, p. ii.

51 Parker, Allan (1976) *Consumer Law in Canada*. Vancouver: International Self-Counsel Press Ltd., p. 6.

52 Reich and Micklitz 1980, p. 67.

53 Jahnke, L. (1973) *The Canadian Consumer Handbook*. Toronto: Self-Counsel Press, p. 58.

54 In Canada, provinces have legislative control over referral sales. See, for example, *British Columbia Consumer Protection Act*.

55 Reich and Micklitz 1980, p. 80; Canada, *Combines Investigation Act*. Sec. 36.3.

56 Epstein 1976, pp. 26-27.

57 Epstein 1976, p. 27.

58 Reich and Micklitz 1980, p. 71.

59 Adamo, Guy (1985) "Mail-order law successful in crackdown on deceptive practices," *Marketing News*, August 16, p. 16.

60 *Consumer Reports* (1986) "Mail Order Scams: Shearing the Suckers," (Feb.), pp. 87-94.

61 Reich and Micklitz 1980, p. 72.

62 Reich and Micklitz 1980, p. 72.

63 Canada, *Combines Investigation Act*, Sec. 37.2.

64 Sinclair, Upton (1906) *The Jungle*. New York: Viking Press edition, 1946.

65 *Official Journal of the European Communities,* Council Directive of 25 July 1985 (85/374/EEC), The Council of the European Communities, No. L210/29.
66 Reich and Micklitz 1980, p. 79.
67 Reich and Micklitz 1980, p. 81.
68 Gordon, Gavin (1966) "The Mechanism of Thalidomide Deformities Correlated with the Pathogenic Effects of Prolonged Dosage in Adults," *Developmental Medicine and Child Neurology,* 8, pp. 761-767; Lenz, W. (1966) "Malformations Caused by Drugs in Pregnancy," *American Journal of Diseases of Children,* 112 (Aug.), pp. 99-106.
69 Layde, Peter M. (1983) "Pelvic Inflammatory Disease and the Dalkon Shield," *Journal of the American Medical Association,* 250:6 (Aug. 12), p. 796.
70 Smith and Swann, p. 119.
71 Reich and Micklitz 1980, pp. 83-84.
72 United States, *Flammable Fabrics Act,* 1953, amended 1967.
73 See Day, M., Milton, M. T., and Wiles, D. M. (1985) "Textile Flammability Regulation and Test Methods: A Guide to the Present Canadian Scene," *Canadian Textile Journal,* (Feb.), pp. 12-14; Canada,, *Hazardous Products Act,* Sec. 3, and Amendments to the Schedule, Orders in Council PC 1971-2276 and PC 1971-2277, Secs. 4, 5, and 13.
74 Dickerson, K. G., Hesten, S. B., and Purdy, R. S. (1982) "How Much Federal Protection can Consumers Afford? The Case of TRIS," *Journal of Home Economics,* 74:1 (Spring), pp. 15-19.
75 Association Europeenne D'Etudes Juridiques et Fiscales (1975) *Product Liability in Europe.* The Netherlands, London: Kluwer-Harrop Handbooks. p. 23.
76 Reich and Micklitz 1980, p. 96.
77 Reich and Micklitz 1980, p. 95.
78 *Official Journal of the European Communities* (1985) Council Directive L210/29, (25 July); Reich, Norbert (1986) "Product Safety and Product Liability -- An Analysis of the EEC Council Directive of 25 July on the Approximation of the Laws, Regulation, and Administrative Provisions of the Member States Concerning Liability for Defective Products," *Journal of Consumer Policy,* 6, pp. 133-154; and Schmitz, Bob (1986) *EEC Council Directive, 25 July 1985, Liability for Defective Products: A consumer viewpoint.* Brussels: Bureau Europeen des Unions de Consommateurs, Feb. 27.
79 Dworkin, Terry Morehead, and Sheffet, Mary Jane (1985) "Product Liability in the '80s," *Journal of Public Policy & Marketing,* 4, p. 70.
80 Dworkin and Sheffet 1985, pp. 72-74.
81 Morishima, Akio, and Smith, Malcom (1986) "Accident Compensation Schemes in Japan: A Window on the Operation of Law in a Society," *UBC Law Review,* 20, pp. 519-521.
82 Association Europeene... 1975, p. 15.
83 24 Cal. 2d 453 P.2d 436 (1944).
84 Epstein, Richard (1980) *Modern Products Liability Law.* Westport, CN: Quorum Books, pp. 36-37.
85 Reich and Micklitz 1980, p. 99.
86 In fact, a Supreme Court decision in the late 1970s in Canada based this upper limit on a famous "trilogy" of

cases. See Charles, W. H. R. (1982) "The Supreme Court of Canada Handbook on Assessment of Damages in Personal Injury Claims," in John Irvine, ed., *Canadian Cases on the Law of Torts*, 18. Agincourt, Ontario: The Carswell Company.
87 Abbott, Howard (1980) *Safe Enough to Sell?* London: The Design Council, p. 56.
88 See, for example, Association Europeene... 1975, pp. 79 and 111; *O'Connor v. Altus* (17 NJ Super 298 335A Ed 545, (1975); Owles, Derrick (1978) *Development of Product Liability in the U.S.A.* Andover, MA: Holmes & Sons (Printers) Limited, p. 83.
89 Dworkin and Sheffet 1985, p. 72.
90 (1973) Q.B. 233.
91 *Tippett v. I.T.U., Loc. 226* [1976] 4 W.W.R. 460 and *U.S.A. v. Radio Shack*, 80 C.L.L.C. 16, 003, are examples.
92 Reich and Micklitz 1980, p. 105.
93 Abbott 1980, p. 59.
94 New York Times, Sept. 1, 1979, p. 16.
95 Association Europeene..., 1975, p. 21.
96 *Beshada vs. Johns Manville Corp.* (1982) 90 N.J. 191, 447 A. 2d. 539.
97 Dworkin and Sheffet 1985.
98 Committee on Consumer Policy (1977) *Consumer Protection in the Field of Consumer Credit.* Paris: Organisation for Economic Cooperation and Development; For a discussion and the actual experience of a sample of U.K. consumers with credit see Ison, Terence G. (1979) *Consumer Marketing and Credit Protection.* London: Croom Helm.
99 Committee on Consumer Policy 1977, p. 22.
100 See, for example, Drury, R. W., and Ferrier, C. W. (1984) *Credit Cards.* London: Butterworths; Walker, G. (1979) *Credit Where Credit is Due.* New York: Holt Rinehart and Winston.
101 Reich and Micklitz 1980, pp. 158-159.
102 Vancouver City Savings Credit Union (1985) *VanCity -- Hertz Used Car Sale.* Vancouver, B. C., (Sept.), printed brochure.
103 Committee on Consumer Policy 1977, p. 28.
104 Committee on Consumer Policy 1977, p. 31.
105 Duggan, A. J., and Darvall, L. W., eds. (1972) *Consumer Protection Law and Theory.* Sydney: Law Book, p. 109.
106 Walker 1979, p. 10.
107 Reich and Micklitz 1980, p. 141.
108 Trebilcock, Michael (1978) *Help.* Toronto: Canadian Broadcasting System, p. 28.
109 Committee on Consumer Policy 1977, p. 37.
110 Committee on Consumer Policy 1977, p. 39.
111 Committee on Consumer Policy 1977, p. 41.
112 Committee on Consumer Policy 1977, p. 41.
113 *Canadian Commercial Law Guide* (1983) Don Mills, Ontario: CCH Canadian Limited.
114 Reich and Micklitz 1980, p. 136.
115 Reich and Micklitz 1980, p. 136.
116 *Canadian Commercial Law Guide*, 1983.
117 Harvey, Brian W. (1978) *The Law of Consumer Protection and Fair Trading.* London: Butterworths, p. 63.

118 Reich, Norman, and Micklitz, H. W. (1981) *Consumer Legislation in Germany*. Berkshire: Van Nostrand Reinhold Company, Ltd. p. 269.
119 Ramsay, Iain, personal communication, 23 June 1986.
120 Calais-Auloy et al (1981) *Consumer Legislation in France*. New York: Van Nostrand Reinhold Co., p. 117.
121 Calais-Auloy et al 1981, p. 118.
122 Cranston, Ross (1978) "Access to Justice for Consumers: A Perspective from Common Law Countries," *Journal of Consumer Policy*, 3, pp. 291-299.
123 Mironowicz, Margaret (1986) "Dispute over flight delays makes for holiday hangover," *The Globe and Mail*, Jan. 4.
124 Calais-Auloy et al 1981, p. 119.
125 Ramsay, Iain D. C. (1981) "Consumer Redress Mechanisms for Poor-Quality and Defective Products," *University of Toronto Law Journal*, 31, p. 117. Professor Ramsay's article is also a good starting point for an analysis of the problem and direction to more details.
126 Cranston, Ross (1984) *Consumers and the Law*. 2nd ed. London: Weidenfeld and Nicholson, pp. 70-71.
127 Cranston 1984, p. 71.
128 Forbes, J. D., Tse, David K., and Taylor, Shirley (1985) "Towards a Model of Consumer Post-Choice Response Behaviour," in Richard J. Lutz, ed., *Advances in Consumer Research*, 13, Provo, UT: Association for Consumer Research, pp. 658-661.
129 J. Calais-Auloy et al 1981, pp. 166-167.
130 Reich and Micklitz 1981, p. 319.
131 Harvey 1978, pp. 121-122.
132 Calais-Auloy et al 1981, p. 174.
133 Calais-Auloy et al 1981, p. 174.
134 Reich and Micklitz 1981, p. 370.
135 Harvey 1978, p. 129.
136 Gerbrant, J. R., Hague, T., and Hague, A. (1972) "Preliminary Study of the Small Claims Court Procedure in Manitoba." Winnipeg: Faculty of Law, University of Manitoba, study supervised by J. Debicka. Only 31 percent of suits were by individuals; Samuels, J. W. (1968) "Small Claims Procedure in Alberta." Edmonton: Institute of Law Research and Reform, University of Alberta. Only 24.5 percent of suits were by individuals.
137 Cranston 1984, pp. 88-89, describing Roscoe Pound's idealistic dream circa 1913.
138 Reich and Micklitz 1981, p. 370.
139 *General Motors of Canada Limited v. Helen Naken et al*, unreported decision of the Supreme Court of Canada, Feb. 8, 1983.
140 Williams, Neil J. (1975) "Consumer Class Actions in Canada -- Some Proposals for Reform," *Osgoode Hall Law Journal*, 13 (June), p. 52.
141 Williams 1975, p. 56.
142 Williams 1975, p. 59.
143 Reich and Micklitz, 1980, p. 196; See also, O'Grady, M. James, (1982) "Consumer Remedies," *Canadian Bar Review*, 60:4 (Dec.), pp. 573-578.
144 BEUC (1985) "Product Liability in Europe at Last."

Brussels: Bureau Europeen des Unions de Consommateurs, press release, May 22.

145 Ferguson, Peter (1983) "Working Paper on Consumer Redress." Ottawa: Consumer Services Branch, Consumer and Corporate Affairs Canada,, (June), mimeo, pp. 11-12.

146 Ison 1979, pp. 248-251.

147 Horrocks, Russell L. (1982) "Alternatives to the Courts in Canada," *Alberta Law Review*, 20:2, pp. 333-334.

148 Harvey 1978, p. 126.

149 Calais-Auloy et al, 1981, p. 167.

150 Widdows, Richard, and Jobst, Kenneth (1986) "Consumer Arbitration of Consumer-Seller Disputes over Automobile Purchases: Has it Achieved what it Set Out to Achieve?" *Proceedings of the 15th Annual Conference for the Southwestern Regional Association Family Economics -- Home Management.* Akron, OH, (Feb.), pp. 124-127.

151 Lowe, Robert, and Woodroffe, Geoffrey (1980) *Consumer Law and Practice.* London: Sweet and Maxwell Ltd., p. 204.

152 Reich and Micklitz 1981, p. 359.

153 Lowe 1980, p. 153.

154 Cranston 1978, p. 234.

155 Cranston 1978, p. 234.

156 Cranston 1978, p. 235; Stanbury 1976, p. 571.

157 Cranston 1978, p. 165.

158 Maitland-Walker, Julian, ed. (1984) *International Anti-trust Law, Volume II.* Oxford: ESC Publishing Limited; Goyens, Monique, ed. (1985) *E. C. Competition Policy and the Consumer Interest.* Louvain-la-Neuve, Belgium: Cabay; MacCrimmon, M. T. (1983) "Controlling Anticompetitive Behaviour in Canada: A Contrast to the United States," *Osgoode Hall Law Journal*, 21, pp. 569-608; Bellis, J-F. (1979) "International Trade and the Competitive Law of the European Economic Community," *Common Market Law Review*, 16 (Nov), pp. 647-683; Smit, H. (1980) "Recent Developments in the EEC: Antitrust and the Court of Justice," *American Journal of Comparative Law*, 28, pp. 334-338; Van der Esch, B. (1980) "EEC Competition Rules: Basic Principles and Policy Aims," *Legal Issues of European Integration*, 2, pp. 75-85.

7. CONSUMERS AND THE POLITICAL PROCESS

Every day a spokesperson for some consumer group, such as the Consumers' Association in the U.K., or OCU in Spain, or the Consumers' Cooperative of Berkeley (California), is reported in the media commenting on some aspect of the consumer interest. Because of their activities on behalf of consumers, these consumer groups are probably the most visible evidence of consumerism to most people. And, over the past twenty or thirty years, these groups' numbers and activities have increased significantly. A short history of the consumer movement was presented in Chapter 1. In this chapter that movement, its organizations and their organizational and political dimensions are examined in greater detail. While, "you might not be interested in politics, ... politics is interested in you."[1]

Consumers are only one of many interest groups whose representational activities have increased since the end of World War II. While interest groups have operated since people first started to govern themselves, their activities in the last several decades have increased to the point that some persons question whether present day politicians can effectively govern in the public interest because of all the special interest groups seeking benefits for their narrower range of concerns.[2]

There is no doubt that interest groups are a fact of life and an integral part of governance in Western Europe and North America. The evidence favors the hypothesis that if citizens do not organize to have their interests formally represented, those interests are in jeopardy of being eroded in the governing process. At least some of this increased political activity is the result of the expansion and increasing complexity of governing. Domestic governments are faced with the problem of obtaining an adequate understanding and representation of its citizens' desires. Further, the evolution of supra-national governments, such as the European Community and the United Nations, and of international regulatory bodies, such as the General Agreement on Tariffs and Trade (GATT) and the International Air Transport Association (IATA), puts decision makers farther away from the individual being governed than ever before. Feeling to some degree disenfranchised, which indeed they are, individuals form groups to collectively make their interests known.

Governing institutions, on the other side of the coin, are liable to lose touch with the governed without a variety of sources of information for decision making. Interest groups are a vital source of information to help them govern. This chapter is divided into three main parts. The first traces the evolution and outlines the range of consumer representation institutions in the OECD countries. The second part uses theories from a broad range of academic disciplines to discuss and analyze the formation and operation of consumer interest groups. The last part of the chapter discusses and presents examples of a variety of consumer representational problems.

This chapter and Chapter 8 draw out the tension between the technocratic model of policy making, the idea that with reasoned analysis policy makers should design the ideal instrument to achieve a particular policy goal, and policy making as essentially a political bargaining process, where policies evolve in the rough and tumble of interest group and power politics. In the end, the reader will see that we believe the reality is an amalgam of the two, but that both sides need to be understood if we are to make better consumer policy; better, meaning achieving policy goals at lower economic and social cost.

CONSUMER GROUPS IN THE OECD

A wide variety of institutions represent, in varying degrees, consumer interests in OECD countries.

However, the broad and ubiquitous nature of the consumer interest, its pervasive and frequently contradictory nature, even for a given individual -- that is, we are both consumers and producers at the same time -- is in evidence when one tries to define consumer groups. While we would all agree that Consumentenbond in the Netherlands is a consumer group, how does one classify a labour union, a cooperative food store or *Good Housekeeping* magazine, who, in some of their activities, champion the consumer interest. In other of these organizations' activities the consumer interest may not be well served. For example, when labour unions call for import restrictions which raise the prices of domestic products to all consumers, when a cooperative food store receives a government subsidy which puts consumers who are not Coop members at a disadvantage, or when *Good Housekeeping* lobbies for a subsidy on mailing costs for magazines, the general consumer interest may not be served.

Table 7-1 presents a classification scheme which aids in understanding the range of institutions which are involved in representing consumer interests in the OECD countries. The scheme was devised using the criteria of government versus nongovernment, ministry versus lower level government organization, directness of mandate or goal to represent consumers, and profit versus non-profit as a source of funding. In addition to these criteria one could include the size of the organization, the multiplicity and complexity of goals, i.e., this scheme does not classify single purpose groups, such as those who represent the interests of homeowners, and there are other possible criteria. However, it does include the vast majority of those groups who appear to have had the major impact on consumer policy in the OECD countries. A more detailed classification was suggested by Maurice Healy of the National Consumer Council in London.[3] Indeed, there are a number of criteria which would allow for more detailed classification. However, for our purposes, the present classification is sufficiently detailed to illustrate the numerous types of institutions which have evolved to represent consumers' interests in a variety of institutional settings.

An analysis was made of the formation of, and significant changes in, OECD consumer institutions. We have called this data a measure of consumer organizational activity. An analysis of that information is graphed in Figure 7-1. The analysis shows that there was a rapid rise in consumer organizational activity during the late 1960s and the 1970s.

To provide the flavour of what types of changes the graph represents, a selection of the more important ones was made and this information is presented in Table 7-2. The organizations presented in the Table represent the major consumer organizations, government and non-government, and their names are in many cases indicative of their functions.[4]

An analysis of the number of institutions in each of the countries indicated that a few countries have relatively few consumer institutions (Greece, Iceland, Ireland, Italy, Turkey, Yugoslavia). Another group of countries had many and varied institutions (Australia, Canada, Denmark, Finland, France, Germany, Japan, Netherlands, Norway, Sweden, Switzerland, U.K., U.S.). Although we have not discovered any comparative measures of the effectiveness of consumer policy among countries, from my interested but non-statistical evaluation of how well consumers fare in the OECD countries and from the evaluation of people interviewed for this study, I have to conclude that consumers are better off in the latter group of countries. While that group has more consumer groups, they are also more affluent, have higher education levels and are generally more developed. So, while representation may be a factor in higher levels of consumer protection and rights, one is not sure whether it is cause or effect. However, a study of consumer law in Europe and the United States concluded that, "A strong and legitimate public constituency is essential ..... if the consumer movement in Europe is to have more input in the Community structure." The authors of that study believe that the stronger the consumer representation institutions, the

Table 7-1 Classes of Consumer Representation Institutions, OECD Countries, 1986

A. Government Consumer Ministry - A government department at the ministerial level which is directly involved in the legislative process and deals exclusively with consumer issues as a major part of its legislative mandate, e.g., Ministry of Consumer Affairs and Government Administration (Norway).

B. Government Ministry, Some Consumer Responsibility - A government department at the ministerial level with consumer interests as only a part of many responsibilities, e.g., The Department of Industry, Commerce and Tourism (Ireland) is in charge of consumer issues.

C. Government Consumer Agencies - Governmental bodies, not at the ministerial or departmental level, whose mission is to deal primarily with consumer issues. Often are called agencies, boards, commissions, committees, crown corporations, etc., e.g., National Institute for Consumer Research (Norway).

D. Government Agencies, Some Consumer Responsibility - Similar to Governmental Consumer Agencies but with consumer interests as only a part of many responsibilities, e.g., Environmental Protection Agency (U.S.).

E. Independent, Non-profit Consumer Organizations - Organizations which have public membership and involvement (voting, etc.) with no government control, although possibly government funded. Consumers are their principle interests, e.g., Consumer Association (U.K.), Consumers Union (U.S.).

F. Independent, Non-profit Organizations, Some Consumer Interests - Organizations that have some consumer interest representation as a result of representing their primary constituency - Some standards organizations, cooperatives, e.g., The League of Christian Women Workers (LOFC) (Belgium), poverty, women's, and senior citizens groups.

(Continued)

---

better off are consumers in the jurisdiction because of the greater effectiveness in developing and enforcing consumer policy.[5] One should add that this is not a conspiracy. Rather, it is simply a matter of numbers and that without a specific mandate to articulate consumers' interests that interest gets lost in the

Table 7-1 Continued

G. Independent, Non-profit Consumer Groups, Federations, Umbrella Groups, etc. - Organizations which usually have no direct, private consumer members. Organizations that are operated as nonprofit private companies, and umbrella organizations, e.g., Council of Consumer Organizations (AGV) (Germany), Consumer Federation of America (U.S.), and BEUC (EEC).

H. Profit-making Consumer Oriented Institutions - Companies that are profit oriented, but whose markets are consumer groups and whose interests are served in supporting consumer interests, e.g., *Good Housekeeping* (U.S.).

SOURCE: J. D. Forbes (1986) "Institutions Representing the Consumer Interest in OECD Countries - 1986." Vancouver, BC: Faculty of Commerce and Business Administration, University of British Columbia, Working Paper No. 1046, p. 6.

babble of other groups representing other interests.

In the research which enabled the production of Table 7-2 we noted that in a number of instances several institutional changes occurred in a country in the same or adjacent years. This illustrates the reality that laws enabling the establishment of consumer institutions or revising existing ones pass in packages of legislation which span several years. For example, federal activities in many countries, for example Australia and Canada, resulted in the establishment of a number of state or provincial institutions within a few years of each other. While institutional activity has fallen in the 1980s, one should not necessarily conclude that consumer interests are not being represented as well now as in the previous decade. If a sufficient number of effective organizations are in place, adding more may be counterproductive. What is important is understanding how such organizations function. Once that goal is achieved, one may be able to measure the effectiveness of their representation efforts. The balance of this chapter is devoted to these two areas, understanding consumer organizations

Figure 7-1 Occurrence of Consumer Institution Events, OECD Countries

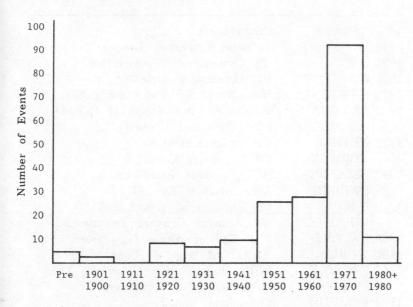

SOURCE: Forbes 1986.

and, to a lesser extent, describing and evaluating some of their activities.

ORGANIZATIONAL DIMENSIONS OF CONSUMER GROUPS

With both public and private interests clamouring for action, a number of organizations, representing many voters with similar policy objectives, can more effectively bring pressure to affect government and business policy than can an uncohesive gaggle of organizations with conflicting and ill-defined goals. In the case of consumers, businesses, faced with a large, coordinated consumer lobby, are more likely to be influenced by consumer demands than if the opposite obtains. If a statute change is needed, a government ministry charged to represent the consumer interest,

Table 7-2 Selected Examples of Consumer Institution Events, 1809-1982

1809	SWEDEN	Ombudsman
1899	U.S.	National Consumer League
1925	U.S.	CR Consumers' Research Inc.
1936	U.S.	CU Consumers' Union
1940	SWEDEN	Natl Board for Consumer Policy
1947	CANADA	Consumers' Association of Canada
	DENMARK	FDR Consumer Council
1953	NETHLDS	CB Consumentenbond
	NORWAY	FR Consumer Council
1957	BELGIUM	AC Consumer Association
	SWEDEN	KR Consumer Council
	U.K.	CA Consumers' Association
	YUGOSLAV	UP Assn of Cons of Yugoslavia
1959	SWITZLD	FRC Fed of Woman Consumers
1960	WORLD	IOCU Intl Orgn of Cons Unions
1962	EEC	BEUC Bur Europn Union des Cons
	FRANCE	ORCO Orgn of Consumers
1964	BELGIUM	Consumer Council
	SWITZLD	SKB Swiss Consumers Union
1965	FINLAND	KK Consumer Council
	LUXEMBG	Consumer Council
1966	GERMANY	Assn for Consumer Protection
1973	EEC	CCC Cons Consultative Committee
	PORTUGAL	DECO Assn for Cons Protection
1974	AUSTRLA	Australian Fed Consumer Orgns
1975	DENMARK	Cons Ombudsman, Complnts Bd
	SPAIN	OCU Orgn de Consumidores y Usuarios
	U.K.	NCC National Consumer Council
	TURKEY	Cons Protection Association
1981	JAPAN	Cons Products Guidance Office

SOURCE: Forbes 1986.

backed by an active consumer lobby, is much more likely to successfully obtain the desired legislation than if no governmental advocate department exists and if the consumer lobby groups are weak, have conflicting goals and are fighting amongst themselves.

The major reasons for the rise of consumer pressure groups were identified in Chapter 2 and consumerism was defined as, "the organized reaction of individuals to inadequacies, perceived or real, of marketers, the marketplace, market mechanisms, government, government services, and consumer policy." The key words in the definition for the purposes of this chapter are "organized reaction". Individuals can and do exercise a variety of avenues of redress when they attempt to exercise their consumer rights. However, in a sustained redress action, the individual consumer is almost always at a disadvantage to sustain that activity than the seller, who almost always has more resources to contest the action. The next course of action is to organize collectively with other consumers to pool resources and to pursue redress.

HOW CONSUMER GROUPS START

Consumer groups arise in a variety of ways. It appears that their formation is a complex, multi-dimensional phenomenon, for which at least four patterns have been described -- disturbance, entrepreneurship, purposive and historical.[6]

Disturbance theory holds that pressure groups form as the direct result of an event or series of events.[7] The theory on disturbances stems from observations during student riots in Berkeley, California in the early 1960s. However, while a disturbance, which is descriptive of an eruption of concern by persons with similar attitudes and values, may bring persons together, most would agree that there needs to be leadership and organization to focus those concerns over the longer time period, once the original disturbance has subsided.[8] Therefore, most observers of consumer groups' formation would probably agree that "spontaneous" formation presupposes leadership to capitalize on the opportunity to develop a functioning organization.

Entrepreneurship theory holds that the drive and organizational activities of a particular individual or individuals are at the root of successful pressure groups.[9] As will be discussed shortly, entrepreneurs organize and provide benefits to members in exchange for their support within the organization. An entrepreneur in public interest groups is characterized by dedication and, quite frequently, shoulders substantial costs, economic and non-economic, for remaining as group leader against odds and costs most persons would consider unacceptable. Examples of entrepreneurs include Ralph Nader, Colston Warne, Carol Foreman and Joan Claybrook in the United States, Phil Edmonston in Canada, and Michael Young, Caspar Brook and Elizabeth Schadee in Europe. These individuals organized groups, whose histories have been described by other authors.[10]

A more recent example of the disturbance and entrepreneur theories is that of OCU in Spain. For a number of years the Spanish consumer movement had limped along, a loose grouping of a housewives' organization, several professional and other groups with relatively little overall direction. One visible person in the melange was a lawyer, Antonio Garcia-Pablos, who published a book in 1975 titled *35 Million Consumers.*[11] In December of that year, Garcia-Pablos was instrumental in forming the Organisacion de Consumidores y Usuarios (OCU) and was elected its first president by the some 100 to 150 persons, mainly professionals, who constituted the founding membership. The organization limped along, supported in part by small grants from more developed consumer groups. With that financial support and encouragement, plus promotional efforts which expanded membership to around 2,000, a consumer magazine, *OCU*, was started in 1981.

This example could be called the reverse disturbance ploy. An entrepreneur, Garcia-Pablos, along with the interested board of directors of OCU, had formed an organization but were having problems expanding it to a viable size. Just then, 1981, an unfortunate disturbance, the discovery of poisoned cooking oil which killed several hundred people and made several thousand ill, provided the disturbance which aroused public interest in consumer matters. These higher levels of concern, OCU's filing of a class action suit on behalf of all the victims of the poisoning, and other activities resulted in a rise in membership from about 2,000 in 1980 to 35,000 in 1985. About 70 percent of its budget is from membership and magazine revenues, 25 percent from government grants, and 5 percent from IOCU, BEUC and the Consumers' Association. While this example may not fit the theoretical models of disturbance and entrepreneurship theory perfectly, it is a real life example of the start of a consumer interest group which has within it many aspects of the theories.[12]

Purposive is a classification I have coined to describe groups purposely created to represent interests. They are frequently the outcome of interaction among consumer groups and governments to specifically represent the consumer interest in the policy process. They may also be the result of the interaction of consumer and business interest.

Examples of the first type of group include the Norwegian Consumer Council, an amalgam of consumer groups representing interests to the Norwegian government and a number of groups in the U.K., such as the National Consumer Council.[13] Such groups are formed in consultation or at the urging of consumer groups when it is felt such an association can better organize to represent the consumer interest. The Bureau European des Consommateurs (BEUC), is an association of consumer groups representing consumers' interests in the European Economic Community. It was formed and is financed mainly by the national consumer organizations of countries in the European Community and by grants from the Community.[14] An example of a purposive group formed by consumers and business is the Canadian Advertising Council whose purpose is to evaluate media advertising according to rules of behaviour established in a code designed and administered by the Council and by national and regional councils.[15]

Organizations of this type exist in a number of European countries.[16]

The *historical* classification has been used for those groups whose existence cannot be explained by the other theories. This does not mean that a pressure group may not have formed from a disturbance or from the activities of an entrepreneur, only that such has not been identified. An example of an historical group is the Consumer's Association of Canada. The group's origins are not well documented, even though it appears to have started during World War II.[17]

WHY JOIN CONSUMER GROUPS?

Two types of consumer group members have been identified, general and activist. The motivation of each type to become and remain members of the organization is discussed below in terms of the benefits exchanged between and among members of consumer groups and the consumer organization in return for that membership.[18]

General Membership Motivation

Consumer group members usually receive their membership status when they subscribe to consumer magazines for the buying information they contain. Indeed, the large consumer organizations know that this is the major incentive for group membership and devote most of their budgets to product testing and buying advice in order to publish authoritative and useful information in their magazines, e.g., *Consumer Reports* in the U.S., *Which?* in the U.K., *Taenk* in Denmark, and *Canadian Consumer* in Canada, *50 Millions de Consummateurs* and *Que Choisir?* in France, *Der Test*, in Germany, etc.[19] Their benefits to subscribers include buying advice on a wide range of goods and services, delivered on a regular basis. Most public libraries have these magazines and their accompanying annual summary books available for the non-subscriber. However, public library systems are not well developed in some of the OECD countries so that in order to have access to them people must subscribe. Even in those that are well served by them, people subscribe for convenience. In addition, some general members feel that joining a consumer group helps the group better represent consumer interests and believe that this help is added incentive to join. How widespread this attitude is among consumer group general membership is not well documented, if it has been studied at all.

There is a body of theory which provides some insight into general membership in interest groups. Mancur Olson, an economist at Harvard University, developed a compelling set of hypotheses to explain the evolution of special interest groups. He observed that small groups of individuals with "special interests" band together to provide themselves with collective goods; those goods which individuals not acting collectively are unlikely to obtain. Examples of "special interest" groups are professional bodies, such as associations of physicians, lawyers, and other guild-like organizations, labour unions, agricultural marketing boards and the like which are coercive, frequently legislated by statute, and which almost always provide services not available to non-members, such as malpractice insurance, technical journals, fee and price setting mechanisms, lobbying activities and the like.

Olson singles out business groups as a special interest which he fits into his classification scheme as follows:

The high degree of organization of business interests, and the power of these business interests, must be due in large part to the fact that the business community is divided into a series of (generally oligopolistic) "industries", each of which contains only a fairly small number of firms.[20]

The collective incentives for membership in such small groups include the association and interaction with others in the same industry, lobbying activities and the industry newsletters and similar material which membership confers. However, many such groups have coercive policies conferred by law which force membership. Consumers, on the other hand, do not have such power. Therefore, their main membership incentive is in their magazine, the collective good they can provide their members. Knowledge of the consumer group's activity in representing interests usually comes from media reports on the organization's efforts in a particular policy area, such as air fares, false advertising, tariff policy and the like. It is important, therefore, that the group receive media coverage to show both members as well as business and government that the organization has the ability to legitimately represent a broad constituency.

The benefits exchanged between members and consumer organizations is a two way street. Leaders of consumer organizations know that they must maintain and recruit members to provide the resources necessary to continue their testing and advice activities as well as income to support lobbying efforts *and* a base of political legitimacy to demonstrate political power to politicians and business leaders. Political legitimacy is the concept that politicians and bureaucrats are more influenced by large groups whose goals are widely accepted. Small groups, whose goals may nonetheless be widely supported by voters, have less legitimacy and political power.

Activist Member Motivation

Why individuals become consumer activists is neither well studied nor well understood. Activist members are defined as individuals who provide leadership and actively work in the organization. Most of the large, national consumer groups have professional staffs who would not fall under this classification, although there is evidence that even professionals in public interest lobbying groups are not as strongly motivated by material and economic benefits as are professionals in other more narrowly focussed industrial pressure groups.[21] In the consumer groups with which the author is more familiar -- Consumers Association (U.K.), Consumers' Association of Canada and Consumentenbond -- activist members number fewer than one or two percent of total membership. Often they are confined to the Boards of Directors since staff is employed to perform all day-to-day functions. An apparent anomaly is the Consumers' Association of Canada, where volunteer members actively participate in day-to-day operations of consumer advice, lobbying and similar activities. Even in this case, a number of professional are employed, especially lawyers and policy analysts. Many of the Public Interest Research Groups (PIRGs), fostered by Ralph Nader and some of his organizations, have a higher proportion of active members but they are frequently much narrower in focus and interest than general consumer groups.

Studies of pressure groups show that the leadership have to provide incentives to members in exchange for their initial joining and continuing support of both the leadership and the organization. The marketing literature dealing with consumer activists is characterized by the identification and comparison of the demographic characteristics of consumer organization members. These studies compare the demographics of members of consumer groups to the population as a whole in terms of age (younger), education (higher), income (higher), and social class (higher).[22] People who participate in voluntary organizations, groups similar in many respects to consumer groups, exhibit demographic patterns quite similar to those in the marketing studies. Motivations for volunteering include altruism, public service, desire to feel useful, self-fulfillment and personal development.[23] Maynes suggests moral outrage and a sense of injustice in the marketplace as a specific motivation for consumerist activity.[24]

The expanding literature on motivation of active members in industrial special interest groups as well as in voluntary action groups and labour unions all show that only a small proportion of the members

are activists. They also show that activists in all
these organizations participate more for non-monetary
incentives and for social and ideological reasons than
do the largely economically motivated general
membership.[25] The only study of which I am aware
which directly investigates consumer activist motivation
is a study of the motivation of activist members of
the Consumers' Association of Canada which a
colleague and I have completed.[26] It showed that
consumer activists participate for the same reasons as
previous studies and expect no economic rewards from
their activities. Indeed, they cite significant monetary
and non-monetary costs as a result of their active
participation.

Berry, in a detailed study of a number of
public interest pressure groups in the United States,
has provided food for thought about the motivation of
members of consumer and similar pressure groups. He
was able to provide a description of the behaviour of
activists which has been intuitively satisfying and to a
number of consumer professionals and activists to
whom I have spoken.[27] He incorporated Clark and
Wilson's theory of three kinds of incentives to be
secured from organizational membership -- material,
solidary and purposive -- to explain the attraction of
public interest pressure groups. Material incentives
"relate to tangible goods" and may be equated with
Olson's economic incentives. These types of incentives
are characterized by the material benefits derived from
information in consumer publications. Solidary
incentives are the incentives derived from the
"socializing and friendships involved in actual group
interaction." Purposive incentives are those benefits one
receives from the pursuit of "nondivisible goods,"
which are the result of the groups' activities which
benefit all members, such as the passage of legislation
or the removal of an onerous tax. Of special
importance for consumer groups, which Berry equates
to public interest groups, is that purposive incentives
are the ideological satisfactions associated with efforts
to obtain collective goods which do not benefit active
members in any significant tangible way.[28] However,

there has been little empirical testing of Olson's original theory, and no testing of the more recent theoretical embellishments of his theory.

Closing this section on activist's motivation, Pearce provides some evidence that joining behaviour in voluntary organizations may be significantly different from other types of groups.[29] Swept along by the enthusiasm of friends, with almost no joining costs and with a desire to contribute service to these types of groups goals which characterize them, individuals join with little thought. This behaviour contrasts with the significant joining costs associated with changing jobs or joining organizations with substantial membership fees. As a result of the low joining costs, their new membership turnover rate is well over fifty percent in the first several months following joining. It is during this period where the real decision on joining takes place. This pattern seems logical because the cost of quitting is equally as low as the cost of joining and when the individual is faced with significant time and commitment costs to remain an active member and contribute to the organization the real choice is forced.

We can conclude that motivation for membership in consumer pressure groups range from those who join out of a sense of moral outrage or an inability to solve an individual problem through a spectrum to persons who join on a whim and leave as easily. There is obviously much we do not know and further study of consumer and similar groups should shed light on the subject.

ORGANIZATIONAL STRUCTURE

The environment within which an organization functions greatly influences its structure and operation. Indeed, pressure groups are adaptive instruments of political communication; they tend to work within the framework established by government, rather than impose their own structures and procedures on the power centres they deal with.[30] Consumer organizations are no exception. Many consumer organizations have the multiple functions of influencing both business and government on behalf of consumers while providing benefits for members to maintain a membership base and generate operating revenues.

Canada - U.S. Example of Function and Structure

Differences in attitudes toward the function and structure of government between Canada (and many European countries) and the United States are instructive in pointing out potential differences in the structure of consumer organizations and their use of resources in the two countries.

Under the parliamentary system of government in Canada, power resides in the Cabinet.[31] Committees of the two houses of the federal Parliament and the single houses at the provincial level have little power. Individual members of the legislatures (the federal Senate has no real legislative power) must follow the direction of the party whips and vote the party position or risk serious discipline. With a parliamentary majority the government in power can, within reason, pass the laws it wants. In addition to politicians, the bureaucracy and elites of various pressure groups are influential in the development of policy and the drafting of legislation. Elites are the influentials, the politicians, bureaucrats and pressure group members and staff professionals, who actually wield power and are able to influence legislation, or, frequently and as important, stifle its introduction.[32]

Canadian pressure groups, therefore, devote the majority of their resources to influencing cabinet members (who are the heads of the various departments), senior bureaucrats, and members and employees of regulatory bodies. Relatively few resources are devoted to influencing various parliamentary committees and individual legislators.[33]

Attitudes about the function of government, and the more formal, legalistic policy development process in the United States, lead to different consumer organization structures and resource use. The importance of Congressional and Senate committees, the frequent chairing of these committees by opposition party members, the lower level of whip control over party members' voting, the separation of the executive from the legislative arm of government, the frequent opposition party control of the legislative branch, and the highly structured legal process for legislation, are generally acknowledged to result in relatively more resources being expended on lobbying individual legislators and legislative committees by U.S. consumer organizations than is the case in Canada. Two recent descriptions of the activities of consumer lobbying activities in the United States, by Michael Pertschuk and Erma Angevine, provide excellent examples of this phenomenon.[34]

The European case is similar, in that the pressure groups relate to government structure. In the European Economic Community, the Bureau European des Unions de Consommateurs (BEUC), the umbrella consumer organization, is made up of national consumer groups for EEC member countries. Located in Brussels, where the community has its headquarters, it structures its inputs into the policy process along the lines of the structure of the Economic Community's committee system and departments. In addition, it attempts to aid consumer groups in the member countries in presenting a unified set of policies when they try to influence their local members to the European Parliament and thereby increase support for BEUC in Brussels.[35]

Rose's analysis of differences in consumer representation between Norway and the United States presents an even greater contrast than the situations described above in that a statutory group represents consumers in Norway. None of the previous groups discussed have statutory, guaranteed access or legitimacy in the policy process -- although BEUC probably has *de facto* and guaranteed access. Rose classifies the ways consumer's interests are represented in society on a continuum from individuals representing themselves without organization, to independent consumer organizations, to government ministries charged specifically with representing consumers in government. The classification scheme presented previously in Table 7-1 is based in great degree on Roses's. He classifies Norway as representing and protecting consumers with a combination of organizations of consumers, including statutory access to the government by consumer organizations and a government ministry. He contrasts this classification of Norway with that of the United States which is mainly free market, with several large consumer organizations, and with a relatively low level, sub-ministerial department charged with representing consumers. The U.S. does not have a ministry with consumer representation as its primary mission.[36]

The Norwegian situation is an example or variant of the concept of "corporatism". This interest accommodation mechanism, much more prevalent in Western Europe than in North America, has as its basis governments providing direct access to the policy-making process for major societal interest groups. For example, labour and business have frequently been given the right to consult with government in the development of national incomes and economic policy. These groups have at times been given a statutory mandate to collect dues or membership fees from all organizations in a sector to finance these representation activities. In return, the interest groups operate very much like an arm of government. At least open criticism of the government is frequently lower and cooperation with government greater than in pluralistic systems where interest groups are treated in a much more arm's length manner and have few if any statutory assists in generating resources to influence policy development.[37]

Differences in Structure of Representation

It is instructive to consider the wide range of consumer representation systems which exist in the OECD countries, because they are quite different. The U.S. is, as described, relatively unstructured at the federal level without a ministry responsible for consumers. Canada has a relatively active federal and provincial ministry system with provincial consumer groups and with one strong private national organization. France has a ministry, has a government supported consumer magazine as well as a private and competing system and magazine funded privately. Germany and Scandinavian countries have government financed testing and a relatively weak consumer organization, but, from what we could determine, consumers have quite an active input into those government systems. The U.K. seems to have the best of both worlds. They have a strong, private consumer organization. In addition the National Consumer Council operates as a government financed consumer advocate within the government, staffed in many areas, at least until recently, by persons who have previously been trained, in large measure, in the private organization. This situation appears to provide a double shot at representing consumers from both within and without the government.

In spite of the differences, and recognizing that in one particular area consumers in these countries may fare slightly better or slightly worse, one is hard pressed to say that one system is better than another. It is doubtful that the system in one country could be transferred to the other because of the differences in attitudes and institutions of government for which each country is unique. There just has not been enough study of the way in which influence works nor what kinds of institutions can be transferred across jurisdictional and cultural lines and still be effective to be able to say which system or combination of systems will work.

ORGANIZATIONAL OPERATIONS

Consumer groups generally have had a more limited base of resources on which to draw, given the broad range of matters with which their mandates require them to be concerned, than have industrial, professional and similar economic pressure groups. That is, the range of concerns which affect consumers is much wider than more narrowly focussed special interest pressure groups, and, per capita and per issue, they are not highly funded. This fact has an effect on how such organizations operate.

Compare the concerns of a consumer pressure group to those of a business pressure group whose members are interested in promoting the welfare of only a small subset of consumption possibilities. In Chapter 1, consumer concerns over electronic funds transfers were discussed. A national consumer organization would consider that it had a mandate to be sure consumers' interests are represented in the development of these EFT systems as only one of many concerns. The national association of banks in a country mainly concerns itself with the EFTS issues and matters directly affecting banking. Further, each member of the industry group often receives direct financial and other benefits from their group membership. While large national consumer groups provide members with the material benefits of buying information, activist members receive little except the solidary and purposive or non-direct benefits and satisfactions of participating described earlier. And, while business organizations can deduct a large proportion of their lobbying expenditures from taxes, as can professionals and persons such as farmers, consumers must use after tax funds to support their efforts.

Three additional points help understand the resource problems faced by consumer and other "large, latent interest groups." First, the larger the group seeking a collective good, the greater the suboptimality of the collective good available to distribute to individual group members. That is, the less exclusive the group, the less value of the collective benefit it provides.[38]

Second, large groups normally need a means for coercive membership, such as the closed shop or professional licensing, to be effective and to solve the free rider problem. The free rider problem is the phenomenon that if an organization obtains a benefit which is distributed to members and non-members alike, there is little economic incentive to join the organization to obtain the benefit and the benefit becomes a "free ride" for non-members because of the "public goods" nature of the benefit.[39] The latter surely characterizes all large consumer groups I have observed; consumers do not have to join to receive many of the benefits the group generates.

For example, the Regulated Industry Program (RIP) of the Consumers' Association of Canada was responsible for securing low cost "advance booking" airline fares for Canadian consumers (RIP).[40] These low rates were available to all Canadians, CAC member and non-member alike. Securing these benefits used a significant proportion of that organization's budget for several years. Similarly, BEUC and the national consumer organizations in Europe are in the process of trying to deregulate the very high cost European airline industry.[41] When -- or if -- deregulation happens, the benefits will go to all individuals flying in Europe, not just members of the various consumer groups. Obvious questions of equity arise from such activities by consumer and similar interest groups. Should such groups not be reimbursed in some manner for their activities which benefit the general public? More on this matter elsewhere.

The third point is Olson's "by-product" theory, which states that interest groups provide collective political lobbying benefits as a by-product of individuals joining a group to obtain individual, non-collective benefits. Olson cites as an example the Farm Bureau in the United States, which started because the government required the formation of county organizations of farmers before the county could receive funds for a county agricultural agent and other educational and technical benefits. ".…. the [collective benefit of lobbying efforts which resulted in] the passage of much legislation that was popular among (and helpful to) the farmers" was a by-product of the requirement to join the Farm Bureau for an individual benefit.[42] Indeed, the "by-product" theory explains to some degree the lobbying activities of consumer organizations in Europe and North America. Each of the organizations that publish a consumer testing magazine provides a private benefit to its readers but their joining also results in a "by-product" lobbying capability brought about by the economic resources generated by the magazine and by the political legitimacy a large membership confers on such groups.

Benefits to Members and Employees

As stated earlier in the chapter and given emphasis above, it is critical for the leadership of consumer organizations to provide its general and activist members plus its professional staff with sufficient benefits to motivate them in each of their important organizational roles. Because interests of activists in large general consumer groups are so diverse, maintaining activist interest may result in spreading the organization's limited resources so thinly that only minimal activity is possible in any area and overall organization effectiveness is reduced. The other possibility is that activities in important policy areas must be postponed. More narrowly focused groups may not have as difficult a problem in providing benefits to their active members, especially if they are of one mind and only have one main area of concern. Members join these types of groups for their specific interests. Researchers have recognized that groups with as diverse interests as consumers are bound to have conflicting interests within their organizations.[43]

Some small consumer advocacy groups have no publications or other sources of material benefits with which to motivate members. However, since all members are activists, they appear to derive their motivation from the non-material benefits of being able to have an active and influential voice in the organization. Public Interest Research Groups (PIRGs) in the U.S. and Canada, started by Ralph Nader with money won in a suit against General Motors, are an example of this type of group.[44] However, they have problems of political legitimacy which may offset some of the benefits of highly involved and influential activists. Even though their cause may be one widely supported by a large segment of society, they are not tied to, nor can they purport to represent in a direct way, a large group of consumers as can groups such as BEUC, the Consumers Association, or Consumentenbond. What small groups gain in activist motivation and increased organizational efficiency they appear to lose in political legitimacy and the resource base to hire professional staff.

Problems of Bigness

An obvious paradox which confronts the leadership of public interest groups in that as the organization expands, as it must if it is to have the expertise to effectively move forward on a variety of policy issues, individual members are more distant from the nexus of priority setting and power. The leadership must devise ways of providing not only for action on policy issues for the diverse set of interests of its membership but also provide a channel for members to voice their preferences in directing the organization. This is true for continuing activist commitments to the organization and to the general membership. But this is also a problem with all large organizations, business, government as well as political parties.

The largest and oldest of the consumer organizations are now staffed almost exclusively by professionals. Their motivations may not always be in concert with the general or more activist members. All the national organizations do report to a management board of some sort which directs the activities of the organization. These boards are composed of persons who in earlier days would probably have been non-paid activists. Needing to satisfy the conflicting priorities of these members appears to have within that process elements of the problem involved in providing benefits to activist members of organizations where non-professionals still have an active day-to-day role. Many organizations are mixed, in that professionals and staff do many of the functions but resources of member activists are also used in significant amounts. From observation and detailed questioning of both members of boards and professional staff, there is often some conflict. However, we have not been able to find information on the problems this mixture of professional and volunteers may cause, if any, in the operation of consumer groups.

Populist-Elitist Conflict

In an analysis of conflicts in populist and elitist pressure groups, Danet hypothesized that advocates of populist groups, defined as totally member run, highly democratic groups, provide satisfaction in exchange for member participation "whereas the elitists argue that [wide] participation only frustrates clients and reduces efficiency ..... [Furthermore], consumer organizations are generally governed by boards in which ordinary members have weak representation."[45] That is, they are elitist. A similar tendency in consumer organizations in the Federal Republic of Germany has been described.[46] While this may be true, we have seen no research to determine whether the interests -- collective and individual -- of ordinary members are better or more poorly served by either populist or elitist types of groups. In fact, Olson's and Moe's work cited earlier would indicate that, except in the case of individuals where solidary benefits are extremely important, populist organizations are not terribly rational in that the costs of marshalling and organizing non-expert contributions in lobbying activities, which usually involve highly technical matters, are greater than the benefits. Of course, it is vital that consumer organizations maintain large memberships in order to have the political legitimacy and to generate resources, discussed previously.

Volunteer-Professional Conflict

The benefits of participation by consumer group members may be at the root of what the author and Pearce have observed in quite a few instances in voluntary organizations, including consumer groups.[47] Namely, the use of paid professionals -- lawyers, scientists, media personnel, managers, organizers -- is probably never completely accepted by the governing group or, if accepted, retains an aura of non-legitimacy. Even though governing boards of consumer organizations are usually not composed solely of lay activists, i.e., they have a number of professional members, they appear to have problems dealing with professionals. While we have seen no quantification of these casual observations, I have seen many examples in Canada of paid professionals, especially when they appear to be developing expertise, come into conflict with boards and end up leaving or being fired by the organizations. This may be characteristic of an organizational form in one country, but interviews with professionals in large consumer organizations in Europe indicate that the volunteer-professional conflict exists to some degree there as well.

More research is needed to understand the problems of using expertise in pressure group activities. Some problems may stem from power conflicts between paid professionals and boards, some may stem from professionals being vocal and newsworthy and taking some of the non-material publicity benefits from the volunteers who compose the directorate, and some of the problems may derive from individual conflicts of personality and ideology. This is a particularly important area for research because government and business have capable and experienced persons on their side in the political bargaining process, the life blood of advocacy activities.[48] Consumers, without effective, experienced,

professional expertise on their side are behind from
the start. The conjecture and hypothesizing in this
paragraph is just that and indicates another void of
knowledge.

INTERACTION WITH OTHER ORGANIZATIONS

Consumer groups must interact with a variety of
organizations in order to effectively influence
governments and other organizations. This interaction
process is designed to develop and maintain
interorganizational networks and agreements to ensure
that consumer interests are represented in the political
process.[49] Pressure groups are, in reality, engaged in
gaining access, legitimacy and resources to influence
and change economic and political relationships to their
members' benefit.

Professor Pross has coined the term "policy
community" to describe the major institutions and
influence groups which participate in the policy process
in a particular area.[50] In the consumer case this
would include the various government ministries
representing consumers, consumer groups, and business,
labour and professional groups, depending on the issue.
For example, in the U.S. during the battle for the
Consumer Protection Agency described previously, one
can see the House of Representatives and the Senate,
the President, the U.S. Chamber of Commerce and
National Association of Manufacturers and the various
consumer groups as the main members of that policy
community. Discussions in the EEC on airfares would
include another group of institutions. However, the
concept of a policy community is useful to reinforce
the reality that there are always a number of groups
involved in these types of policy questions and that
the interaction among the groups is the reality of
policy making.

Organizationally mature and effective pressure
groups carry out a wide range of functions. These
functions include pursuing multiple, broadly defined,
collective and selective objectives, having extensive

human and financial resources, conducting an effective public relations program with access to the news media, and regular contact with policy makers and membership on advisory and policy making boards.[51] Consumer organizations such as Consumentenbond, Consumers' Association, Consumers Union, BEUC and a number of others fall into this classification. Other consumer groups approach this level of organizational maturity and sophistication. However, in some countries, these functions are only beginning to develop. Pressure groups are only a part of, albeit an important adjunct to, representative government.

Therefore, with increasingly complex interrelationships between business, government and other interests in society, it is only natural for consumers to want their interests adequately represented in the political process.[52] Furthermore, competition among groups for political influence and a hypothesized natural political advantage of business groups over other types of groups, only reinforce this felt need by consumers for adequate representation.[53] With the increase in the size and importance of government shown in Chapter 5, the need for adequate consumer representation in relationships with government and other groups appears to be even greater than even a decade or two ago.[54]

Regulatory activity, frequently instituted by the regulated group in their own interests, or regulatory capture of the regulators by the regulated, provide further reasons to represent consumers and to ensure that this large societal group's interorganizational agreements and interaction networks do not deteriorate.[55] One of the major thrusts of consumer political activity in the last ten to twenty years has been intervening before regulatory bodies of all types to insure the interests of consumers are taken into account in the regulatory process. In listening to the rhetoric about regulation, I have the feeling that even those who decry it the most are really saying, "Deregulate everything that prevents me from doing as I would like but keep those regulations which benefit me." However, there is little sign that deregulation, even in the United States and the U.K. which tout it highly, is decreasing in any significant degree. Therefore, consumer groups quite properly realize that regulation is endemic and that they must represent effectively their constituency or have these interests suffer in the long run.

Using Canada as an example, only because I know of no other listing as exhaustive, researchers identified 111 federal regulatory statutes which existed in 1978.[56] These regulations affected all manner of economic, social, health and welfare matters of Canadians. About the same time, a group of students and professors at the University of Toronto Law School identified 292 regulatory statutes and regulatory bodies in the Province of Ontario.[57] It is mind boggling to think of the number of regulations affecting both consumers and businesses when one counts federal, provincial and then includes municipal regulations. The regulatory jungle of European countries and, superimposed on domestic regulations, those of the European Community in Brussels, are no less complex than in Canada.

Examples of Regulatory Success and Failures

Consumer activists with whom I have spoken believe that consumer interests in all political jurisdictions are seldom represented with the same vigour as those who have large and direct financial benefits to gain from the matters in question. Such anecdotal observations are just that, since it is difficult to measure the effectiveness of any lobby group. As well, there is still much to be learned in the area, both regarding measurement and in identifying the many groups involved in the political influence process. However, consumer groups win some of their regulatory fights but lose some as well, as the examples below illustrate.

Agriculture and Food Policy - A prime example of relative consumer impotence in the policy process through lack of access and legitimacy is documented in aspects of food policy in the United States,

Canada, and the European Community. For some commodities in North America and for most food products in the EEC under Common Agricultural Policy (CAP), price supports and other regulatory regimes result in farm prices higher than equilibrium levels. This results in excessive revenues to big farmers, who produce the large majority of output, and the placing of a relatively greater burden of costs on low income consumers who spend a larger portion of their income on food than do the general population if higher food costs result. While the EEC subsidizes consumer food prices to some degree, thereby alleviating some of the burden on low income consumers, the tax costs and the inefficiencies introduced by the CAP are counter-productive on any measure one wishes to use. They continue to exist because of the political power of farmers and the political problems that politicians in the member states face in changing the regime to one that was more equitable and efficient.

A number of authors have shown that, for Canada and the EEC respectively, that the lack of access to the policy process, and an apparent lack of legitimacy in food matters, leave consumers with little influence in this important policy area.[58] The U.S. case is too complex to develop here and consumers there are less seriously affected than in the EEC or Canada, but only in degree. Suffice it to say that there are large monetary transfers to producers of some food commodities which appear unjustified from the U.S. consumers' viewpoint.[59]

Air Fares - The deregulation of airlines and air fares in the United States and Canada is an example where consumer and other groups have been effective in their lobbying activities. That deregulation saves North American consumers over $6 billion annually (in 1977 dollars).[60] That battle is just commencing to bear fruit in Europe in the face of what appears to be more governmental opposition than was experienced in North America.[61] That is, many of the governments involved have vested economic and egoistic interests in the continuance of the highly restrictive and monopolistic routes and fare structures.[62] Political pressure from many interest groups and economic pressures from the now deregulated trans-Atlantic and charter business within Europe will provide an interesting scenario to observe over the next few years. The consumer lobby groups, especially BEUC, are pressing even harder for rationalization now that the EEC Court of Justice has decided that airlines are not exempt from prosecution for anti-competitive practices.[63]

Consumer Protection Agency Battle - There is no better or as well documented political situation which illustrates consumer lobbying efforts and those of opposing interests than does the defeat of a bill that would have set up a Consumer Protection Agency in the United States.

About 1970, then President Nixon appointed a number of individuals to federal regulatory agencies whose sympathies were widely held to be strongly pro-industry. President Nixon had, in effect, made the industries self-regulating. Ralph Nader, as a result of this flurry of self-interest appointments, proposed the establishment of a government agency to represent consumer interests before regulatory agencies in the U.S. federal government.[64] While this may be overstating the case, it does not do so by much. Following several liberal presidents, a number of consumer successes, such as the truth in lending bill, President Carter supported the establishment of a Consumer Protection Agency which would centralize the more than twenty consumer type agencies in the federal government and provide the power to intervene in the consumer interest before regulatory bodies. It would also have provided the funds to present the consumer side of issues in front of congressional committees in the development of legislation at the federal level.

Business groups in the United States had been relatively somnolent during the period when consumers had been making legislative advances during the 1960s and early 1970s. In the proposed bill they saw their power being further eroded. Members of their major

ced their feeling that President Carter
was committed to the bill, they started a campaign to
bring pressure on members of the U.S. House of
Representatives and Senate to defeat the bill.[65]
Through their efforts, "Thousands of letters poured
into the National Chamber [of Commerce offices in
Washington] from business people who said they were
opposed to creating another government agency."[66]
These letters were in response to a letter writing
campaign promoted by business groups with a good
deal of support from some sectors of the news media.
The goal of the campaign was for people to inform
the politicians of the excessive government "in their
lives -- too much protection, too much of what other
people think is good for them ....." as Dr. Richard L.
Lesher, president of the Chamber of Commerce of the
United States, saw the problem and promoted the
defeat of the bill.[67] On the day before the vote on
the bill in the House of Representatives, the National
Association of Manufacturers put the following recorded
message out to its members across the country:

> Yesterday the House began consideration of ..... the
> bill ..... Administration lobbyists crowded the House
> halls yesterday and the president himself is making
> calls to wavering representatives. With a hard
> administration push, what looked like a sure defeat
> for the consumer bill is now looking like an
> exceedingly close vote today. NAM members should
> make personal calls immediately to their
> representatives to make sure that they do not
> cave in to administration pressure to create a new
> bureaucracy. Your efforts are crucial to defeat any
> version of the bill today.[68]

A cartoon by Ben Sargent, Figure 7-2, quite
nicely reflects the feelings of consumer activists about
the battle and is probably quite realistic about the
relative magnitude of the resources available to the
two sides in mounting their respective campaigns.

Figure 7-2 Cartoon About Consumer Protection Agency Fight

Reprinted by permission.

The business lobby was successful and defeated the bill by a 38 vote margin, 227 to 189. While consumer advocates were disappointed, several commented on the fact that it came so close to passage. The *New York Times* quoted a Democratic supporter of the bill to the effect that the bill was designed to make existing legislation work by putting consumers in a more equitable position in commenting on legislation where the advantage to business interest is, "50 to 1; 100 to 1 on most issues."[69] There was obviously much support for it. This coincides with an observation by Michael Pertschuk, removed by President Reagan as Chairman of the Federal Trade Commission because of his proactive public interest bias, that U.S. consumers may have felt a general, non-specific aversion to bureaucracy and regulation, but, when quizzed on specifics, were supportive of consumer protection through legislation and many types of regulation. "Overwhelming majorities [of U.S. consumers] continue undaunted to support continued regulation of industrial safety, auto emissions and safety standards, and environmental restraints, and to call for even more regulation designed to strengthen consumer rights and remedies."[70]

The Professional Gladiators

One of the most stimulating areas of interest in the influence process is how influence activities by stakeholders in a particular jurisdiction actually occur. How are networks of influence developed, nurtured and utilized in the influence process called governance?

Maurice Healy, of the National Consumer Council in the U.K., has coined the term "professional gladiators" to describe those individuals that, through a variety of contacts with other gladiators, actually create and maintain the networks among organizations. These individuals, who work for interest groups and governments, are members of the political elite described earlier. They frequently sit in the interminable meetings which characterize the influence process. A telephone call from one of them may help set the agenda for such meetings and pave the way for agreement. They or their bosses may set the political agenda in the media, through press releases, conferences, personal appearances and similar activities which influence the environment within which policy is made. The individuals in the business lobby in the United States, whose activities in the Consumer Protection Agency debate were just documented, were doing their jobs as professional gladiators. They are engaged in all the activities in the political/influence process such as setting out the alternatives which may be considered, defining positions of the parties involved, designing tradeoffs and possible changes in positions which are politically and organizationally acceptable, and then in attempting to sell the agreements to their organizations. They also are involved often in helping the passage and implementation of legislation and in the adoption of non-legislative agreements by the parties involved in a particular issue.

For example, consider the maneuvering surrounding a proposed imposition of a quota on the importation of clothing. Most consumer groups would oppose such measures. However, domestic manufacturers and labour unions would support it, as would the politicians from the constituencies where the clothing is manufactured. The gladiator(s) for consumers would attempt to create support for the consumer position by finding out what other groups and politicians were opposed to the proposed quotas, such as free trade groups and manufacturers of other products who could face countervailing quotas from countries whose exports would be excluded. They would then investigate how the groups could work together to effectively oppose the proposed quotas. This type of activity is the lifeblood of influence activities.

Professor Creighton concluded that

..... consumer representation ..... must share the responsibility of their own failure [to influence legislation and activities under President Roosevelt's New Deal in the U.S. in the 1930s because] ..... they were novices at playing what was essentially a political game.[71]

This cannot be said of today's consumer groups, whose political capabilities and resources become ever more experienced and capable.

SUMMARY AND CONCLUSIONS

Consumer advocacy groups are political pressure groups whose role is to represent consumer interests in the political process. Their numbers increased dramatically in the 1960s and 1970s to the point where consumers in most OECD countries are represented by a wide range of institutions both in and out of government. While these groups may not have the power that they would like, consumers are much better represented in the political process than they were several decades ago. Because of the public goods nature of the things they lobby for, consumer groups will always be less well funded than special interest groups. In spite of this inherent problem, and one which has been alleviated to a degree in a number of countries by government financial support, consumer interest groups have established themselves as legitimate political entities with legitimate claims on the political system. They have, perhaps grudgingly, earned the respect of other interest groups, especially business, through those efforts.

NOTES

1 Holsworth, Robert D. (1980) *Public Interest Liberalism and the Crisis of Affluence: Reflections on Nader, Environmentalism, and the Politics of a Sustainable Society.* Boston: G. K. Hall & Co., p. 1.
2 Lowi, Theodore J. (1969) *The End of Liberalism.* New York: W.W. Norton and Co., Inc.
3 Personal interview, May 1985.
4 A detailed listing of all the organizations identified in the research may be found in Forbes 1986.
5 Bourgoignie, Thierry M., and Trubek, David M. (1984) *Consumer Law, Common Markets and Federalism in Europe and the United States.* Florence: European University Institute, in press, pp. 34-35; 52-55; 405.
6 This section is intended only to present the briefest discussion of organizational genesis. Theories explaining pressure group genesis are in their infancy and are the subject of an expanding body of literature including, Berry, Jeffrey M. (1978) "Origins of Public Interest Groups - Tests of Two Theories." *Policy*, 10:3, pp. 379-399; Moe, Terry M. (1980) *The Organization of Interests.* Chicago and London: The University of Chicago Press; Rose, Lawrence E. (1980) "The

Role of Interest Groups in Collective Interest Policy-Making: Consumer Protection in Norway and the United States," *European Journal of Political Research*, 9, pp. 17-45; Salisbury, Robert H. (1969) "An Exchange Theory of Interest Groups," *Midwest Journal of Political Science*, 13:1 (Feb.), pp. 1-32; Smelser, Neil J. (1963) *Theory of Collective Behavior*. New York: The Free Press of Glencoe; Truman, David B. (1951) *The Governmental Process: Political Interests and Public Opinion*. New York: Knopf.

7 Berry, Jeffrey M. (1977) *Lobbying for the People*. Princeton: Princeton University Press, p. 23; Smelser 1963.

8 In a later paper, Berry (1978) concludes that the entrepreneur theory is more credible than the disturbance theory. This view is also supported by Moe's research, although he also believes that there may be "spontaneous" formation which is similar, if not analogous to, disturbance theory (Moe, Terry M. (1981) "Towards a Broader View of Interest Groups." *Journal of Politics*, 43, p. 537).

9 Moe 1980; Salisbury 1969.

10 Angevine, Erma, ed. (1982) *Consumer Activists: They Made a Difference*. Mount Vernon, NY: National Consumers Committee for Research and Education and Consumers Union; Pertschuck, Michael (1982) *Revolt Against Regulation: The Rise and Pause of the Consumer Movement*. Berkeley: University of California Press, p. 30; Berry 1977, p. 25; Pearce, Michael R., and Green, Alan R. (1982) "Ontario Rusty Ford Owners' Association v. Ford Motor Company of Canada -- The Activists' Version," in Stanley J. Shapiro and Louise Heslop, eds., *Marketplace Canada: Some Controversial Dimensions*. Toronto: McGraw-Hill Ryerson Limited, pp. 32-58; Roberts, Eirlys (ca 1982) *International Organization of Consumers Unions: 1960 1981*. The Hague: International Organization of Consumers Unions.

11 Garcia-Pablos, Antonio (1975) *35 Millones de Consumidos*. Madrid: Mateu Cromo, S.A.

12 OCU (ca 1985) "Breve Nota Sobre el Desarrollo de la OCU." Madrid: OCU, mimeo, and personal interview, Carlos Sanchez Reyes, Director, OCU, Madrid, June 10, 1985.

13 Rose 1980, pp. 17-45; Shanks, Michael (1983) "Comment on the Paper by Nelles," *Journal of Consumer Policy*, 6, pp. 279-283.

14 Mitchell, Jeremy (1978) *Marketing and the Consumer Movement*. Maidenhead, Berkshire, England: McGraw-Hill Book Company (UK) Ltd., pp. 272-273; Personal interview, Tony Venables, Director, BEUC, Brussels, May 1985.

15 Advertising Standards Council (1982) *The Canadian Code of Advertising Standards*. Toronto: Advertising Standards Council, (May); Boddewyn, J. J. (1984) "Outside Participation in Canadian Advertising Self-Regulation," *Canadian Journal of Administrative Sciences*, 1:2, pp. 214-237.

16 Boddewyn, J. J. (1983) "Outside Participation in Advertising Self-Regulation: The Case of the Advertising Standards Authority (U.K.)," *Journal of Consumer Policy*, 6:1, pp. 77-93; Boddewyn, J. J. (1983) "Belgian Advertising Self-Regulation and Consumer Organizations: Interaction and Conflict in the Context of the Jury d'Ethique Publicitaire

(JEP)," *Journal of Consumer Policy* 6:3, pp. 303-323; Boddewyn, J. J. (1984) "Outside Participation in Advertising Self-Regulation: The Case of the French Bureau de Verification de la Publicite (BVP)," *Journal of Consumer Policy*, 7:1, pp. 45-64.

17 Dawson, Helen Jones (1963) "The Consumers' Association of Canada," *Canadian Public Administration*, 6 (March), pp. 92-118; Morningstar, Helen J. (1977) "The Consumers' Association of Canada -- The History of an Effective Organization," *Canadian Business Review*, 4:4, pp. 30-33.

18 Social exchange theory, as analyzed in Bagozzi, Richard P. (1974) "Marketing as an Organized System of Exchange," *Journal of Marketing*, 38 (Oct.), pp. 77-81, and (1975) "Marketing as Exchange," *Journal of Marketing*, 39 (Oct.), pp. 32-39; Emerson, Richard M. (1976) "Social Exchange Theory," *Annual Review of Sociology*, 2, pp. 335-362; and Thibaut, J., and Kelley, H. H. (1959) *The Social Psychology of Groups*. New York: Wiley, have been used to explain the concepts underlying the exchange of benefits for joining groups. Clark and Wilson's 1961 theory on incentives is useful in explaining the exchange of benefits which membership in a consumer organization confers (Clark, Peter B. and Wilson, James Q. (1961) "Incentive Systems: A Theory of Organizations," *Administrative Science Quarterly*, 6 (Sept.), pp. 129-166).

19 Both *50 Millions de Consummateurs* and *Der Test* are partially funded by the French and German governments, respectively. This public funding does not appear to have affected their popularity and quality as they continue to attract subscriptions. Their public funding is an indication that both of those governments recognize the public goods nature of such publications.

20 Olson, Mancur (1971) *The Logic of Collective Action: Public Goods and the Theory of Groups*. Cambridge, MA: Harvard University Press, p. 143.

21 Berry 1977, Chap 4.

22 Bourgeois, Jacques C., and Barnes, James G. (1979) "Viability and Profile of the Consumerist Segment," *Journal of Consumer Research*, 5:4 (Mar.), pp. 217-228; Chandon, Jean-Louis, and Strazzieri, Alain (1980) "Who are the European Consumerists?" Paper presented to the European Association for Advanced Research in Marketing, Edinburgh, March 25-28; Jolibert, Alain J-P., and Baumgartner, Gary (1981) "Toward a Definition of the Consumerist Segment in France," *Journal of Consumer Research*, 8 (June), pp. 114-117; Thorelli, Hans, Becker, Helmut, and Engledew, Jack (1975) *The Information Seekers*. Cambridge, MA: Ballinger Publishing Co.

23 Anderson, John C., and Moore, Larry F. (1978) "The Motivation to Volunteer," *Journal of Voluntary Action Research*, 7:3-4, pp. 120-129; Pearce, Jone L. (1983) "Comparing Volunteers and Employees in a Test of Etzioni's Compliance Typology," *Journal of Voluntary Action Research*, 12, pp. 22-30; Smith, David Horton (1975) "Voluntary Action and Voluntary Groups," *Annual Review of Sociology*, 1, pp. 247-270.

24 Maynes, E. Scott 1983, personal communication.

25 Anderson and Moore 1978; Berry 1977; Smith 1975, p. 250; Moe 1980, pp. 168-180; Moe 1981, pp. 535-537; Marsh, David (1976) "On Joining Interest Groups: An Empirical Consideration of the Work of Mancur Olson, Jr.," *British Journal of Political Science*, 6, pp. 257-271; Grant, W. (1979) "On Joining Interest Groups: A Comment," *British Journal of Political Science*, 9, pp. 126-128; Grant, W., and Marsh, D. (1976) *The Confederation of British Industry*. London: University of London Press; Marsh, David (1978) "More on Joining Interest Groups," *British Journal of Political Science*, 8, pp. 380-384.

26 Forbes, J. D., and Punnett, Trent (1985) "Who Are the Consumer Activists?" Vancouver, B.C.: Faculty of Commerce and Business Administration, University of British Columbia, (May), mimeo.

27 Berry 1977.

28 Berry 1977, p. 21.

29 Pearce, Jone L., telephone interview, 24 January 1984.

30 Pross, A. Paul (1986) *Group Politics and Public Policy*. Toronto: Oxford University Press, p. 108. This excellent text provides a lucid introduction to the theory of interest groups. It also provides a useful analytical framework with which to study them. Also see, Adams, J. Stacy (1980) "Interorganizational Processes and Organization Boundary Activities," *Research in Organizational Behavior, Vol. II.* pp. 321-355; Danet, Brenda (1981) "Client-Organization Relationships," in Paul C. Nystrom and William H. Starbuck, eds., *Handbook of Organizational Design, Vol. I.* New York, Oxford: Oxford University Press, pp. 382-428; Pfeffer, Jeffrey (1982) *Organizations and Organization Theory*. Marshfield, MA: Pitman Publishing Inc.; Presthus, R. (1974) "Preface," in R. Presthus, ed., *The Annals of the American Academy of Political Social Science: Interest Groups in International Perspective*. p. x.

31 Van Loon, R. (1981) "Stop the Music: The Current Policy and Expenditure Management System in Ottawa," *Canadian Public Administration*, 24:2 (Summer), pp. 75-199.

32 See Lijphart, Arend (1968) *The Politics of Accommodation*. Berkeley: University of California Press, for a study of elitism in The Netherlands, and Presthus, R. (1973) *Elite Accommodation in Canadian Politics*. Toronto: Macmillan, for an analysis of elitism in Canada.

33 Presthus 1973; Van Loon 1981.

34 Pertschuk 1982; Angevine, Erma (1982) "Lobbying and the Consumer Federation of America," in Erma Angevine, ed., *Consumer Activists: They Made a Difference*. Mount Vernon, NY: National Consumers Committee for Research and Education and Consumers Union Foundation, pp. 331-342.

35 Mitchell 1978, pp. 272-273; personal interviews with J. Sheehan, Consumers Service, Commission of the European Communities, and Tony Venables, Director, BEUC, Brussels, 15 May 1985; Koopman, Joop (1986) "New Developments in Government Consumer Policy: A Challenge for Consumer Organizations," *Journal of Consumer Policy*, 9, p. 280.

36 Rose 1980, pp. 20-23.

37 Lowi 1969; Schmitter, Phillipe C. (1982) "Reflections on Where the Theory of Neo-Capitalism Has Gone and Where

the Praxis of Neo-Capitalism May Be Going," in Suzanne Berger, ed., *Organizing Interests in Western Europe: Pluralism, Corporatism and the Transformation of Politics in Western Europe.* New York: Press Syndicate of the University of Cambridge, pp. 285-327.

38 Olson 1971, pp. 22-43.

39 Olson 1971, p. 133.

40 Regulated Industries Program (various years) *Annual Report.* Ottawa: Consumers' Association of Canada.

41 BEUC 1985.

42 Olson 1971, p. 149-150

43 Medawar, Charles (1983). "Comment on the Paper by Shanks," *Journal of Consumer Policy*, 6:2, p. 146.

44 Berry 1977, p. 68; Creighton 1976, p. 55; Goldstein, Jonah (1979) "Public Interest Groups and Public Policy: The Case of the Consumers' Association of Canada," *Canadian Journal of Political Science*, 13:1 (March), pp. 137-155.

45 Danet 1981, p. 411

46 Rock, Reinhard, Biervert, Bernd, and Fisher-Winkelmann, Waf F. (1980) "A Critique of Some Fundamental Theoretical and Practical Tenets of Present Consumer Policy," *Journal of Consumer Policy*, 4:1, p. 98.

47 Pearce 1983.

48 Pertschuk 1982, pp. 26-28, provides a particularly insightful description of the value of a competent staff in helping Senator Magnuson's Commerce Committee develop consumer legislation in the U.S.

49 Gottfredson, Linda S., and White, Paul E. (1981) "Interorganizational Agreements," in Paul C. Nystrom and William H. Starbuck, eds. *Handbook of Organizational Design.* 1, New York, Oxford: Oxford University Press, pp. 471-486; Koopman 1986, p. 272.

50 Pross, A. Paul (1981) "Pressure Groups: Talking Chameleons," in M. Whittington and G. Williams, eds., *Canada in the 1980's.* Toronto: Methuen, pp. 221-242.

51 Pross 1986.

52 Chatov, Robert (1981) "Cooperation Between Government and Business," in Paul C. Nystrom and William H. Starbuck, eds., *Handbook of Organizational Design, Vol. I.* New York, Oxford: Oxford University Press, pp. 487-502; Danet 1981; Economic Council of Canada (1979) *Responsible Regulation, An Interim Report.* Ottawa: Supply and Services Canada; Eisenstadt, Shmuel N. (1981) "Interactions Between Organizations and Societal Stratification," in Paul C. Nystrom and William H. Starbuck, eds., *Handbook of Organizational Design, Vol. I.* New York: Oxford University Press, pp. 309-322; Lehmbruch, Gerhard (1983) "Interest Intermediation in Capitalist and Socialist Systems", *International Political Science Review*, 2, pp. 153-172; Lowi 1969; Paltiel, Khayyam Z. (1982) "The Changing Environment and Role of Special Interest Groups," *Canadian Public Administration*, 25:2 (Summer), pp. 170-182; Peters, Guy (1977) "Insiders and Outsiders: The Politics of Pressure Group Influence on Bureaucracy," *Administration and Society*, (Aug.), pp. 191-218; Pross, A. Paul (1982) "Governing Under Pressure: The Special Interest Groups -- Summary of Discussion," *Canadian Public Administration*, 25:2

(Summer), pp. 170-182; Shanks 1983; Stanbury, W. T. and Fred Thompson (1980) "The Scope and Coverage of Regulation in Canada and the United States: Implications for the Demand for Reform," in *Government Regulation: Scope, Growth, Process.* W. T. Stanbury, ed., Montreal: The Institute for Research on Public Policy, pp. 17-68.

53 Becker, Gary S. (1983) "A Theory of Competition Among Pressure Groups for Political Influence," *Quarterly Journal of Economics.* 48:3 (Aug.), pp. 371-400; Lindblom, Charles E. (1977). *Politics and Markets.* New York: Basic Books, Inc., Chapter 13.

54 Koopman 1986.

55 Scherer, F. M. (1980) *Industrial Market Structure and Economic Performance.* Boston: Houghton Mifflin Company, p. 483; Stigler, George (1971) "The Theory of Economic Regulation," *Bell Journal of Economics and Management Science,* 22 (Spring), pp. 3-21.

56 Priest, Margot, and Wohl, Aaron (1980) "The Growth of Federal and Provincial Regulation of Economic Activity, 1867-1978," in W. T. Stanbury, ed., *Government Regulation: Scope, Growth, Process.* Montreal: The Institute for Research on Public Policy, pp. 69-150.

57 Bresner, Barry, Roberts, J., Pritchard, S., Trebilcock, Michael J., and Waverman, Leonard, (1978) "Ontario's Agencies, Boards, Commissions, Advisory Bodies and Other Public Institutions: An Inventory (1977)," *Government Regulation: Issues and Alternatives 1978.* Toronto: Ontario Economic Council, pp. 207-275.

58 Averyt, William F., Jr. (1977) *Agropolitics in the European Community: Interest Groups and the Common Agricultural Policy.* New York: Praeger Publishers; Forbes, J. D. (1982) "Societal Control of Producer Marketing Boards," *Journal of Macromarketing,* 2:1 (Spring), pp. 27-32; Forbes, J. D. (1985) *Institutions and Influence Groups in Canadian Farm and Food Policy.* Toronto: Institute of Public Administration of Canada; Forbes, J. D., Hughes, David, and Warley, T. K. (1983) *Economic Intervention and Regulation in Canadian Agriculture.* Ottawa: Economic Council of Canada and The Institute for Research on Public Policy; Harris, Simon, Swinbank, Alan, and Wilkinson, Guy (1983) *The Food and Farm Policy of the European Community.* New York: John Wiley and Sons.

59 Duncan, Marvin, and Borowski, Marla (1984) "Agricultural Policy: Objectives for a New Environment," *Economic Review.* Kansas City: Federal Reserve Board of Kansas City, (June), pp. 20-36.

60 Morrison, Steven, and Winston, Clifford (1986) *The Economic Effects of Airline Deregulation.* Washington, DC: The Brookings Institution, p. 1.

61 BEUC 1985.

62 National Consumer Council (1986) *Air Transport and the Consumer: A Need for Change?* London.

63 *European Report* (1986) "Air Transport: Consumers Urge Commission Action in Wake of Court Ruling," No. 1221, Sec. 111 (May 14), p. 2.

64 Rowse, Arthur E. (1978) "The Consumer Agency Bill: Time for a Recall?" *Washington Post,* Feb. 5, p. B7.

65 Cohen, Stanley E. (1977) *Advertising Age*, 48, July 18, p. 10.
66 *Nation's Business* (1978) "How Business Won a Major Washington Victory," Mar., p. 86.
67 *Nation's Business* 1978, p. 86.
68 Johnson, Haynes (1978) "Losing," *Washington Post*, Feb. 12, p. A3.
69 Shabecoff, Philip (1978) "House Rejects Consumer Agency," *New York Times*, Feb. 9, p. B10.
70 Pertschuk 1982, p. 48.
71 Creighton 1976, p. 26.

8. A CONSUMER POLICY FRAMEWORK

The breadth and complexity of the consumer interest that has been demonstrated in the previous seven chapters indicates that an analytical and conceptual consumer policy framework is needed if one is to be able to assess current policy effectively and rationally, develop priorities and prepare legislative agendas in new policy areas.

The problems in creating such a framework are numerous. As we have seen, interpretation of the consumer interest can be made from the point of view of various disciplines, such as economics, political science, the law and from the philosophy of the moral values held by a society. Furthermore, the consumer interest cannot be looked at independently of other societal interests, such as those of owners of capital or laborers. Finally, the assessment of consumer issues, as in other policy areas, cannot be done "objectively". In any evaluation there are normative judgements which must eventually be made, but which do not readily fit into any framework that has been developed from the various theoretical perspectives presented so far.

Figure 8-1 depicts the four elements of the consumer policy framework which are used as the structure for the chapter. Its first element revolves around the problems of detecting and evaluating consumer problems. Second is a discussion of the rationales for consumer policy. A description of the types of governing instruments which may be used to address consumer problems and the forces affecting instrument choice comprise the third part of the chapter. The final section discusses policy questions of consumer funding and representation.

Figure 8-1 Elements of a Consumer Policy Framework

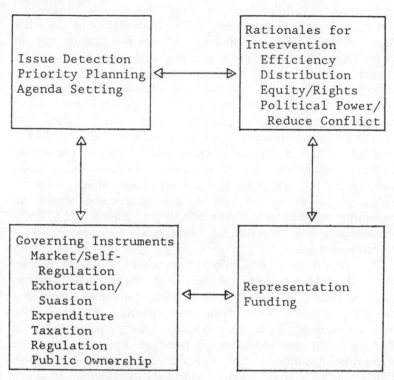

ISSUES, PRIORITIES AND AGENDAS

Government and private consumer institutions face the problem of deciding the how, what, when, where and why of their activities, as do all other interest representation groups in a society. For a single interest consumer group, such as one dealing with tenants' rights, their focus may be narrow, but they still have the problem of allocating resources and setting priorities. For a large consumer ministry in an OECD government, the problems are larger, but can still be reduced to some simple basics.

The detection of consumer problems comes about in a range of structured and unstructured ways.

Something which affects enough consumers in sufficient magnitude to cause them to complain to their leaders and seek remedial action has been the historical source of issue detection. The establishment of the first weights and measures standards thousands of years ago no doubt sprang from just such complaints. Health and safety regulations of all kinds had similar histories and this avenue of issue detection will continue. In addition, both government and non-government investigations have been used to evaluate the nature and magnitude of consumer problems in a more systematic way. Consumer surveys, using a variety of data collection techniques, has been the general methodology for these efforts.[1] While these types of efforts are extremely useful in providing overviews of consumer problems, they are expensive, time consuming, and are not done on a continuing basis.

A number of activists to whom I spoke during research for this book stated that they would like to have an on-line system to record consumer problems as they arise and to help set agendas and priorities for legislation. Such a system exists informally in Europe with the Consumer Interpol network whereby consumer groups in the various countries, along with BEUC and IOCU, report consumer problems to each other on a regular basis. "There exists in England and Wales a system know as HASS (Home Accident Surveillance System) which systematically picks up data from emergency departments in hospitals on home accidents. This is used by the Consumer Safety Unit to help determine priorities."[2] Similar networks, established by food and drug ministries in various countries to discover problems with products in their particular areas of responsibility, could be considered consumer issue detection devices. However, such systems do not appear to be in use in all countries.

Systems which detect consumer problems through recording complaints are not the only systems which should be used to identify issues, since a number of studies have shown that only a small percentage of people who are dissatisfied actually complain. Indeed, although we all have preconceived ideas about how and when people complain, there has been only a limited amount of research on the factors behind consumer complaining behaviour.[3] Therefore, consumer groups and agencies often use studies and other means to, in a proactive way, identify consumer problems which need attention.

However, most consumer problems are more general than day-to-day occurrences and, because all consumer groups are relatively poorly funded, the major problem facing policy makers is setting priorities and allocating resources to those concerns which they feel are the most needed. The decision is really one of cost/benefit analysis and involves a number of considerations which can only be outlined briefly here. The first question which must be addressed is the magnitude and severity of the problem. For example, the passage of consumer product liability legislation, whose absence may cost consumers millions of pounds, or francs, or Deutchmarks annually, would have greater benefits than improving the present labelling regulations regarding ingredients in canned food products. However, any benefits should be weighed against the costs of achieving them. Improved canned food labelling may be relatively inexpensive and easily attainable while, because of intense business resistance and lack of committment by governments, product liability legislation may be extremely costly, perhaps even impossible to obtain in the short run.

Another example is the setting and allocating of finite budgets across the multiple tasks of medium to large consumer organizations. What these tasks are will be dictated by the governing bodies of the organizations, such as the head of a ministry, the board of directors of a consumer organization, and so forth. For example, Consumentenbond, the Dutch consumer organization, reports to a governing group composed of representatives of the eighty local consumer organizations and other groups. That group discusses problems and sets policy goals on a periodic basis for the one hundred and fifty staff employees of the organization.[4] BEUC engages in a similar policy planning process when its Council, composed of representatives of its member organizations, meet and put together a *Programme of Activities*, which is in reality an eighteen month to two year resource and issue planning document.[5]

Agenda setting is the term used for attempting to have particular issues raised by governments and put into the legislative stream. It is often used in a more general sense, that of raising a particular issue to the attention and discussion of the public. Whether or not a particular issue is put on the public agenda and, from the advocate's viewpoint, into the legislative process, if that is the goal, depends on a number of circumstances, many of which may not be controllable. The government must be receptive, the public's interest must be obtained, the case must be prepared and ready for presentation, and the like. To use a current but non-consumer example, the nuclear accident at Chernobyl in the Soviet Union put the nuclear power question at the top of the agenda, whether or not any of the concerned parties were ready. Similarly, as described in the previous chapter, contaminated cooking oil provided the impetus for the expansion of the Spanish consumer organization, OCU, as well as for the establishment of increased government institutions and commitment by the Spanish government.

Therefore, as well as performing the cost/benefit analysis and the priority planning, getting particular issues put on political agendas must be considered as part of the planning process. As well, using resources to highlight the issues, such as media activities, letter writing campaigns, dissemination of information in publications and ensuring speeches and appearances on behalf of the institutions involved, all of which involve lobbying and influence management, must be considered in agenda setting. And this is true for both government and private groups. Just as business groups in the United States were able to set their agenda and successfully defeat the bill to establish a Consumer Protection Agency, members of the European Economic Community consumer policy community have brought pressure on a number of governments and institutions to develop product liability legislation.[6] To attempt to pass consumer legislation in the face of the business onslaught in the U.S. in 1978, given the tenor of the federal government, would have been poor agenda setting. Consumer groups diverted their efforts to state governments who appeared more open to considering consumer policy questions.[7]

Issue detection, priority planning and agenda setting are highly interrelated. This brief introductory section is designed to illustrate that a policy framework is not a cut and dried affair. Benefit-cost analysis is a useful tool to help set priorities, but its users know that it is a only a tool, subject to many problems of judgement, measurement and estimation.[8] As will be discussed shortly, benefits for consumers frequently are costs for other groups, including politicians, who may not view the consumer interest in the same light as do its advocates. Budgets may be tight, ideology against new legislation or enforcement of existing legislation in the consumer interest may be at its zenith, or a number of more important items may appear on the political agenda to thwart efforts to address pertinent consumer issues. On the other hand, events frequently unfold so that the environment suddenly changes in the positive direction. But, unless the issues are understood and policy positions prepared and ready to enter the public debate, an opportunity may be lost. Indeed, those wishing an issue's advancement may not recognize that the time is fortuitous unless they have done the necessary planning and preparation. That is, planning is the "anticipatory decision-making" which allows organizations to take advantage of opportunities when they arise.[9]

RATIONALES FOR POLICY INTERVENTION

This section of the chapter addresses three questions: Why do consumers need protection, when should the government intervene, and when intervening, what governing instrument(s) should be used.[10]

Rationales for intervention on behalf of consumers have been divided into four areas to facilitate discussion. The first three to be discussed have been standard classifications for a number of years in the academic literature. The fourth one, reduction of misuse, exploitation and conflict, is added because it is often cited as a rationale for intervention in the real world.

Actions to Improve Economic Efficiency

Many of the concerns discussed in previous chapters have revolved around the negative consequences to consumers which occur because markets have not operated efficiently. The major problems where intervention may be justified include market imperfections caused by lack of or distortions of information, uncompetitive or extortionate prices, lack of market accessibility and monopolistic market structures. High transaction costs, such as in information acquisition and analysis and in obtaining individual redress, are other major consumer concerns. The fact that some goods and services may be more logically treated as public goods, such as education and health care, may also fall under this rationale for intervention. In each of these cases, classical economic analysis says that intervention could increase the economic efficiency of the marketplace. That is, intervention could lead to greater societal wealth from the more efficient use of a given endowment of resources.

Distributional Alterations

Actions to alter wealth, income, or consumption distributions are based on various concepts of justice and equity that are held within a particular society. They are highly cultural in their roots, in that they are based on widely accepted beliefs that there are basic human needs to be met and that income, wealth and consumption of some goods and services are the basic right of all members of the particular jurisdiction. The goals of policies under this rationale heading include redistributing income, ameliorating poverty and providing basic services such as education, health care, housing and transportation, to those who cannot pay for them, or cannot acquire sufficient quantities of them in market transactions. Such distributional questions are usually contentious in their implementation, even if their goals are widely shared in principle, because they involve taking from one group and giving to another.

It is often difficult to separate distributional from equity and rights rationales, since both are based on societal judgement. However, rights created are more clear cut than are the transfers of wealth and income among individuals, which the distributional rational involves.

Actions to Affect Equity or Create Rights

Rights are non-market goods granted to individuals and groups by the government. *Rights are what governments define them to be and which governments are willing to enforce when called upon to do so by individuals.*[11] The demand of consumer groups for the establishment of a consumer bill of rights, described in Chapters 1 and 2, has been a campaign to obtain government agreement that policies should be developed to articulate, create and protect those rights. Similarly, obtaining an agreement that consumers should, by right, be placed on government and professional regulatory bodies to represent consumer interests is another important right being sought by consumers. These "social rights" for consumers represent a general understanding within the legal and other professions that without guaranteed access to justice in its broadest sense, the ideals of democracy for a wide number of people are meaningless. That they are in "legal poverty."[12]

Many rights may be widely accepted in one group of societies when in others they may be highly controversial. For example, many OECD countries endorse universal medical care. Other countries, especially the United States, have a much more market-oriented, highly variable level of medical care and a wide range of attitudes about the appropriateness of universal care which most other OECD countries accept as a matter of right. [13]

Intervention for Political Reasons

Some intervention rationales are not measurable in economic terms but are clearly justifiable on their political goals. As balancers of interests, governments, which in the final analysis are run by politicians, react to political desires to power and to the need to reduce conflict among groups within their jurisdictions. The three previous categories have been developed by economists who tend to force rationales into categories which fail to reflect the very real need to react to political goals and to reduce conflict.

A number of the most ethical and far reaching rationales for intervention is "part of the continuing process of deciding what sort of a society we shall be -- how risk averse, how hospitable to entrepreneurial change, how solicitous of the vulnerable..." [14]

At a more pragmatic level, and while policy makers may only infrequently admit to it in public, it is widely agreed to in private that political power and a need to reduce conflict among groups in society is a common rationale for intervention. It is hard to find good consumer examples of this rationale because consumers are not a powerful political group. However, a number of business and other interest examples can be found for each OECD jurisdiction and are left to the reader to supply. Examples in previous chapters of electronic funds transfer systems, agricultural policy and the defeat of the Consumer Protection Agency bill illustrate reaction to political power. And while such may be the rationale for intervention relating to immediate political pressure from special interest groups, the society may wish for greater consumer equity and decide to implement truth-in-lending or any other measure with wide support from the electorate for that type of societal environment.

Seldom are interventions based on only one of these four rationales. More generally, intervention is based on a combination of them.

Recognizing the bases which exist for intervention, the government must go through the following reasoning process:

- Is there a basis for intervention?
- If yes, are there instruments available which will rectify the problem?
- If yes, what other (political) objectives are pertinent, and will any of the available instruments satisfy those objectives?
- If yes, do we actually use the instrument(s)?

GOVERNING INSTRUMENTS

If the government is convinced that there is a need for intervention then they have available to them, at least in theory, a number of methods or "governing instruments," with which to attempt to attain the goals of intervention. The choice of a particular instrument is usually not simple because its use will often have ramifications or side-effects outside of the particular focus of the original policy goal. It will also be shown that instrument choices are not made in a vacuum; rather they are iterative, involving complex nestings and priorities of objectives and considerations of what is politically possible. More on this shortly.

The concept of governing instruments is an important one in policy making, since it attempts to structure and consider the effects of using a particular instrument or group of instruments before their use, instead of implementing a policy and only after the fact recognizing their conflicting and often deleterious and unanticipated side effects. Yet, the use of the governing instrument approach will not answer all the concerns of policy makers. First, it would be naive to suggest that policy makers are able to identify and weigh all the effects of the instruments chosen. In particular, there is not perfect information about what is desired, nor what market failures exist, nor how the population might want wealth and rights distributed. In reality, there are competing interests providing slanted, incomplete information in order to influence policy and instrument choice. Second, there is a good case for suggesting that those involved in the policy process do not act solely with "public" or "societal" interests in mind. Self-interest is a common motivation for all parties involved.

In spite of their problems, the use of governing instruments provides an attractive starting point for policy making. Their use require the attempt to provide concrete, identifiable, measurable outcomes of the policy intervention. The attempt to determine how their use will achieve a goal, or in the case of hindsight, how effective their use has been, provides a much better approach than the *ad hoc* methods used previously. In addition, governing instruments are both a means and an end in the policy process. That is, certainly they are techniques to carry out a policy objective, but at the same time they represent an outcome of the process itself and indicate what was politically possible at the time they were passed. This provides insight into the difficulties of intervention which may help in future decisions. In other words, they provide a structured approach to the complex business of policy making which, until recently, was thought not amenable to structured planning and analysis.

Definitions of Governing Instruments

Table 8-1 outlines the range of governing instruments available to policy makers. They are arranged on a spectrum of the degree of legitimate coercion which each instrument implies. They range from the least coercive forms of self-regulation and exhortation/suasion to the most coercive measures of regulation and public ownership. Where coercion increases, the instruments usually involve sanctions or penalties to back the desire by government to elicit certain behaviour. While a complete discussion of each of the governing instruments is out of the scope of this book, a consideration of the major governing instruments affecting consumers in OECD countries will serve to illustrate the concept. Interested readers are directed to the sources cited on the table for more details. Joop Koopman, Director of Consumer Policy in The Netherlands, suggests three levels of instruments which range from governments providing for basic rights, self-regulation and actions between consumer groups and business.[15]

Self-regulation - Self-regulation and letting the market operate implies no government intervention. However, these instruments still must operate in an environment which has a number of rules, such as weights and measures, health and safety regulations, and the various laws regarding information disclosure, fraud and the like. Since there are many rules in force, one tends to evaluate this governing instrument classification in the context of the environment of rules in which an additional governing instrument is to operate. In the case of self-regulation, such as that for professional bodies and labour unions, where coercive legislation requires membership and dues payment of some kind plus members conforming to rules set by the governing body, consumers have a real concern that they have little say in the operation of these bodies, whose rules frequently have profound effects on the consumer interest. Self-regulation implies a good deal of freedom for the regulated group to manage its own affairs, but it usually insulates the group from many market forces and, except in rare cases, from effective political control.

Exhortation and Suasion - Exhortation and suasion are a commonly used form of intervention which runs the gamut from simple exhortation by politicians to the corporatism, described in Chapter 7, whereby governments have permitted a close relationship and liaison with labour and business in Europe in the planning of economic development,

Table 8-1 Governing Instruments

SELF-REGULATION	market operates or self-regulation
EXHORTATION/ SUASION	pure political leadership, mass suasion, consultation leading to co-option, use of confidential information, monitoring and information disclosure, suasion with inducements (corporatism)
EXPENDITURE	as an employer, monetary and fiscal policy, grants, tax expenditures, loan guarantees, social programs and transfers, subsidies
TAXATION	non-tax revenues (e.g., royalties), taxes, tariffs, rules, (e.g., quotas, standards), fines, guidelines
REGULATION	restrictions, guidelines, rules, fines, sanctions
PUBLIC OWNERSHIP	government agencies, crown corporations

SOURCES: Trebilcock, M. J., Hartle, D. G., Prichard, R. S., and Dewees, D. N. (1982) *The Choice of Governing Instruments.* Ottawa: Economic Council of Canada; Doern, B. G., and Phidd, R. W. (1983) *Canadian Public Policy, Ideas, Structure, Process.* Toronto: Methuen; Stanbury, W. T., and Fulton, Jane (1984) "Suasion as a Governing Instrument," in Allan M. Maslove, ed., *How Ottawa $pend$, 1984: The New Agenda.* Toronto: Methuen, pp. 319-324.

incomes, employment and social policy. Consumers have been trying to obtain the right to more consultation in these matters, but they are also concerned that by too close cooperation that they may be co-opted by government.

Expenditure - As an employer, governments expend tax money for consumer purposes through the funding of government institutions which represent and protect consumers -- consumer ministries, safety and health enforcement and the like. Some governments, such as France, Germany, Denmark and Sweden, finance government testing and information programs to a much greater extent than do other OECD countries. Many countries, in one way or another, subsidize private consumer groups in a variety of ways. The problem of co-option is a concern of many consumer activists, but the funds are welcome and they are hard to resist.

Taxation - Taxation has usually affected consumers' interest representation and policy advocacy in a negative way. Consumers' major adversaries, business and other special interest groups, are permitted by the tax laws in most countries to deduct most advertising and lobbying expenses from before tax income. Consumers, on the other hand, support their groups with after tax revenues. Further, laws governing tax exempt or charitable institutions, which provide for tax credits on donations, have restrictions on lobbying activities in most jurisdictions, controlling the advocacy efforts of consumer groups funded by these types of donations. It appears that, while there are some restrictions on the tax deductibility of resources expended on lobbying activities for business and professional groups, these restrictions are less circumscribing for these organizations than for public interest advocacy groups, such as consumers.

Regulation - Many of the measures sought by consumer ministries and consumer organizations involve the passage of legislation which regulate and restrict the behaviour and activities of manufacturers and sellers on the one hand or, on the other hand, require them to do certain things which help consumers make better purchase decisions. Weights, measures, safety and health legislation, information disclosure rules and the restriction of anti-competitive behaviour are all intervention instruments which fall into this classification. Many of them are designed both to improve economic efficiency as well as to ensure consumer rights. Where sectors of society are regulated, either by governments or by self-regulatory bodies, consumers want to ensure that their interests are included in regulatory considerations. Experience

has shown consumer groups that effective power --
voting rights and more than token membership -- plus
the resources to develop their case is a prerequisite to
any real influence in regulatory matters.

Public Ownership - Whether through government
agencies or government corporations, consumers are
vitally concerned with their ability to influence the
recognition of the consumer interest when the
government decides that public ownership is the
appropriate governing instrument to achieve a
particular policy goal. State run or owned
telecommunications and transportation systems,
broadcast media, postal services, power utilities and a
variety of country-specific public ownership situations
may provide areas of concern for consumers. The
immediate situation consumers desire to remedy is
frequently similar to that of regulation, providing for
effective consumer interest input. In the long run,
consumers may advocate for a level of privatization or
institutional modernization which attempts to obtain
goods or services more appropriate to consumers'
needs and to changing conditions. This has been
exhibited in the air transport and some
telecommunications situations. However, attempting to
change established government institutions is frequently
volatile and controversial, fraught with ideological
conflict even within many consumer organizations. I
hasten to point out that many public enterprises are
valued by consumers and appear to have stood the
test of time as effective governing instruments.

Even with the very brief illustrations provided
here, it is clear that the choice of instruments and
the bases or criteria on which their use could be
compared and evaluated is difficult and complex. How
the criteria are weighted in comparing alternative
governing instruments will obviously depend upon the
parties involved in a particular issue -- voters,
politicians and interest groups -- as discussed below.

The Governing Instrument Choice Process

The motivations influencing the choice of governing

instruments are decidedly political in nature as is the process of choice. It is assumed that the actors in the choice process -- politicians, voters and other interests -- act in their rational self-interest. That is, the normative goals of economic efficiency, a just distribution of wealth and income, and so on, are not directly goals of the actors, although they may very well end up as outcomes or by-products of the process. This drive of self-interest, in combination with imperfect knowledge of the costs of obtaining and analyzing information, results in a bargaining process for information and policy favours analogous to economic markets. This is, of course, a simplistic and limiting view of the process, but it is worthwhile looking at its implications before broadening the decision process to include ideological and equity goals.

Rational self-interest means for the various actors that: politicians have as a primary goal their re-election; political parties wish to maximize their votes, particularly by focussing on marginal voters in swing ridings; voters maximize their utility, viewing political activity as an investment in future benefits, basing their decisions on past performance and; interest groups focus on the magnitude and permanence of the benefits and on the costs to obtain them. Information on how policy decisions affect voting is the valuable commodity sought by politicians and political parties. However, except for very special issues which are usually not the normal fare of advocacy activities, it is almost impossible to relate policy decisions to voter behaviour. In this regard, those interests with resources have more political power and will use that power to increase their resource base. Hence, over time, the lobbying and electoral processes will tend to increase inequalities in bargaining power and the distribution of wealth. Second, voter ignorance on an individual level becomes rational, because the costs of informing oneself on issues or of participating actively in the process are greater than the benefits received from a single vote. However, recognizing the collective benefits to efficient information use in the policy process, individuals join or support influence groups to use their collective power to influence policy. This was the subject of the previous chapter.

Factors Affecting Choice of Governing Instrument(s)

A variety of factors affect the choice of governing instruments. They vary from cost factors of all kinds to the more difficult to measure, but no less important, judgemental and political considerations. Table 8-2 presents a listing and comments about factors which affect governing instrument choice. The factors are presented with those factors usually considered most important first. However, depending on the particular situation, any one or a combination of them could be foremost in the decision calculus.

Given the complex process which determines how the various parties in a governing instrument choice decision view the use of specific instruments, instrument choice can often be a complex political bargaining process. Furthermore, the outcome may be less than optimal once the tradeoffs among the parties involved are completed. However, those are the facts of life in representative democracies. Politicians, faced with conflict between opposing groups, for example consumers and business firms, best satisfy their own political goals if they can find a solution which satisfies both groups. Of course, explicit goals may be mutually exclusive and thereby in conflict. But, if a solution can be found which symbolically satisfies the objectives or goals of one group without affecting the other group negatively, the politician would have satisfied his or her own goals. It is hypothesized that regulatory bodies do just that: consumers perceive the body as protecting them, while regulatory capture of the regulators by the regulated protects the regulated group. Everyone feels they have won; of course, somebody may have to lose, and in too many cases in consumer policy it seems to be the consumer, at least in the short run.

Table 8-2 Factors Affecting Choice of Governing Instruments

Criteria	Comment
Costs	monetary, non-monetary, social, political, administrative
Efficacy	does it work, can goals be achieved
Targetability	selectivity of cost/benefit distribution
Signalling Capacity	ability to show economic or political value of the instrument
Symbolic Capacity	symbolic/ideological content; role of government in society, party ideology, electorate ideology
"Fog Factor"	ability to disguise true objective, avoid political flak
Reversibility	ability to withdraw
Modifiability/ Flexibility	re: targets, scale, cost/benefit distribution
Speed of Implementation	
Accountability	budget, committees, etc.
Monitoring Cost	
- Politician	
- Voter	
Legality	
Constitutionality	

SOURCE: Adapted from Stanbury, W. T., and Fulton, Jane (1984) "Suasion as a Governing Instrument," in Allan M. Maslove, ed., *How Ottawa $pend$, 1984: The New Agenda*. Toronto: Methuen, pp. 319-324.

The way in which ideology affects the choice of instrument can be seen at two levels. On a broad level we can see that there are differences between countries in the perception of the role of government in the marketplace. The U.S., France and the U.K. in recent years, tend to believe less government as better. In Canada, Germany, Sweden and other European countries, however, there is much less concern about government intervention where apparent justification for such intervention is perceived. Of course, I expect many would disagree with these generalizations and I would not always quarrel with them, since they are generalizations.

Even within a country, we cannot overlook the ideology of individuals and, most importantly, political parties. Hence, although we recognize that the U.S. is less inclined to government intervention, the Democrats are somewhat less concerned about this than are the Republicans. A further complication to this is the role that the political system itself plays. In a parliamentary system, such as that in Canada and the U.K., the party line is strictly followed, and the party in power has the ability to pass, within reason, whatever legislation it introduces. In the U.S., where the split of executive and legislative powers and the complex committee system lead to a considerable amount of bargaining between even the individual politicians involved, the party ideology may be less important than that of the individual legislators who occupy pivotal power positions.

Finally, there are various constitutional, legal, and administrative constraints on the choice of instruments. Most actions, for instance, face constraints because of the separation of federal (national), state and provincial and local governmental power and the jurisdictional disputes which inevitably result. Further, even within and between government departments and agencies, jurisdictional disputes occur. Not only do these types of problems put constraints on the instruments which might legally or realistically be implemented, they also put limits on the effectiveness of policy coordination. These problems are multiplied many times in the case of supra-national governments and organizations, such as the EEC and the United Nations. The various levels of government and their respective departments and bodies must work together and, at times, anticipate each other's actions. The best laid plans and policies may be thwarted by simultaneous actions elsewhere in the bureaucracy or outside one's national borders.

GROUP REPRESENTATION AND FUNDING

Consumer group funding and representation are critical policy matters which should be discussed in this policy framework chapter. Most discourses of policy frameworks stop with the three sections presented above. However, such discussions usually are from the government or business viewpoint, where funds to support operations are generated by taxes or where the benefits from their expenditures can be relatively well understood.

Businesses, in general, do not expend lobbying and influence resources without expecting they will receive value for those expenditures. Professional groups and trade unions are more similar to business groups than to consumers in that they almost always have some type of coercive power to generate operating revenues. Their activities are designed to provide benefits, mainly to their members, and generally not to non-members. They do not face the free rider problem or, in the case of labour unions, have coercive legislation to prevent it through compulsory membership.

Consumer groups, on the other hand, produce "public goods" financed by their members, who are a relatively small portion of the total society they represent. Throughout the book evidence of the "public goods" nature of consumerism's efforts to represent consumers' interests has been pointed out. Further, especially in Chapter 4, it was pointed out that a relatively few active searchers for price, quality and service put great pressure on the market to operate efficiently. Dunn and Ray, in a major study of the benefits and costs of local consumer information systems commissioned by the National Science Foundation in the U.S., estimated that savings in that country of one hundred billion dollars annually (1979 prices) from an improved local consumer information system. Costs for such a system were estimated to be only a "small fraction of the benefits."[16] The potential savings of such a system, even if Dunn and Ray's estimates are high by even fifty or one hundred percent, and the fact that they have not been instituted by the market system, except in a few minor, subsidized instances, attest to the public goods nature of the issue.

However, this type of funding question is highly ideological in nature and, since all governments have finite resources and many conflicting demands on them, only portions of some consumer information, advocacy and representation activities receive government funding. This is due to a variety of reasons. The structure of consumer representation in the OECD countries is highly variable, a result of history and of the political practice of the country or institution involved. The range of organizational forms and funding vary across the spectrum from no private consumer groups, with government organizations representing the consumer interest, as in Denmark, Sweden and Germany, to little government support, with almost completely privately funded consumer groups, as in the United States, to ineffective or non-existent consumer representation of any form as in Greece and Portugal. France, the United Kingdom and Canada fall in the middle with a mix of private and government organizations and funding. I cannot resist from commenting on the Dunn and Ray report which so clearly recognizes the public goods nature of local consumer information systems but does a number of machinations to try to show how the private sector could fund such a program. The ingrained ideology (not the reality) of the pariah-like nature of government intervention of any kind in their country appears to have stopped them from even voicing the obvious conclusion of an efficiency rationale for government funding in their otherwise excellent analysis.

In some countries, there has been a recognition that if public goods result from the efforts of consumer pressure groups then some means to reimburse such groups for the costs of these activities is fair. For example, the costs of interveners in some regulatory hearings in Canada and the United States may be reimbursed by the regulatory agency.

However, this type of funding is far from universal and is open to changes in government attitudes.

Closely bound up in the source of funding is the question of the most effective institutions to properly represent the consumer interest. In research for this book, we encountered a variety of opinions about how consumers could best be represented. Consumer advocates, especially those who had long been associated with a national consumer group, felt that any government aid or involvement with private groups was inappropriate and suspect since it tainted the organization's independence. Several, but surely not all, government officials believed that they were perfectly capable of representing the "real" consumer interest and that non-governmental lobby groups, with their "unrealistic" demands, only clouded the situation. Single interest consumer groups (for example, homeowners), felt that their particular interest was not adequately represented by the larger, more broadly based consumer groups whose resources were widely spread over many issues. Younger consumer advocates, frequently those working for both government and non-government funded consumer groups, evidenced much less concern over source of funding as long as the funds were forthcoming.

The question one would like to have answered is whether or not the source of funding and the effectiveness of consumer representation are related. My conclusions, based on my casual observation and on comments by people who I have interviewed and who have been active in national and international consumer organizations for a number of years, is that how well off consumers are is a function of the effectiveness of consumer institutions and adequate funding, rather than their institutional form or funding source. The form of institution is very much dictated by attitudes regarding the role of interest groups and government within a specific country and by established institutions and policy processes. The Scandinavian countries and Germany seem to be well served but lack a private consumer advocacy group. France has both private and publicly funded groups which seems to work. Britain has a very active private group, a government funded internal organization and a government ministry with a good deal of consumer clout. One could believe, given the story of the defeat of the bill to establish a Consumer Protection Agency in the U.S. detailed in the last chapter, that U.S. consumers suffered. In fact, while federal legislation did stop, advocacy groups concentrated on state legislation and on maintaining safeguards of consumer rights which had been in place previously. Consumers appear well served in that country.

That is not to say that consumers in all countries are equally well served nor that there are not problems still to be solved. Rather, it attests to the fact that viable organizations and institutions adjust to their environment. Consumer organization have done just that, but organization and source of funding will continue to be important policy questions to be addressed by policy makers. It is also an area of research which is relatively untouched.

CONCLUSIONS

As consumer representation groups become more mature, they stand to benefit from planning agendas and from developing support for rationales to substantiate the need for government intervention, or, conversely, non-interference, on their behalf. Cost/benefit analysis and analyzing policy interventions on a governing instruments continuum applied to consumer policy issues has the potential for better understanding how different policy alternatives affect the attainment of consumer policy objectives. A continuing topic for policy debate will be the appropriate mix of private and public funding of consumer activities, especially for those activities with a large public goods component to them. Further, how to properly represent the broad consumer interest in the OECD countries is an issue far from settled. It will be the subject of debate and conflict for the foreseeable future, if it ever will or can be decided once and for all.

NOTES

1 National Consumer Council (1981) *An Introduction to the Findings of the Consumer Concerns Survey.* London: National Consumer Council; Best, Arthur, and Andreasen, Alan R. (1977) "Consumer Response to Unsatisfactory Purchases: A Survey of Perceiving Defects, Voicing Complaints and Obtaining Redress," *Law and Society,* 12 (Spring), pp. 701-742; Claxton, John D., and Ritchie, J. R. Brent (1981) *Consumers' Perceptions of Prepurchase Shopping Problems and Solutions: Major Findings and Directions for Action.* Ottawa: Consumer and Corporate Affairs Canada.

2 Ramsay, Iain, personal correspondence, June 23, 1986.

3 Forbes, J. D., Tse, David K., and Taylor, Shirley (1985) "Towards a Model of Consumer Post-Choice Response Behaviour," in Richard J. Lutz, ed., *Advances in Consumer Research, Vol. XIII.* Provo, UT: Association for Consumer Research, pp. 658-661; Ison, Terance G. (1979) *Credit Marketing and Consumer Protection.* London: Croom Helm Ltd., especially Chapters 6 and 15.

4 Thomas Recter, Consumentenbond, The Haag, personal interview, May 14, 1985.

5 BEUC (1984) *Programme of Activities.* Brussels: Bureau Europeen des Unions de Consommateurs, Oct. 5.

6 See Chapter 7 for an explanation of these terms and situations.

7 *International Management Review* (1980) "The Consumer Movement Finds Going Tougher," July, pp. 34-35. Interview with Ralph Nader.

8 Mishan, E. J. (1982) *Cost-benefit Analysis.* 3rd ed., London: George Allen & Unwin, provides a general discussion of the technique. Sugden, R., and Williams, A. (1978) *The Principles of Practical Cost-Benefit Analysis.* Oxford: Oxford University Press, Chap. 16, has an insightful discussion of cost-benefit analysis in the social decision making context.

9 Ackoff, Russel L. (1970) *A Concept of Corporate Planning.* New York: Wiley-Interscience, p. 2.

10 The material in this section benefited greatly from the insightful work of Ramsay, Iain D. C. (1984) *Rationales for Intervention in the Consumer Marketplace.* London: Office of Fair Trading, (Dec.); and Stanbury, W. T. (1984) "The Normative Bases of Government Action," Background Paper (Vol. 2), for testimony to the Ontario Commission of Inquiry Into Residential Tenancies. Vancouver, BC: Faculty of Commerce and Business Administration.

11 Adapted from Stanbury 1984.

12 Cappelletti, Mauro, and Garth, Bryant (1978) "Access to Justice: The Newest Wave in the Worldwide Movement to Make Rights Effective," *Buffalo Law Review,* 27, p. 183.

13 Evans, R. G. (1984) *Strained Mercy: The Economics of*

Canadian Health Care. Toronto: Butterworths, Chap 14; Abel-Smith, Brian (1985) "Who is the Odd Man Out?: The Experience of Western Europe in Containing the Costs of Health," *Milbank Memorial Fund Quarterly,* 63:1, pp. 1-17.

14 Stewart, Richard B., and Sunstein, Cass R. (1982) "Public Programs and Private Rights," *Harvard Law Review,* 95:6, p. 1238.

15 Koopman, Joop (1986) "New Developments in Government Consumer Policy: A Challenge for Consumer Organizations," *Journal of Consumer Policy,* 9, pp. 273-277.

16 Dunn, Donald A., and Ray, Michael L. (1980) "A Plan for Consumer Information System Development, Implementation and Evaluation," in Jerry C. Olson, ed., *Advances in Consumer Research, Vol. VIII.* University Park, PA: Association for Consumer Research.

9. PERSPECTIVES AND PROSPECTS

Most of us should be happier being a consumer today than we should have been twenty years ago. The number of wild and exaggerated claims advertised for products which do not live up to their billing appear fewer, the labels on products we buy contain much more information than they did even a few years ago, when we borrow money interest terms are specified in intelligible and comparable terms, and when our local utility company wants to raise its rates there may be access for consumer advocates to make our interests known in an effective way. However, if we encounter a problem with a product or service there are still few avenues for effective and fast redress. When we buy an insurance policy, experienced as we may be in buying intelligently, we still may feel somewhat naked in the marketplace. In short, we've come a long way as consumers but nirvana is still to be reached.

This chapter first discusses the major forces which should have important effects on consumers and consumerism between now and the year 2000 A.D. It then takes stock of where consumers are today and looks towards the future in each major area discussed in the book. The final section addresses the potential for the evolution of consumer power as a political force over the next several decades.

CONSUMERISM TO 2000 A.D. AND BEYOND

There are three forces which will most likely affect consumers and maintain consumerism as a necessary force in policy making in the future. These forces are increasing world interdependence, the increasing complexity of life, and an exploding information technology.

As the world increases in population and as pressures are put on the finite resources of the planet, political jurisdictions will become even more interdependent than they are today. There will be less room for the stronger countries to impose negative externalities on to the weaker countries than there has been in the past. For example, there will be greater pressure from all countries to resist the exportation of pollution and other forms of environmental degradation. The circumvention of national laws by exporting goods and services, which are unsalable domestically, to other countries with less stringent laws, should decline. As is already happening, there should be an increase, although slow and probably never dramatic, of bilateral and multilateral agreements against the violation of the laws and rights of consumers in one country by another.

The complexity of products, services and organizations within a society, which gave rise to some aspects of consumerism in the first place, have not lessened. Indeed, their complexity will continue to increase. Citizens, individually and in groups, will continue to experience difficulty in coping with this increased complexity and they will put pressure on their respective governments to help them function effectively in this environment. Indeed, thoughtful politicians see the problem more clearly than most and do not see simple solutions. If they did, such problems would have been solved. However, changes in educational systems, in information collection and analysis, and in effective use of governing instruments are some of the responses we already see happening to meet these challenges.

Prediction is a chancy business, but we are only at the beginning of the explosion of the information storage and transmission technology which has been so widely heralded as a characteristic of the future. An example of one of the first applications of this technology was used in Chapter 1 to show the possible consumer concerns in electronic funds transfer systems. A large scale, nation-wide experiment in France is rapidly expanding our knowledge of the possibilities of such technology.[1] As more individuals become integrated into an increasing number of information networks, the possibility of both increased exploitation through these networks as well as increased consumer protection and information technologies are possible. Not only will people be able to buy products and services instantaneously, both at home and at work, but there should be an expansion of the use of these technologies to assist in better buying decisions. The potential for real time access to information could provide an entirely new and expanded dimension to consumer education. By reducing the cost of information acquisition and analysis consumers may be able to use and learn at the point of purchase, when and where the motivation is high to do so. The possibilities are much more complex than we can do justice to here, but only more exciting because of their number and the potential opportunities they present.

These world forces may not affect each of us in the same way, that is, the goat herd on the Peloponnesus in Greece or the subsistence farmer on a mountain in the centre of Calabria in Italy will probably be affected differently than will residents of Paris, Stockholm or New York. However, the majority of the countries and consumers in the OECD will feel the effect of these forces and have available to them the power to use or misuse these technologies, with all the good or evil they may engender.

The observations which follow generally have what has been called "a north/south bias." That is, in the OECD countries the most extensive and effective consumer rights and protective legislation is found in Northern Europe and North America. As one proceeds further south to the Mediterranean countries there is less legislation, less awareness of consumer problems, less acceptance of them as a force and less effective consumer advocacy. For example, consumer groups are weak in Greece, Italy and, until the last ten years, in Spain. Ireland has its problems in that it has a ministry representing consumers but, according to all reports, little legislation or enforcement. Japan can probably be classed somewhere in the middle, although even here generalization is hazardous. However, the north/south distinction is generally appropriate to the broad statements made in this final chapter.

Safety and Health

Legislation and organization to protect consumer safety and health has significantly improved over the last several decades. At the very best, there is legislation, inspection and enforcement of laws to ensure that, intelligently used, consumers can be relatively assured of safe products, or at least products where the risk of health damage through normal use is minimal. While a number of countries have recall mechanisms where, if a product is found to be unsafe or injurious to health, it can be quickly removed from the market, many do not.

While the least progressive countries have minimal standards and very unsophisticated safety and health problem detection systems, most seem to be improving. As the European Economic Community expands its jurisdiction, almost in spite of themselves, some of the countries have to improve their safety and health measures if they are to export into the very lucrative common market.

Changes in the safety area will probably not be dramatic but will be incremental. A number of individuals and consumer organizations are concerned that, with the imposition of more stringent safety and health regulations, firms will export the products which are unsalable at home to countries where there are less stringent safety health regulations and enforcement. There are moves afoot to monitor such activities but these activities are relatively new and the rewards for enforcement have little monetary return or incentive to those who are trying to police the situation. It would appear that these measures are more suited to supra-national organizations such as the EEC and the United Nations and its affiliate organizations.

Information

This broad ranging and important area of consumer policy has been broken down into three sections to facilitate exposition.

Weights, Measures and Labelling - This, one of the oldest areas of consumer concern dating back many millennia, is in relatively good order. Weights and measures have been standardized across the world except that the United States and Canada are still being dragged screechingly into the metric world. Still, in Canada all packages are labelled in metric, and in the U.S. many packages have metric equivalents on them. World pressure for metric measurement and pressure from the scientific community in all countries, who recognize the logic of such a simple system, means the writing is on the wall that the world should be metric by 2000 A.D.

Labelling has some way to go to please a number of critics. Content details and the lucidity of labels is much better than in the past. Still, many countries require what is considered by consumer advocates as barely minimal labelling information. The most positive measures in this area have to do with food where ingredients lists, and in many jurisdictions age-dating, have improved consumers' knowledge of what they are buying. There have been mistakes in labelling as well. Nutrition labelling in the United States, which requires detailed technical labelling information, unusable even by trained nutritionists, have lent ammunition to those who would rather put less than more information on a label. However, these types of mistakes lead to more common sense legislation, with an increased ability to implement and enforce provisions of labelling laws which result in providing really useful information to buyers.

In many countries, consumers and other interest groups are consulted regularly on improvements on labelling, package size and other types of requirements which assist consumers in buying. There is no reason to believe that, through cooperation between industry, government and consumers, these positive steps in labelling will not continue to provide consumers with more useful and timely information.

Standards and Contract Terms - It is becoming recognized by many consumer groups that properly designed standards can be one of the most effective consumer protection measures. These include minimum standards for a wide range of products as well as minimum standards for the disclosure of information about services and products to be provided and contract terms, such as those for credit or purchase agreements. Proper standards, if enforced, prevent many problems from occurring and often are easier and less expensive to enforce than other types of governing instruments. While the question of standards is too complex a subject to do more than make broad generalizations about here because of their effect on industries and their positive benefits to both industry and consumers, there are a number of organizations working to standardize product characteristics and interchangeability in a number of product areas. In addition, there is some standardization of services, but this is less advanced than with products.

Activities supported by many legal groups have attempted to standardize the terms of credit agreements and contract terms. Goaded by consumers' organizations, lawyers and legal associations, governments and lawyers are working on this problem. Standard disclosure information laws in a number of countries have made the consumers' law in these countries much better through the requirements to disclose contract terms and interest rates in an intelligible manner.

However, there is much left to be done in the area. There are many jurisdictions and areas where there is still a need for useful standardized terminology and performance requirements, and more information and experience is needed to provide standards which do not restrict creativity and innovation. As with many other concerns, properly drafted legislation with sufficient administrative license, coupled with guaranteed access for consumers to the policy process and discussions amongst the parties involved, appears to be assisting in charting the way for interesting developments in this area.

Testing and Usage Information - This is an area where prediction is difficult. There have been significant strides in the amount and quality of consumer testing and usage experience through information contained in consumer magazines. The number of tests conducted on both products and services has increased. Furthermore, the quality of testing and evaluation methods in consumer organizations has improved greatly since the end of World War II. The government funds testing in some Scandinavian countries, Germany and France. Elsewhere, government involvement in the testing and dissemination of consumer information for buying specific products is minimal to nonexistent. A thorn in the side of many consumer organizations is the fact that in some countries governments continue to resist releasing information to the public on tests they have performed on commercial products for government use. The consumer logic for releasing this information is that since taxpayers funded the tests, taxpayers have a right to use it. Government responses of unfairness to those businesses who fared poorly in the tests by releasing this information are hard to understand, except when one realizes the political pressure from business not to disclose such data.

However, some improvement of testing and decision advice will probably result from the increasing power of information technology discussed previously. Many consumers to whom I spoke about the problems of information acquisition and analysis expressed the belief that for most of the products which they now purchase, if they try hard enough, they are able to make adequately informed decisions. However, they also generally agree that for some types of information, acquisition is still not simple, quick and easy, especially when the product or service must be used before it can be properly evaluated. Even here, usage experience published by consumer magazines for nationally distributed goods and services helps.

However, locally produced products, services and sellers are not evaluated and will remain a major problem in the foreseeable future.

We should observe increased real time relevance of information. That is, it should be easier and less expensive to record problems with new products and compile experience records for old products. The results of these collection activities will be made available faster and at less expense because of collection and analysis with the new, lower cost information technology. The biggest problem will continue to be the local consumer information systems, i.e., information on the performance of firms and the provision of services in local markets which are not amenable to national testing and evaluation. A few local systems are operable today, but they have been restricted by the lack of a funding source. Further, while there may be information on a number of consumer products, that information is highly diffused with no funding available to develop a general directory to help locate it. With a limited amount of funding a better information system for both national and local products could be developed by simply collecting and organizing data already in existence. However, one hesitates to predict the direction local and national information systems will take in the future because it is hard to see a centralized source of pressure for developing funding for this classic public goods type of information. Given the pressures on governments and their funds, no dramatic developments appear on the horizon. However, consumer groups will continue pressuring for expansion of publicly financed, effective consumer information systems.

Advertising

Advertising has been the *bete noire* of consumers for years. However, it is not the "good advertising" that provides unbiased, timely information about products being offered for sale that angers consumers. Rather, the culprit is that portion of advertising which distorts, misleads and obfuscates.

There have been a number of recent developments in consumer policy regarding advertising which include restrictions on advertising aimed at children, passage of legislation outlawing false and misleading advertising, and a number of advertising regulatory bodies, both self-regulating and legislatively backed institutions, which monitor advertising content. The most effective programs we have uncovered are those where the government funds investigators to enforce properly drafted legislation. Where actively enforced, there is a noticeable improvement in the level of truth in advertising. In Canada, as an example, in the late 1960s and early 1970s both federal and provincial legislation was enacted which provided enforceable and common sense rules for identifying false and misleading advertising. This was actively enforced by both levels of government and had a noticeable effect on the improvement in the quality of advertising. The Canadian experience also illustrates the kinds of problems that arise when governments choose not to enforce legislation. For example, in the Province of British Columbia, as funds were withdrawn from the consumer ministry in the 1980s, the level of enforcement of consumer protection legislation went down, leaving only the federal government operating in this area. This occurrence points out the fact that legislation not enforced results in consumers' rights not being protected. The casual evidence is that many consumer grievances now go uncontested.

Consumer groups will continue to push for more legislation which restricts the abuses of advertising. However, they will find that advertisers will continue to resist controls over the messages they transmit to potential buyers. Businesses in several countries are financing university and other researchers to counteract pressure for legislated advertising restriction. The question is as much ideological as it is economic. Consumers ask that truth not be distorted and feel that this, in and of itself, is an adequate rationale for truth in advertising. The problem remains one of long standing acceptance of the right of sellers to hyperbole in the presentation of their offerings and this attitude is hard to change. However, there are some jurisdictions where much higher levels of truth is in evidence. Consumer groups in other jurisdictions will continue to demand greater truth and less distortion in advertising. As well as a political problem it will remain a question of cultural values within each country.

Deceptive Practices

A good bit of legislation against deceptive selling practices has been passed in the last several decades. Included in this legislation are restrictions on door-to-door sales, pyramid selling schemes, bait and switch advertising, unsolicited goods, and questionable mail order schemes. However, the range of practices worthy of legislation is wide and in many countries only a few undesirable practices have legislative sanctions against them. Very often, consumer groups have had the support of business in restricting such practices, since many of the practices are widely despised by legitimate sellers. Government enforcement in many of the countries has been high and some deceptive practices have declined. However, there appears always to be a person who wants to misuse the market to his or her own advantage and as soon as one scheme is squashed others arise.

One can predict further efforts from consumers to reduce deceptive practices and, with proper support of the business community, this is probably an area that will engender less rancour and conflict than will legislation concerning improved information dissemination and the restriction of undesirable advertising practices.

Product Liability

There have been major advances in consumers' rights in consumer product liability. In many jurisdictions, both the manufacturer and members of the channels of distribution may be liable for products which cause injury or loss to consumers. It is less easy for manufacturers to fob their liability off to employees who were at fault. That is, manufacturers must take responsibility for their employees. It also appears that a long running battle for product liability laws in the EEC may have crossed a major hurdle in 1985/86. However, developments in this area are still unfolding. Unfortunately, in a number of countries, product liability laws are still unclear and consumers have little recourse if they suffer loss or injury from faulty products.

Individuals and groups will continue to push for improved product liability legislation in the future. It is a major area of consumer concern. One may see this area joined with improved product standards and testing to ensure that fewer products reach the market which have the potential of harming or causing damage. Many lawyers, consumer activists and businesses involved in the area feel that melding standards and liability should be the focus for future developments.

Redress

The area of consumer redress is one where people have had high hopes but where the achievements and prospects are disappointing. The regular legal system does not cope well with the majority of consumer redress needs. If you have a new home built on a foundation which gives way, and if the contractor is still in business, then a court proceeding is possible. However, if your automatic coffee maker is defective and if the manufacturer fails to honour the warranties, there is little that one can realistically do. The amount of loss will not justify court action and other redress systems do not work well. Granted that warranties have improved immensely in the past years, and granted that there is a wide range of information about how to complain, but if these activities are not fruitful the courts are of limited value to individuals.

Consumers frequently lack knowledge of their rights. Even if they do know them, the courts are not set up to handle small claims because the costs of hiring a lawyer and the threat of having to pay damages to the defendant if one's claim is not upheld severely restricts the court's use for the majority of consumer purchases. In addition, sellers are able to set up continuing systems, for example putting a lawyer on retainer, and thereby gain scale economies in protecting their rights. Consumers, on the other hand, have relatively infrequent need of the courts and when they do need them the costs outweigh any possible benefits except for large claims.

There have been some advances in this area. Door-to-door selling arrangements in many countries provide a cooling off period where the buyer can cancel the transaction within a specified number of days -- usually three or more. There have been small claims courts established where one does not need a lawyer and can attempt to obtain redress. However, the majority of cases taken to small claims courts are sellers obtaining orders for payment from consumers rather than consumers obtaining redress from sellers. In fact, it is not overstating the situation to say that small claims courts have become inexpensive debt collection mechanisms for sellers, which was not their intended goal when first established.

Another development is the use of arbitration and conciliation services, frequently set up by an industry, such as the automobile industry, to adjudicate claims. These have been positive in some respects but still do not appear to be the panacea which people hoped they would be at their inception.

A further innovation was the use of a class action where buyers could form together and bring joint suits against firms. While these have been quite successful in some jurisdictions for a few specific types of problems, their generalized use has been bogged down by some serious legal problems regarding the need to protect the rights of the sellers. Knowledgeable persons in the law are not optimistic about dramatic or even significant changes from the present state of affairs in class action activities. In a similar vein, there has been an increase in suits to protect and enlarge consumers' rights by advocacy groups. These suits will continue and may further expand the broad notion of consumers' rights.

While many consumer advocates, with legal training and otherwise, would like to extend the range of consumer redress mechanisms, many to whom we spoke believed that forms of legislation and regulation which prevented problems from occurring would be more effective in the long run than trying to make the system of the courts more amenable to redress. That does not mean that there has not been a tremendous increase in the number of suits brought by individuals and groups against sellers. It does mean that, except in specific instances, such as when consumers can band together in a class action type suit or when the magnitude of the loss of the individual consumer is large enough, the legal route is not of much consequence. Reducing the number of faulty products and poorly functioning services reaching consumers is probably more cost effective and should result in fewer suffering damages and incurring individual costs. Having said that, efforts will continue to be made to expand the availability and usefulness of legal redress as well as non-legal conciliation and arbitration measures for situations where all else has failed.

Consumer Education

There is no doubt that, at least in North America, consumer education has developed rapidly since the 1920s and 1930s. This includes not only the establishment of schools of home economics in a number of universities but a wide ranging understanding that good buying and consuming habits can be taught. Indeed, research has shown that good consuming traits are passed on in the family through the child-rearing process. However, it is also recognized that education is a complex phenomenon and that leaving things just to the family may not be the best solution. Throughout North America there has been an increase in the number of secondary educational institutions teaching consumer skills in a variety of courses with names such as homemaking, consumer education, consumer economics, home economics and the like. In the past several decades there has been a burgeoning of good teaching materials and a commitment by governments to support this type of education at the secondary school level.

There is no reason to believe that these courses will decline in number. Rather, one would expect them to increase, especially in those jurisdictions where they are not now available. However, education is not just an activity for the schools. The skills of consumer decision-making carrying on into later life and the knowledge of the need for information and evaluation which starts in the schools carries over into all other areas of consuming behaviour. Mass communications media, such as newspapers, magazines, radio and television, have played a major role in expanding consumers' knowledge and consuming expertise as well as of their rights and possible avenues for redress. They have also played a significant role in providing a positive environment for improved consumer legislation. With a trained population which understands the value of improved information systems and with consumer groups, media and governments providing an expanding range of information and decision making expertise, education to reduce poor experiences is probably more cost effective than the process of redress after the fact.

Representation

Of all the aspects of consumerism, the burgeoning of consumers' ability to have their interests represented in government, in regulation activities and with business has been its greatest gain. It also will be its greatest legacy to the future, because without representation, given the complexity of modern governments and the activities of special interest groups, consumers will take a backseat in the halls of governance. It is hard to foresee this happening. Literally hundreds of institutions, from consumer ministries to national and international consumer representation organizations, to single interest local consumer advocacy groups, now represent consumer interests on a broad scale. Indeed, while some observers of the consumer scene have viewed the decline in the last decade or so of the number of changes in consumer organizations as a reduction of consumer influence, one has to seriously question if there are not already too many and too fragmented, small, unorganized groups. While large groups serving many interests may not be as energetic in promoting every interest as would a smaller, more narrowly focussed group, there is also great value in larger organizations and their ability to take advantage of scale economies in developing the resources and expertise to represent consumers' interests. Further, through proper planning and organization the larger group can overcome many of their size problems.

Consumer groups have gained experience and expertise in identifying issues, quantifying their magnitudes, and presenting feasible and workable solutions to both business and government. They are becoming ever more skillful in planning their resource use, setting agendas and having their views and ideas presented to the public. As Steven Brobeck, Executive Director of the Consumer Federation of America so aptly recognized, the reason consumer groups continue to have the power they do with the public is that they put their case to their constituency through the press in a very effective way. They get their facts straight and, because of this, have been effective to a degree much greater than their limited resources would lead people to expect.

While consumers are now included on many advisory and legislatively sanctioned regulatory bodies, consumer groups still do not feel that they have the representational power that they deserve, given the importance of the interest they represent. A major thrust for consumer organizations in the next little while will be expanding their inclusion in, and participation on, these types of bodies as well as in expanding their influence and expertise on the councils in which they now have membership. These consumer groups will become more and more aware of the need to integrate activities among themselves so that the fragmentation which is a detriment today can be changed into a beneficial use of resources in the future.

A FINAL COMMENT

There is increased recognition of the legitimacy of consumerism's desire and right to represent people's interests in their consuming roles. While such recognition may be grudgingly given, governments, through the establishment of ministries to represent consumer interests and business, which in some areas of activities and in some countries are including consumers on advisory bodies, attest to this expanded legitimacy. Professional bodies are less inclined to recognize consumers' rights to be involved in decision making regarding professional matters. But, where consumers' interests appear to be of legitimate concern, if business professional bodies have not allowed access, governments have established other institutions and regulatory bodies to remedy the situation. Hospital and public utility boards are cases in point. More government intervention will occur if legitimate consultation is denied consumers.

There is a recognition that perhaps Adam Smith oversimplified the case when he stated that the purpose of all production is consumption. He recognized when he looked at the preponderance of concern in mercantile England for production and producers' rights that without considering consumption, production was an empty vessel. As the world becomes more interdependent, one would expect that that insightful Scotsman would agree with a slight modification of his oft-quoted remarks to the effect that what we are looking for is a balance between our interests as producers and laborers and our interests and roles as consumers. We are faced with a political power situation in which governments, considering the many interests they represent, are looking for ways to balance the powers of producers and laborers with the powers of the consumers.

I began this book with a comment that the way people perceive consumers and consumerism is very much like the four blind men trying to describe an elephant, each touching one of the very diverse parts of that magnificent animal and coming away with a different description. As this long-term project closes, I perceive the problem of consumerism as being made up of many parts, but in the final analysis it is a political power situation of representation in modern governance. Where consumers have the luxury of democratic representation and the affluence to spend their energies in representing consumer interests, I think we are all better off for those efforts. Over the next several decades consumer organizations in the developed countries, as they have started already to do, will be devoting more and more of their resources and energies to helping establish representational groups for consumers in the developing nations, where consumers' rights and protection is a mere shadow of what prevails in the countries of the OECD.

NOTES

1 Mayer, Robert N. (1986) *Videotex in France: The Other French Revolution.* Salt Lake City, UT: Family and Consumer Studies, University of Utah.

REFERENCES

Aaker, David A., and Day, George S. (1978) *Consumerism: Search for the Consumer Interest.* New York: The Free Press.

Abbott, Howard (1980) *Safe Enough to Sell?* London: The Design Council.

Abel-Smith, Brian (1985) "Who is the Odd Man Out?: The Experience of Western Europe in Containing the Costs of Health," *Milbank Memorial Fund Quarterly,* 63:1, pp. 1-17.

Ackoff, Russel L. (1970) *A Concept of Corporate Planning.* New York: Wiley-Interscience.

across the board (1977) "The consumer confronts the business man," (Nov.), pp. 81-83.

Adamo, Guy (1985) "Mail-order law successful in crackdown on deceptive practices," *Marketing News,* August 16, p. 16.

Adams, J. Stacy (1980) "Interorganizational Processes and Organization Boundary Activities," *Research in Organizational Behavior, Vol. II.* pp. 321-355.

Adamson, Colin (1982) *Consumers in business: How business has responded to the consumer interest - some case histories.* London: National Consumer Council.

Advertising Standards Council (1982) *The Canadian Code of Advertising Standards.* Toronto: Advertising Standards Council, (May).

Alberta Consumer and Corporate Affairs (1979) "What Price Quality?" *Market Spotlight,* (March).

Alford, Robert R., and Friedland, Roger (1975) "Political Participation and Public Policy," *Annual Review of Sociology* pp. 429-479.

Anderson, John C., and Moore, Larry F. (1978) "The Motivation to Volunteer," *Journal of Voluntary Action Research,* 7:3-4, pp. 120-129.

Andreasen, Alan R., and Manning, Jean (1980) "Information Needs For Consumer Protection Planning," *Journal of Consumer Policy,* 4:2, pp. 115-125.

Angevine, Erma (1982) "Lobbying and the Consumer Federation of America," in Erma Angevine, ed., *Consumer Activists: They Made a Difference.* Mount Vernon, NY: National Consumers Committee for Research and Education and Consumers Union Foundation, pp. 331-342.

Arrow, K. J. (1967) "Values and Collective Decision Making," in E. S. Phelps, ed. (1973) *Economic Justice.* Baltimore, MD: Penguin Education, pp. 117-136.

Association Europeenne D'Etudes Juridiques et Fiscales (1975) *Product Liability in Europe*. The Netherlands, London: Kluwer-Harrop Handbooks.

Averyt, William F. Jr. (1977) *Agropolitics in the European Community: Interest Groups and the Common Agricultural Policy*. New York: Praeger Publishers.

Bagozzi, R. P. (1974) "Marketing as an Organized Behavioral System of Exchange," *Journal of Marketing*, 38 (Oct.), pp. 77-81.

Bagozzi, R. P. (1975) "Marketing as Exchange," *Journal of Marketing*, 39 (Oct.), pp. 32-39.

Bauer, Raymond A. and Greyser, Stephen A. (1968) *Advertising in America: The Consumer View*. Boston: Graduate School of Business Administration, Harvard University, as cited in Day and Aaker 1970.

Baumol, William J., Panzar, John C., and Willig, Robert D. (1982) *Contestable Markets and the Theory of Industry Structure*. New York: Harcourt Brace Jovanovich, Inc.

Beales, Howard, Mazis, Michael B., Salop, Steven C., and Staelin, Richard (1981) "Consumer Search in Public Policy," *Journal of Consumer Research*, 8:1 (June), pp. 11-22.

Becker, Gary S. (1983) "A Theory of Competition Among Pressure Groups for Political Influence," *Quarterly Journal of Economics*, 48:3 (Aug.), pp. 371-400.

Bellis, J. F. (1979) "International Trade and the Competitive Law of the European Economic Community," *Common Market Law Review*, 16 (Nov.), pp. 647-683.

Berry, Jeffrey M. (1977) *Lobbying for the People*. Princeton: Princeton University Press.

Berry, Jeffery M. (1978) "Origins of Public Interest Groups - Tests of Two Theories," *Policy*, 10:3, pp. 379-399.

Beshada v. Johns Manville Corp. (1982) 90 N.J. 191, 447 A. 2d. 539.

Best, Arthur (1981) *When Consumers Complain*. New York: Columbia University Press.

Best, Arthur, and Andreasen, Alan R. (1977) "Consumer Response to Unsatisfactory Purchases: A Survey of Perceiving Defects, Voicing Complaints and Obtaining Redress," *Law and Society*, 12 (Spring), pp. 701-742.

Bettman, J. R. (1979) *An Information Processing Theory of Consumer Choice*. Reading, MA: Addison-Wesley Publishing Co.

BEUC (1984) *Programme of Activities*. Brussels: Bureau Europeen des Unions de Consommateurs, Oct. 5.

BEUC (1985) "Product Liability in Europe at Last." Brussels: Bureau Europeen des Unions de Consommateurs, press release, May 22.

BEUC (1985) *Report on Air Fares*. Brussels: Bureau Europeen des Unions de Consommateurs, July 11.

Bickerstaffe, George (1980) "A New Direction for Consumerism," *International Management*, (Oct.), pp. 35-41.

Biehal, Gabriel, and Chakravarti, Dipankar (1986) "Consumers' Use of Memory and External Information in Choice: Macro and Micro Perspectives," *Journal of Consumer Research*, 12 (Mar.), pp. 382-405.

Bishop, James, and Hubbard, Henry W. (1969) *Let the Seller Beware*. Washington, DC: The National Press.

Blomquist, Ake, Wonnacott, Paul, and Wonnacott, Ronald (1983) *Economics: First Canadian Edition*. Toronto: McGraw-Hill Ryerson.

Bloom, Paul N., and Greyser, Stephen A. (1981) "The Maturing of Consumerism," *Harvard Business Review*, (Nov.-Dec.), pp. 130-139.

Boddewyn, J. J. (1979) *Decency and Sexism in Advertising: An International Survey of Their Regulation and Self-Regulation*. New York: International Advertising Association.

Boddewyn, J. J. (1983) "Belgian Advertising Self-Regulation and Consumer Organizations: Interaction and Conflict in the Context of the Jury d'Ethique Publicitaire (JEP)," *Journal of Consumer Policy*, 6:3, pp. 303-323.

Boddewyn, J. J. (1983) "Outside Participation in Advertising Self-Regulation: Nature, Rationale and Modes." New York: Baruch College, mimeo.

Boddewyn, J. J. (1983) "Outside Participation in Advertising Self-Regulation: The Case of the Advertising Standards Authority (U.K.)," *Journal of Consumer Policy*, 6:1, pp. 53-70.

Boddewyn, J. J. 1984) *Advertising to Children: An International Survey of Its Regulation and Self-Regulation*. New York: International Advertising Association.

Boddewyn, J. J. (1984) "Outside Participation in Advertising Self-Regulation: The Case of the French Bureau de Verification de la Publicite," *Journal of Consumer Policy*, 7:1, pp. 45-64.

Boddewyn, J. J. (1984) "Outside Participation in Canadian Advertising Self-Regulation," *Canadian Journal of Administrative Sciences*, 1:2 (December), pp. 215-237.

Boddewyn, J. J. (1985) "Advertising Self-Regulation: Private Government and Agent of Public Policy," *Journal of Public Policy & Marketing*, 4, pp. 129-141.

Bourgeois, Jacques C., and Barnes, James G. (1979) "Viability and Profile of the Consumerist Segment," *The Journal of Consumer Research*, 5:4 (Mar.), pp. 217-228.

Bourgoignie, Thierry M., and Trubek, David M. (1984) *Consumer Law, Common Markets and Federalism in Europe and the United States*. Florence: European University Institute, (Aug.).

Bresner, Barry, Roberts, J., Pritchard, S., Trebilcock, Michael J., and Waverman, Leonard, (1978) "Ontario's Agencies, Boards, Commissions, Advisory Bodies and Other Public Institutions: An Inventory (1977)," *Government Regulation: Issues and Alternatives 1978.* Toronto: Ontario Economic Council, pp. 207-275.

British Columbia (1976) *General Advertising Guidelines.* Victoria, B.C.: Ministry of Consumer Services.

Bruce, Marian (1972) "Giant-killer tells how," *Vancouver Sun.* Nov. 10, p. 43.

Buchanan, James M. and Tullock, Gordon (1962) , *The Calculus of Consent.* Ann Arbor, MI: The University of Michigan Press.

Burstein, Paul (1981) "The Sociology of Democratic Politics," *Annual Review of Sociology,* 7, pp. 291-319.

Buskirk, Richard H., and Rothe, James T. (1970) "Consumerism An Interpretation," *Journal of Marketing,* 34 (October), pp. 61-65.

Calais-Auloy, J., et al (1981) *Consumer Legislation in France.* New York: Van Nostrand Reinhold Co.

Canada, *Broadcast Act.*

Canada, *Consumer Packaging and Labelling Act.*

Canada, *Combines Investigation Act.*

Canada, *Hazardous Products Act* (1971) Sec. 3, and Amendments to the Schedule, Orders in Council PC 1971-2276 and PC 1971-2277, Secs. 4, 5, and 13.

Canadian Commercial Law Guide (1983) Don Mills, Ontario: CCH.

Canadian Society of Consumer Affairs Professionals -- CSOCAP (ca1985) "Membership List." Toronto: Box 6338, Station A, M5W 1P7.

Caplovitz, David (1963) *The Poor Pay More.* New York: The Free Press.

Capon, Noel, and Lutz, Richard J. (1979) "A Model and Methodology for the Development of Consumer Information Programs," *Journal of Marketing,* 43 (Jan.), pp. 58-67.

Cappelletti, Mauro, and Garth, Bryant (1978) "Access to Justice: The Newest Wave in the Worldwide Movement to Make Rights Effective," *Buffalo Law Review,* 27, pp. 181-292.

Cave, Martin (1985) "Market Models and Consumer Protection," *Journal of Consumer Policy,* 8, pp. 335-351.

Caves, Douglas W., Christensen, Laurits R., Tretheway, Michael W., and Windle, Robert J. (1985) "An Asessment of the Efficiency Effects of U.S. Airline Deregulation Via an International Comparison." Madison, WI: Wisconsin Economic Research Institute, University of Wisconsin, (Dec. 1), mimeo.

Chandon, Jean-Louis, and Strazzieri, Alain (1980) "Who are the European Consumerists?" Paper presented to the European Association for Advanced Research in Marketing, Edinburgh, March 25-28.

Charles, W. H. R. (1982) "The Supreme Court of Canada Handbook on Assessment of Damages in Personal Injury Claims," in John Irvine, ed., *Canadian Cases on the Law of Torts*, 18. Agincourt, Ontario: The Carswell Company.

Chatov, Robert (1981) "Cooperation Between Government and Business," in Paul C. Nystrom and William H. Starbuck, eds., *Handbook of Organizational Design, Vol. I.* New York, Oxford: Oxford University Press, pp. 487-502.

Chetley, Andrew (1986) "Not Good Enough for Us but Fit for Them -- An Examination of the Chemical and Pharmaceutical Export Trades," *Journal of Consumer Policy*, 9, pp. 155-180.

Clark, Peter B. and Wilson, James Q. (1961). "Incentive Systems: A Theory of Organizations," *Administrative Science Quarterly*, 6 (Sept.), pp. 129-166.

Claxton, J. D., and Ritchie, J. R. Brent (1979) "Consumer Prepurchase Shopping Problems: A Focus on the Retailing Component," *Journal of Retailing*, 53:3 (Fall), pp. 24-43.

Claxton, John D., and Ritchie, J. R. Brent (1981) *Consumers' Perceptions of Prepurchase Shopping Problems and Solutions: Major Findings and Directions for Action.* Ottawa: Consumer and Corporate Affairs Canada, RG23-56/1980e.

Claxton, John D., Fry, Joseph N., and Portis, Bernard (1974) "A Taxonomy of Prepurchase Information Gathering Patterns," *Journal of Consumer Research*, 1 (Dec.), pp. 35-42.

Cohen, Stanley E. (1977) *Advertising Age*, 48, July 18, p. 10+.

Commission of the European Communities (1977) *Consumer Protection and Information Policy: First Report.* Brussels: Commission of the European Communities.

Committee on Consumer Policy (1977) *Consumer Protection in the Field of Consumer Credit.* Paris: OECD.

Committee on Consumer Policy (1979) *Report on Bargain Prices and Similar Marketing Practices.* Paris: OECD.

Consumer and Corporate Affairs Canada (ca1982) "Retailers' Use of Manufacturers' Suggested List Prices for Comparison Purposes in Advertising." Ottawa: Trade Practices Division, Consumer and Corporate Affairs Canada, mimeo.

Consumer Reports (1978) "Business Lobbying: Threat to Consumer Interest," 43 (Sept.), pp. 526-531.

Consumer Reports (1986) "Mail Order Scams: Shearing the Suckers," (Feb.), pp. 87-94.

Courville, Leon, and Hausman, Warren H. (1979) "Warranty Scope and Reliability under Imperfect Information and Alternative Market Structures," *Journal of Business*, 52:3, pp. 361-378.

Cranston, Ross (1978) "Access to Justice for Consumers: A Perspective from Common Law Countries," *Journal of Consumer Policy*, 3, pp. 291-299.

Cranston, Ross (1978) *Consumers and the Law*. 1st ed. London: Weidenfeld and Nicholson.

Cranston, Ross (1984) *Consumers and the Law*. 2nd ed. London: Weidenfeld and Nicholson.

Creighton, Lucy Black (1976) *Pretenders to the Throne: The Consumer Movement in the United States*. Lexington, MA: D.C. Heath and Co.

Crosby, Lawrence A., and Taylor, James R. (1981) "Effects of Consumer Information and Education on Cognition and Choice," *Journal of Consumer Research*, 8 (June), pp. 43-56.

Dameron, Kenneth (1939) "The Consumer Movement," *Harvard Business Review*, 18:3 (Jan.), pp. 271-289.

Danet, Brenda (1981) "Client-Organization Relationships," in Paul C. Nystrom and William H. Starbuck, eds., *Handbook of Organizational Design, Vol. I*. New York, Oxford: Oxford University Press, pp. 382-428.

Dawson, Helen Jones (1963) "The Consumers' Association of Canada," *Canadian Public Administration*, 6 (Mar.), pp. 92-118.

Day, George S., and Aaker, David A. (1970) "A Guide to Consumerism," *Journal of Marketing*, 34:3 (July), pp. 12-19.

Day, M., Milton, M. T., and Wiles, D. M. (1985) "Textile Flammability Regulation and Test Methods: A Guide to the Present Canadian Scene," *Canadian Textile Journal*, (Feb.), pp. 12-14.

Dickerson, K.G., Hesten, S. B., and Purdy, R. S. (1982) "How Much Federal Protection can Consumers Afford? The Case of TRIS," *Journal of Home Economics*, 74:1 (Spring), pp. 15-19.

Dole, Robert (1975) "Hearings before the Committee on Government Operations." Washington, DC: United States Senate, Ninety-Fourth Congress on S.200, U.S. Government Printing Office.

Domzalski, Yves (1984) *The Interpols of the Consumer Associations*. Brussels: Bureau Europeen des Unions de Consommateurs, May 17-18.

Dornoff, Ronald J., and Tankersley, Clint B. (1975) "Perceptual Differences in Market Transactions: A Source of Consumer Frustration," *Journal of Consumer Affairs*, (Summer), pp. 97-103.

Drucker, Peter F. (1969) "The Shame of Marketing," *Printers' Ink*, 299:8 (Aug.), pp. 60-64.

Drury, R. W., and Ferrier, C. W. (1984) *Credit Cards*. London: Butterworths.

Duggan, A. J., and Darvall, L. W., eds. (1972) *Consumer Protection Law and Theory*. Sydney: Law Book.

Duncan, Marvin and Borowski, Marla (1984) "Agricultural Policy: Objectives for a New Environment," *Economic Review*. Kansas City: Federal Reserve Board of Kansas City, (June), pp. 20-36.

Dunn, Donald A., and Ray, Michael L. (1980) "A Plan for Consumer Information System Development, Implementation and Evaluation," in J. C. Olson, ed., *Advances in Consumer Research, Vol. III*. University Park, PA: Association for Consumer Research.

Dworkin, Terry Morehead, and Sheffet, Mary Jane (1985) "Product Liability in the '80s," *Journal of Public Policy in Marketing*, 4, pp. 69-79.

Economic Council of Canada (1979) *Responsible Regulation, An Interim Report*. Ottawa: Supply and Services Canada.

Eisenstadt, Shmuel N. (1981) "Interactions Between Organizations and Societal Stratification," in Paul C. Nystrom and William H. Starbuck, eds., *Handbook of Organizational Design, Vol. I*. New York: Oxford University Press, pp. 309-322.

Emerson, Richard M. (1976) "Social Exchange Theory," *Annual Review of Sociology*, 2, pp. 335-362.

Epstein, David (1976) *Consumer Protection in a Nutshell*. St. Paul, MN: West Publishing Co.

Epstein, Richard (1980) *Modern Products Liability Law*. Westport, CN: Quorum Books.

Escola v. Coca-Cola Bottling Co., 24 Cal. 2d 453 P.2d 436 (1944).

European Report (1986) "Air Transport: Consumers Urge Commission Action in Wake of Court Ruling," No. 1221, Sec. 111 (May 14), p. 2.

Evans, R. G. (1984) *Strained Mercy: The Economics of Canadian Health Care*. Toronto: Butterworths.

Executive Office of the President (1963) *Consumer Advisory Council, First Report*, Washington, DC: U.S. Government Printing Office.

Federal Trade Commission (1979) *Consumer Information Remedies - Policy Session*. Washington, DC: U.S. Government Printing Office, July 1.

Fennell, Rosemary (1979) *The Common Agricultural Policy of the European Community*. London: Granada.

Ferguson, Peter (1983) "Working Paper on Consumer Redress." Ottawa: Consumer Services Branch, Consumer and Corporate Affairs Canada,, (June), mimeo.

Folkes, Valerie S., and Kotsos, Barbara (1985) "Buyers' and Sellers' Explanations for Product Failure: Who Done It?" Fullerton, CA: School of Business Administration and Economics, California State University, mimeo.

Forbes, J. D. (1985) *Institutions and Influence Groups in Canadian Farm and Food Policy*. Toronto: Institute of Public Administration of Canada.

Forbes, J. D. (1985) "Organizational and Political Dimensions of Consumer Pressure Groups," *Journal of Consumer Policy*, 8, pp. 105-131.

Forbes, J. D. (1987) "Price Dispersion in Consumer Markets: Theory, Empirical Evidence and Policy Implications," in Paul A. Anderson and Melanie Wallendorf, eds., *Advances in Consumer Research, Vol. XIV*. Association for Consumer Research, forthcoming.

Forbes, J. D., Arcus, P. L., Loyns, R. M. A., Oberg, S. M., Ouellet, F., Veeman, M. M., Veeman, T. S., and Wood, A. W. (1974) *Consumer Interest in Marketing Boards*. Ottawa: Canadian Consumer Council, Consumer and Corporate Affairs Canada.

Forbes, J. D., Hughes, David, and Warley, T. K. (1983) *Economic Intervention and Regulation in Canadian Agriculture*. Ottawa: Economic Council of Canada and The Institute for Research on Public Policy.

Forbes, J. D., and Punnett, Trent (1985) "Who Are the Consumer Activists?" Vancouver, B.C.: Faculty of Commerce and Business Administration, University of British Columbia, (May), mimeo.

Forbes, J. D., Tse, David K., and Taylor, Shirley (1985) "Towards a Model of Consumer Post-Choice Response Behaviour," in Richard J. Lutz, ed., *Advances in Consumer Research, Vol. XIII*. Provo, UT: Association for Consumer Research, pp. 658-661.

Friedman, Hershey H. (1984) "Ancient Marketing Practices: The View from Talmudic Times," *Journal of Public Policy & Marketing*, 3, pp. 194-204.

Friedman, Monroe (1967) "Quality and Price Considerations in Rational Consumer Decision Making," *Journal of Consumer Affairs*, 1 (Summer), pp. 13-23.

Friedman, Monroe (1987) "Predicting Frequency of Problems Experienced by Owners of Used Cars: A Statistical Analysis of Six Years of *Consumer Reports* Survey Data for 1979 Model Cars," in Paul A. Anderson and Melanie Wallendorf, eds., *Advances in Consumer Research Vol. XIV*. Association for Consumer Research, forthcoming.

Fuller, John G. (1972) *200,000,000 Guinea Pigs*. New York: G. P. Putnam's Sons.

Fullerton, Ronald A. (1987) "Historicism: What It Is, and What It Means for Consumer Research," in *Advances in Consumer Research, Vol. XIV*, in Paul F. Anderson and Melanie Wallendorf, eds., Association for Consumer Research, forthcoming.

Fulop, Christina (1968) *Consumers in the Market*. London: Institute of Economic Affairs.

Fulop, Christina (1977) *The Consumer Movement and the Consumer*. London: The Advertising Association.

Furuhashi, Y. Hugh and McCarthy, E. Jerome (1971) *Social Issues of Marketing in the American Economy*. Columbus, OH: Grid, Inc.

Gaedeke, Ralph M., and Etcheson, Warren W. (1972) *Consumerism: Viewpoints from Business, Government, and the Public Interest*. San Francisco: Canfield Press.

Garcia-Pablos, Antonio (1975) *35 Millones de Consumidos*. Madrid: Mateu Cromo, S.A.

Gardner, David (1970) "An Experimental Investigation of the Price/Quality Relation," *Journal of Retailing*, (Fall), pp. 25-41.

Generals Motors of Canada Limited v. Helen Naken et al (1983) Unreported decision, Supreme Court of Canada, Feb. 8.

Gerbrant, J. R., Hague, T., and Hague, A. (1972) "Preliminary Study of the Small Claims Court Procedure in Manitoba." Winnipeg: Faculty of Law, University of Manitoba.

Global 2000 Report to the President. (1980) Washington, DC: U.S. Government Printing Office, Vols. I, II and III.

Goldstein, Jonah (1979) "Public Interest Groups and Public Policy: The Case of the Consumers' Association of Canada," *Canadian Journal of Political Science*, 13:1 (March), pp. 137-155.

Gordon, Gavin (1966) "The Mechanism of Thalidomide Deformities Correlated with the Pathogenic Effects of Prolonged Dosage in Adults," *Developmental Medicine and Child Neurology*, 8, pp. 761-767.

Gottfredson, Linda S., and White, Paul E. (1981) "Interorganizational Agreements," in Paul C. Nystrom and William H. Starbuck, eds. *Handbook of Organizational Design*. 1, New York, Oxford: Oxford University Press, pp. 471-486.

Goyens, Monique, ed. (1985) *E. C. Competition Policy and the Consumer Interest*. Louvain-la-Neuve, Belgium: Cabay.

Grant, W. (1979) "On Joining Interest Groups: A Comment," *British Journal of Political Science*, 9, pp. 126-128.

Grant, W., and Marsh, D. (1976) *The Confederation of British Industry*. London: University of London Press.

Harland, David (1985) "Legal Aspects of the Export of Hazardous Products," *Journal of Consumer Policy*, 8 (Sept.), pp. 209-238.

Harris, Simon, Swinbank, Alan and Wilkinson, Guy (1983) *The Food and Farm Policy of the European Community*. New York: John Wiley and Sons.

Harvey, Brian W. (1978) *The Law of Consumer Protection and Fair Trading*. London: Butterworths.

Healy, Maurice (1978) "Advertising: what the consumer

wants," in Jeremy Mitchell, ed., *Marketing and the Consumer Movement*. London: McGraw-Hill Book Company (UK) Limited, pp. 179-189.

Herrmann, Robert O. (1971) "The Consumer Movement in Historical Perspective." State College, PA: Department of Agricultural Economics and Rural Sociology, Pennsylvania State University, (Feb.), as reprinted in Aaker and Day 1978, pp. 27-36.

Hirschman, Albert O. (1970) *Exit, Voice and Loyalty*. Cambridge, MA: Harvard University Press.

Holsworth, Robert D. (1980) *Public Interest Liberalism and the Crisis of Affluence*. Boston: G. K. Hall & Co.

Holton, Richard H. (1967) "Government-Consumer Interest: Conflicts and Prospects," *Changing Marketing Systems*. Chicago: American Marketing Association, Winter Conference Proceedings, pp. 15-17.

Horrocks, Russell L. (1982) "Alternatives to the Courts in Canada," *Alberta Law Review*, 20:2, pp. 333-334.

Howlett, Karen (1985) "B of M joins teller network," *Globe and Mail*, Oct. 17, p. B6.

Howlett, Karen (1986) "Cableshare eyes U.S. market for shopping system," *Globe and Mail*, Feb. 17, p. B8.

Humes, Kathryn H. (1980) "EFT and the Consumer: An Agenda for Research," in Kent W. Colton and Kenneth L. Kraemer, eds., *Computers and Banking*. New York: Plenum Press, pp. 55-65.

Hunter, Mark (1985) "The Smart Card Earns Its Credentials in a French City," *International Herald Tribune*, Electronic Banking: A Special Report, June 11, p. 9.

International Management Review (1980) "The Consumer Movement Finds Going Tougher," July, pp. 34-35.

IOCU (ca1984) *IOCU: Giving a Voice to the World's Consumers*. The Hague: International Organization of Consumers Unions.

Ison, Terence G. (1979) *Credit Marketing and Consumer Protection*. London: Croom Helm.

Jacoby, Jacob, Speller, Donald E., and Berning, Carol Kohn (1974) "Brand Choice Behavior as a Function of Information Load: Replication and Extension" *Journal of Consumer Research*, 1 (June), pp. 33-42.

Jacoby, Jacob, Hoyer, Wayne D., and Sheluga, David A. (1980) *Miscomprehension of Televised Advertising*. New York: American Association of Advertising Agencies.

Jahnke, L. (1973) *The Canadian Consumer Handbook*. Toronto: Self-Counsel Press.

Johnson, Michael D. (1984) "Consumer Choice Strategies for Comparing Noncomparable Alternatives," *Journal of Consumer Research*, 11 (Dec.), pp. 741-753.

Johnson, Haynes (1978) "Losing," *Washington Post*, Feb. 12, p. A3.

Jolibert, Alain J-P., and Baumgartner, Gary (1981) "Toward a Definition of the Consumerist Segment in France," *Journal of Consumer Research*, 8 (June), pp. 114-117.

Kaikati, Jack G. (1984) "Domestically Banned Products: For Export Only," *Journal of Public Policy & Marketing*, 3, pp. 125-133.

Kallet, Arthur, and Schlink, F. J. (1933) *100,000,000 Guinea Pigs*. New York: Grosset and Dunlop.

Kamerschen, David R., and Wallace, Richard L. (1972) "The Costs of Monopoly," *Antitrust Bulletin*, 17:1 (Summer), pp. 485-496.

Kiel, Geoffrey C., and Layton, Roger A. (1981) "Dimensions of Consumer Information Seeking Behavior," *Journal of Marketing Research*, 18 (May), pp. 233-239.

Kinnear, Thomas C., Taylor, James R., and Ahmed, Sadruddin A. (1974) "Ecologically Concerned Consumers: Who Are They?" *Journal of Marketing*, 38 (April), pp. 20-24.

Klein, Gary D. (1982) "A Cross-Cultural Comparison of the Attitudes of Consumers and Business People Towards Consumerism," *Developments in Marketing Science*, 5, Greenvale, NY: C.W. Post Center, Long Island University School of Business, pp. 45-54.

Koopman, Joop (1986) "New Developments in Government Consumer Policy: A Challenge for Consumer Organizations," *Journal of Consumer Policy*, 9, pp. 269-286.

Kotler, Philip (1972) "What Consumerism Means for Marketers". *Harvard Business Review*, (May-June) pp. 48-57.

Kuhlmann, Eberhard (1983) "On the Economic Analysis of the Information-Seeking Behaviour of Consumers," *Journal of Consumer Policy*, 6, pp. 231-237.

Lambie, J. (1979) *Electronic Funds Transfer Systems in Canada*. Ottawa: Consumer and Corporate Affairs Canada.

Layde, Peter M. (1983) "Pelvic Inflammatory Disease and the Dalkon Shield," *Journal of the American Medical Association*, 250:6 (Aug. 12), p. 796.

Lehmbruch, Gerhard (1983) "Interest Intermediation in Capitalist and Socialist Systems", *International Political Science Review*, 2, pp. 153-172.

Leibenstein, Harvey (1966) "Allocative Efficiency vs. X-Efficiency," *American Economic Review*, 56 (June), pp. 392-415.

Leifeld, John, and Heslop, Louise A. (1984) "Reference Prices and Deception in Newspaper Advertising." Guelph, ON: Dept. of Con. Studies, Univ. of Guelph.

Lenz, W. (1966) "Malformations Caused by Drugs in Pregnancy," *American Journal of Diseases of Children*, 112 (Aug.), pp. 99-106.

Lerner, Abba P. (1972) "The Economics and Politics of Consumer Sovereignty," *American Economic Review*, 62 (May), pp. 258-266.

Lewis, Ben W. (1938) "The "Consumer" and "Public" Interests under Public Regulation," *Journal of Political Economy*, 46 (Feb.), pp. 97-107.

Lijphart, Arend (1968) *The Politics of Accommodation.* Berkeley: University of California Press.

Lindblom, Charles E. (1977) *Politics and Markets.* New York: Basic Books, Inc.

Little, I.M.D. (1952) "Social Choice and Individual Values," *Journal of Political Economy*, 60, pp. 422-432.

Lowe, Robert, and Woodroffe, Geoffrey (1980) *Consumer Law and Practice.* London: Sweet and Maxwell Ltd.

Lowi, Theodore J. (1969) *The End of Liberalism.* New York: W. W. Norton and Co., Inc.

Loyns, R. M. A., and Pursaga, Alex J. W. (1973) *Economic Dimensions of the Consumer Interest.* Winnipeg: Department of Agricultural Economics, University of Manitoba.

MacCrimmon, M. T. (1983) "Controlling Anticompetitive Behaviour in Canada: A Contrast to the United States," *Osgoode Hall Law Journal*, 21, pp. 569-608.

Madison, James (ca1788) *The Federalist: No. 10*, in *Great Books of the Western World.* Chicago: Encyclopaedia Britannica, 1952.

Maitland-Walker, Julian, ed. (1984) *International Anti-trust Law, Volume II.* Oxford: ESC Publishing Limited.

Malhotra, Naresh K. (1982) "Information Load and Consumer Decision Making," *Journal of Consumer Research*, 8:4 (March), pp. 419-430.

Markin, Rom J. (1971) "Consumerism: Militant Consumer Behavior - A Social and Behavioral Analysis." *Business and Society*, 1:1 (Fall), pp. 5-17.

Marsh, David (1976) "On Joining Interest Groups: An Empirical Consideration of the Work of Mancur Olson, Jr.," *British Journal of Political Science*, 6, pp. 257-271.

Marsh, David (1978) "More on Joining Interest Groups," *British Journal of Political Science*, 8, pp. 380-384.

Martin, John, and Smith, George W. (1968) *The Consumer Interest.* London: Pall Mall Press.

Mayer, Robert N. (1986) *Videotex in France: The Other French Revolution.* Salt Lake City, UT: University of Utah, Family and Consumer Studies, (Sept.).

Maynes, E. Scott (1973) "Consumerism: Origin and Research Implications," in Eleanor B. Sheldon, ed. *Family Economic Behavior: Problems and Prospects.* Philadelphia: Lippincott, pp. 270-294.

Maynes, E. Scott, and Assum, Terje (1982) "Informationally Imperfect Markets: Empirical Findings and Policy Implications," *Journal of Consumer Affairs*, (Summer), pp. 62-87.

Mazis, Michael B., et al. (1981) "A Framework for Evaluating Consumer Information Regulation," *Journal of Marketing*, 45:1 (Winter) pp. 11-21.

McGuire, E. Patrick (1980) "Consumerism lives ..... and grows," *across the board*, (Jan.), pp. 57-62.

Medawar, Charles (1983) "Comment on the Paper by Shanks," *Journal of Consumer Policy*, 6:2, pp. 145-147.

Methven, John (1978) "Forward," in Jeremy Mitchel, ed., *Marketing and the Consumer Movement*. London: McGraw-Hill Book Co. (U.K.) Ltd.

Mill, J. S. (1972) *Utilitarianism, Liberty and Representative Government*. Edited by J. B. Acton. London: Dent, 1972.

Mironowicz, Margaret (1986) "Dispute over flight delays makes for holiday hangover," *The Globe and Mail*, Jan. 4.

Mishan, E. J. (1982) *Cost-benefit Analysis*. 3rd ed., London: George Allen & Unwin.

Mitchell, George W. (1980) "Problems and Policies in Making EFT Available to the Public," in *Computers and Banking*, Kent W. Colton and Kenneth L. Kraemer eds., New York: Plenum Press, pp. 141-146.

Mitchell, Jeremy (1978) *Marketing and the Consumer Movement*. Maidenhead, Berkshire, England: McGraw-Hill Book Company (UK) Ltd.

Mitchell, Wesley C. (1912) *American Economic Review*, 2 (June), pp. 269-281, as reprinted in Gaedeke and Etcheson 1972.

Moe, Terry M. (1980) *The Organization of Interests*. Chicago: University of Chicago Press.

Moe, Terry M. (1981) "Towards a Broader View of Interest Groups." *Journal of Politics*, 43, pp. 531-543.

Morishima, Akio, and Smith, Malcolm (1986) "Accident Compensation Schemes in Japan: A Window on the Operation of Law in a Society," *UBC Law Review*, 20, pp. 491-533.

Morningstar, Helen J. (1977) "The Consumers' Association of Canada -- The History of an Effective Organization," *Canadian Business Review*, 4:4, pp. 30-33.

Morris, Ruby, and Bronson, Claire (1969) "The Chaos in Competition Indicated by *Consumer Reports*," *Journal of Marketing*, (July), pp. 26-34.

Morrison, James F., and Wagstaff, Stanley W. (1984) "The Videotex Dimension of Marketing." Burnaby, BC: Department of Business Administration, Simon Fraser University, unpublished MBA Research project.

Morrison, Steven, and Winston, Clifford (1986) *The Economic Effects of Airline Deregulation*. Washington, DC: The Brookings Institution.

Moskowitz, Milton (1974) "Social Responsibility Portfolio 1973," *Business and Society Review*, (Jan. 15), p. 1.

Moskowitz, Milton (1974) "46 Socially Responsible Corporations," *Business and Society Review*, (July 2), p. 8.

Moskowitz, Milton (1975) "Profiles in Corporate Responsibilities," *Business and Society*, (Spring), pp. 28-42.

Murray, Edward J. (1968) "Conflict: Psychological Aspects." in David L. Sills, ed., *International Encyclopedia of Social Sciences*. New York: The Macmillan Company and The Free Press, p. 220.

Nadel, Mark V. (1971) *The Politics of Consumer Protection*. Indianapolis: The Bobbs-Merrill Company, Inc.

Nader, Laura (1980) *No Access to Law*. New York: Academic Press, Inc.

Nader, Ralph (1965) *Unsafe at Any Speed*. New York: Pocket Books Special.

Nader, Ralph (1971) *Beware*. New York: Law Arts Publishers Inc.

National Commission on Electronic Fund Transfers (1977) *EFT and the Public Interest*. Washington, DC: U.S. Government Printing Office.

National Consumer Council (1981) *An Introduction to the Findings of the Consumer Concerns Survey*. London.

National Consumer Council (1986) *Air Transport and the Consumer: A Need for Change?*. London.

Nation's Business (1978) "How Business Won a Major Washington Victory," Mar., p. 86.

Nelson, P. (1970) "Information and Consumer Behavior," *Journal of Political Economy*, 78, pp. 311-399.

North, Robert C. (1973) "Conflict: Political Aspects." *International Encyclopedia of Social Sciences*. New York: The Macmillan Company and The Free Press, p. 226.

O'Connor v. Altus (17 NJ Super 298 335A Ed 545, (1975).

OECD (1972) *Consumer Policy in Member Countries*. Paris.

OECD (ca1984) "Quarterly National Accounts." Paris: Department of Economics and Statistics, No. 4.

Office of Fair Trading (1982) *Micro-electronics and Retailing*. London: Office of Fair Trading (Sept.).

Official Journal of the European Communities (1985) Council Directive L210/29, (25 July).

O'Grady, M. James, (1982) "Consumer Remedies," *Canadian Bar Review*, 60:4 (Dec.), pp. 573-578.

Olson, Mancur (1971) *The Logic of Collective Action*. Cambridge, MA: Harvard University Press.

Organisacion de Consumidores y Usuarios (ca1985) "Breve Nota Sobre el Desarrollo de la OCU." Madrid, mimeo.

Owles, Derrick (1978) *Development of Product Liability in the U.S.A.* Andover, MA: Holmes & Sons (Printers) Limited.

Oxenfeldt, Alfred (1950) "Consumer Knowledge: Its Measurement and Extent," *Review of Economics and Statistics*, 32, pp. 300-316.

Packard, Vance (1957) *The Hidden Persuaders*. New York: David McKay Company, Inc.

Packard, Vance (1960) *The Waste Makers*. New York: David McKay Company, Inc.

Paltiel, Khayyam Z. (1982) "The Changing Environment and Role of Special Interest Groups," *Canadian Public Administration*, 25:2 (Summer), pp. 170-182.

Parker, Allan (1976) *Consumer Law in Canada*. Vancouver: International Self-Counsel Press Ltd.

Pearce, Jone L. (1983) "Comparing Volunteers and Employees in a Test of Etzioni's Compliance Typology," *Journal of Voluntary Action Research*, 12, pp. 22-30.

Pearce, Michael R., and Green, Alan R. (1982) "Ontario Rusty Ford Owners' Association v. Ford Motor Company of Canada -- The Activists' Version." in Stanley J. Shapiro and Louise Heslop, eds., *Marketplace Canada: Some Controversial Dimensions*. Toronto: McGraw-Hill Ryerson Limited, pp. 32-58.

Pertschuk, Michael (1982) *Revolt Against Regulation: The Rise and Pause of the Consumer Movement*. Berkeley: University of California Press.

Peters, Guy (1977) "Insiders and Outsiders: The Politics of Pressure Group Influence on Bureaucracy," *Administration and Society*, (Aug.), pp. 191-218.

Pfeffer, Jeffrey (1982) *Organizations and Organization Theory*. Marshfield, MA: Pitman Publishing Inc.

Pollay, R. W. (1986) "The Distorted Mirror: Reflections on the Unintended Consequences of Advertising," *Journal of Marketing*, 50:2 (April), pp. 18-36.

Presthus, R. (1973) *Elite Accommodation in Canadian Politics*. Toronto: Macmillan.

Presthus, R. (1974) "Preface," in R. Presthus, ed., *The Annals of the American Academy of Political Social Science: Interest Groups in International Perspective*.

Preston, Ivan L. (1975) *The Great American Blow-Up: Puffery in Advertising and Selling*. Madison, WI: University of Wisconsin Press.

Preston, Ivan L., and Richards, Jef I. (1986) "The Relationship of Miscomprehension to Deceptiveness in FTC Cases," in Richard J. Lutz, ed., *Advances in Consumer Research*, 13, Provo: UT: Association for Consumer Research, pp. 138-142.

Priest, George L. (1981) "A Theory of the Consumer Product Warranty," *Yale Law Review*, 90:6 (May), pp. 1297-1352.

Priest, Margot, and Wohl, Aaron (1980) "The Growth of Federal and Provincial Regulation of Economic Activity, 1867-1978," in W. T. Stanbury, ed., *Government Regulation: Scope, Growth, Process*. Montreal: The Institute for Research on Public Policy, pp. 69-150.

Prior, Faith (1971) "Today's Consumer Movement," in Loys L. Mather, ed., *Economics of Consumer Protection*. Danville, IL: The Interstate Press.

Pross, A. Paul (1981) "Pressure Groups: Talking Chameleons," in M. Whittington and G. Williams, eds., *Canada in the 1980's*. Toronto: Methuen, pp. 221-242.

Pross, A. Paul (1982) "Governing Under Pressure: The Special Interest Groups -- Summary of Discussion," *Canadian Public Administration*, 25:2 (Summer), pp. 170-182.

Pross, A. Paul (1986) *Group Politics and Public Policy*. Toronto: Oxford University Press.

Ramsay, Iain D. C. (1981) "Consumer Redress Mechanisms for Poor-Quality and Defective Products," *University of Toronto Law Journal*, 31, pp. 117-152.

Ramsay, Iain D. C. (1984) *Rationales for Intervention in the Consumer Marketplace*. London: Office of Fair Trading, (Dec.).

Ratchford, Brian T. (1980) "The Value of Information for Selected Appliances," *Journal of Marketing Research*, 17 (Feb.), pp. 14-25.

Rawls, J. (1971) *A Theory of Justice*. Cambridge, MA: Belknap Press of Harvard University.

Regulated Industries Program (various years) *Annual Report*. Ottawa: Consumers' Association of Canada.

Reich, Norbert (1986) "Product Safety and Product Liability -- An Analysis of the EEC Council Directive of 25 July on the Approximation of the Laws, Regulation, and Administrative Provisions of the Member States Concerning Liability for Defective Products," *Journal of Consumer Policy*, 6, pp. 133-154.

Reich, Norbert, and Micklitz, H. W. (1980) *Consumer Legislation in the EC Countries: A Comparative Analysis*. Berkshire, UK: Van Nostrand Reinhold Company Ltd.

Reich, Norbert, and Micklitz, H. W. (1981) *Consumer Legislation in Germany*. Berkshire, UK: Van Nostrand Reinhold Company.

Riesz, Peter (1978) "Price versus Quality in the Marketplace, 1961-1975," *Journal of Retailing*, (Winter), pp. 15-27.

Rines, Michael (1977) "The Consumer Watchdogs Need Watching," in Fulop, Christina, ed. *The Consumer Movement and the Consumer*. London: The Advertising Association, p. 110.

Roberts, Eirlys (1966) *Consumers*. London: C. A. Watts & Co. Ltd.

Roberts, Eirlys (ca1982) *International Organization of Consumers Unions: 1960-1981.* The Hague: International Organization of Consumers Unions.

Rock, Reinhard, Biervert, Bernd, and Fisher-Winkelmann, Waf F. (1980) "A Critique of Some Fundamental Theoretical and Practical Tenets of Present Consumer Policy," *Journal of Consumer Policy,* 4:1, pp. 93-110.

Rockefeller, David (1971) "Environment: Beyond the Easy Answers," *Wall Street Journal,* July 7, p. 10.

Rose, Lawrence E. (1980) "The Role of Interest Groups in Collective Interest Policy-Making: Consumer Protection in Norway and the United States," *European Journal of Political Research,* 9, pp. 17-45.

Rose, P. S. and Bassoul, H. G. (1978) "EFTS: problems and prospects," *The Canadian Banker and ICU Review,* 85:3 (May-June), pp. 24-28.

Ross, Myron H., and Stiles, Donald (1973) "An Exception to the Law of Demand," *Journal of Consumer Affairs,* 7:2 (Winter), pp. 128-144.

Rowell, Frederick (1970) *An Examination of Deceptive and Unethical Selling Practices In Canada.* Toronto: Canadian Consumer Council.

Rowse, Arthur E. (1978) "The Consumer Agency Bill: Time for a Recall?" *Washington Post,* Feb. 5, p. B7.

Rudd, Joel (1983) "The Consumer Information Overload Controversy and Public Policy," *Policy Studies Review,* 2:3 (Feb.), pp. 465-473.

Russo, J. Edward (1974) "More Information is Better: A Reevaluation of Jacoby, Speller and Kohn," *Journal of Consumer Research,* (Dec.), pp. 68-72.

Ryans, John K., Jr., Samiee, Saeed, and Wills, James (1985) "Consumerist Movement and Advertising Regulation in the International Environment: Today and the Future," *European Journal of Marketing,* 19:1, pp. 5-11.

Salisbury, Robert H. (1969) "An Exchange Theory of Interest Groups," *Midwest Journal of Political Science,* 13:1 (Feb.), pp. 1-32.

Samuels, J. W. (1968) "Small Claims Procedure in Alberta." Edmonton: Institute of Law Research and Reform, University of Alberta.

Sarel, Dan (1983) "A Comment on Capon and Lutz's Model and Methodology for the Development of Consumer Information Programs," *Journal of Marketing,* 47:3 (Summer), pp. 103-107.

Scammon, Debra L. (1977) ""Information Load" and Consumers," *Journal of Consumer Research,* 4:3 (Dec.), pp. 148-155.

Scheffman, David, and Applebaum, Elie (1982) *Social Regulation in Markets for Consumer Goods and Services.* Toronto: University of Toronto Press.

Scherer, F.M. (1980) *Industrial Market Structure and Economic Performance*. Boston: Houghton Mifflin Company.

Schmitter, Phillipe C. (1982) "Reflections on Where the Theory of Neo-Capitalism Has Gone and Where the Praxis of Neo-Capitalism May Be Going," in Suzanne Berger, ed., *Organizing Interests in Western Europe: Pluralism, Corporatism and the Transformation of Politics in Western Europe*. New York: Press Syndicate of the University of Cambridge, pp. 285-327.

Schmitz, Bob (1986) *EEC Council Directive, 25 July 1985, Liability for Defective Products: A consumer viewpoint*. Brussels: Bureau Europeen des Unions de Consommateurs, Feb. 27.

Shabecoff, Philip (1978) "House Rejects Consumer Agency," *New York Times*, Feb. 9, p. B10.

Shanks, Michael (1983) "Comment on the Paper by Nelles," *Journal of Consumer Policy*, 6, pp. 279-283.

Shanks, Michael (1983) "The Consumer as Stakeholder and the Implications for Consumer Organizations," *Journal of Consumer Policy*, 6/7, pp. 133-142.

Silber, Norman Issac (1983) *Test and Protest: The Influence of Consumers Union*. New York: Holmes and Meier.

Simon, Julian L., and Kahn, Herman (1984) *The Resourceful Earth*. Oxford: Basil Blackwell.

Sinclair, Upton (1906) *The Jungle*. New York: Viking Press, 1946 edition.

Smelser, Neil J. (1963) *Theory of Collective Behavior*. New York: The Free Press of Glencoe.

Smit, H. (1980) "Recent Developments in the EEC: Antitrust and the Court of Justice," *American Journal of Comparative Law*, 28, pp. 334-338.

Smith, Adam (1784) *The Wealth of Nations*.

Smith, David Horton (1975) "Voluntary Action and Voluntary Groups," *Annual Review of Sociology*, 1, pp. 247-270.

Smith, Peter, and Swan, Dennis (1979) *Protecting the Consumer: An Economic and Legal Analysis*. Oxford: Martin Robertson & Co., Ltd.

Sproles, George (1977) "New Evidence on Price and Product Quality," *Journal of Consumer Affairs*, 11 (Summer), pp. 63-77.

Stanbury, W. T. (1976) "Penalties and Remedies Under the Combines Investigation Act 1889-1976," *Osgoode Hall Law Journal*, 14:3, pp. 571-631.

Stanbury, W. T. (1984) "The Normative Bases of Government Action," Background Paper (Vol. 2), for testimony to the Ontario Commission of Inquiry Into Residential Tenancies. Vancouver, BC: Faculty of Commerce and Business Administration.

Stanbury, W. T., and Thompson, Fred (1980) "The Scope and Coverage of Regulation in Canada and the United States: Implications for the Demand for Reform," in W. T. Stanbury, ed., *Government Regulation: Scope, Growth, Process.* Montreal: The Institute for Research on Public Policy, pp. 17-68.

Stanbury, W. T., and Fulton, Jane (1984) "Suasion as a Governing Instrument," in Allan M. Maslove, ed., *How Ottawa $pend$, 1984: The New Agenda.* Toronto: Methuen, pp. 319-324.

Stanley, J., and Robinson, Larry M. (1980) "Opinions on Consumer Issues: A Review of Recent Studies of Executives and Consumers," *Journal of Consumer Affairs,* 14:1 (Summer), pp. 207-220.

Stelzer, Irwin M. (1980) "A Policy Guide for Utility Executives: Know When to Hold 'em Know when to Fold 'em," *Public Utilities Fortnightly,* (Oct. 9), pp. 64-65.

Stewart, Richard B., and Sunstein, Cass R. (1982) "Public Programs and Private Rights," *Harvard Law Review,* 95:6, pp. 1195-1322.

Stigler, George (1971) "The Theory of Economic Regulation," *Bell Journal of Economics and Management Science,* 22 (Spring), pp. 3-21.

Sturdivant, Frederick D. (1979) "Executives and Activists: Test of Stakeholder Management," *California Management Review,* 22:1 (Fall), pp. 53-59.

Sugden, R., and Williams, A. (1978) *The Principles of Practical Cost-Benefit Analysis.* Oxford: Oxford University Press.

Thibaut, J. and Kelley, H. H. (1959) *The Social Psychology of Groups.* New York: Wiley.

Thorelli, Hans, Becker, Helmut, and Engledew, Jack (1975) *The Information Seekers.* Cambridge, MA: Ballinger Publishing Co.

Tippett v. I.T.U., Loc. 226 [1976] 4 W.W.R. 460.

Trebilcock, Michael (1978) *Help.* Toronto: Canadian Broadcasting System.

Trebilcock, M. J., Hartle, D. G., Prichard, R. S., and Dewees, D. N. (1982) *The Choice of Governing Instruments.* Ottawa: Economic Council of Canada.

Trubek, David M., Trubek, Louise G., and Stingl, Denis (1984) "Consumer Law in the American Federal System," in Bourgoignie and Trubek 1984, pp. 55-175.

Truman, David B. (1951) *The Governmental Process: Political Interests and Public Opinion.* New York: Knopf.

Tse, David K. C. (1984) "A Model of Consumer Post-Choice Processes." Berkeley: School of Business Administration, University of California, unpublished doctoral dissertation.

United States, *Flammable Fabrics Act,* 1953, amended 1967.

U.S.A. v. Radio Shack, 80 C.L.L.C. 16, 003.

Van der Esch, B. (1980) "EEC Competition Rules: Basic Principles and Policy Aims," *Legal Issues of European Integration*, 2, pp. 75-85.

Van Loon, R. (1981) "Stop the Music: The Current Policy and Expenditure Management System in Ottawa," *Canadian Public Administration*, 24:2 (Summer), pp. 75-199.

Vancouver City Savings Credit Union (1985) *VanCity -- Hertz Used Car Sale*. Vancouver, B. C., (Sept.), printed brochure.

Veblen, Thorstein (1920) *The Vested Interests and the Common Man*. New York: B. W. Huebsch, Inc.

Vermeer, Ruth (1981) "The Consumer Protection Movement." Penang: International Organization of Consumers Unions, draft outline, mimeo.

Vogel, David (1979) "Ralph Naders all over the place: citizen vs. the corporations," *across the board*, (April), p. 30.

Walker, David (1980) *The Oxford Companion to Law*. Oxford: Oxford University Press.

Walker, G. (1979) *Credit Where Credit is Due*. New York: Holt Rinehart and Winston.

Wall Street Journal (1971) "Leaders of Firms Who Pollute to Prison," April 19, p. 23.

Warner, W. Lloyd. (1963) *Yankee City*. New London: Yale University Press, one volume, abridged edition.

Warneryd, Carl-Erik (1980) "The Limits of Public Consumer Information," *Journal of Consumer Policy*, 4:2, pp. 127-141.

Whincup, Michael (1979) *Defective Goods*. London: Sweet & Maxwell.

Widdows, Richard, and Jobst, Kenneth (1986) "Consumer Arbitration of Consumer-Seller Disputes over Automobile Purchases: Has it Achieved what it Set Out to Achieve?" *Proceedings of the 15th Annual Conference for the Southwestern Regional Association Family Economics -- Home Management*. Akron, OH, (Feb.), pp. 124-127.

Wilde, Louis L. (1980) "The Economics of Consumer Information Acquisition," *Journal of Business*, 53:3:2, pp. S143-S158.

Williams, Neil J. (1975) "Consumer Class Actions in Canada -- Some Proposals for Reform," *Osgoode Hall Law Journal*, 13 (June), pp. 1-88.

Winter, Ralph K. (1972) *The Consumer Advocate versus the Consumer*. Washington, DC: American Enterprise Institute for Public Policy Research, as reprinted in Aaker and Day 1978.

AUTHOR/NAME INDEX

SUBJECT INDEX